Illustration
NOW!

Ed. Julius Wiedemann

Illustration NOW!

TASCHEN

KÖLN LONDON LOS ANGELES MADRID PARIS TOKYO

Brad Holland Intro

Shape and Content

Words use time to convey meaning. Pictures use space. The unique value of illustration is its ability to flatten time and compress different states of consciousness into a frozen moment.

Drawing a picture isn't the best way to inventory your feelings. Prose is better at that. And art has surrendered to photography its precision in capturing an instant of real time in its physical detail. But a picture that tells a story can still do what words and photos can't improve upon; It can gather together our loose ends and stray thoughts, put them into a hat and pull out a rabbit.

The secret of making a picture that sticks in the mind is to by-pass reason. To reason with words is to disappear into circles of abstraction. A picture wants to make the abstract visible. And what's visible in the mind is what lingers there when the vividness of the passing scene has gone. The fading memory of shapes and colors, sensations and fleeting thoughts all sit in the memory like a stump in the woods that decays among the leaves, but glows in the dark. This foxfire of memory is something we all share, but for the artist it's a special tool. It lets you recreate dimly the flash of insight that fades with understanding. It gives shape to thoughts. It lets you do something with pictures that you can't do with words.

Words are ideal tools for dissecting experience. But to dissect, you first have to kill the experience and lay it open. Writing consists of giving names to nameless perceptions, then manipulating them to tell a story, convey emotion or set out the facts. Language is a very flexible tool. But to make it work, you have to line up your words and march them out in a certain order; with language, sequence is everything. Try telling a story backwards and see how much sense it makes. Try telling a joke with the punchline first and see how many laughs you get.

Time is the essence of the writer's art. But by abstracting experience into symbols and symbols into the stream of time, your consciousness becomes a figment of the abstraction. What this gives you in depth of understanding, it takes from you in immediacy. A picture that's done well can re-capture the foxfire of a first impression. It can restore to understanding the sense of wholeness we always hope to extract from the passing scene.

Do most illustrations do this? No, over the years, illustration has had different purposes. Traditionally illustrators illustrated. They drew pictures for readers to help them visualize the key scenes in a story, or to brighten dull ideas. Illustrations could color statistics or animate the logic of a tedious argument. But in fact, the word illustration is now an inexact word. It comes from a time when publishers needed pictures to interest readers in an unfamiliar book or to break up pages of gray type. Over the last fifty years that's all changed.

Much of the art that now grows through the cracks in the electronic media has a different claim on our attention. Some people have called this art graphic commentary, but that's a cumbersome word and reminds me of the time in New York when housemaids struck their employers, demanding to be called "domestic engineers." There's no need to re-label this new approach to the way we use pictures, but to understand how and why it's different from Norman Rockwell, it helps to understand the change in attitude that brought it about.

In traditional illustration, you read a manuscript and made a picture to match the writer's point-of-view. But an artist with his own point of view wants to start where the writer starts and deliver his goods in pictures instead of prose.

This kind of picture is pre-literary. It forms in the fog of the mind a second before the Big Bang of consciousness would otherwise start the fog expanding, where gases would otherwise cool into thoughts and thoughts into words. In a picture, the fog will cool into lights and darks and colors and concrete forms. This kind of picture comes from the unconscious. It may not illustrate in the normal sense, because the artist who makes it doesn't have to channel a writer's sensibility. Instead, he can skirt the intellect and draw on memory and association. This kind of independence lets a picture recapture, if it can, the glow of a first impression. This is a different way of giving shape to content, and coming at a time when movies can now do much of what illustration used to do, it's something new in the way of popular art.

Le fond et la forme

Les mots utilisent le temps pour véhiculer un sens. Les images utilisent l'espace. L'intérêt particulier qu'a l'illustration est d'anéantir le temps et de comprimer différents états de conscience en un moment figé.

Créer une image n'est pas la meilleure façon d'inventorier ses sentiments. Pour cela, mieux vaut recourir à la prose. Et l'art a cédé à la photographie sa précision dans la capture d'un instant de temps réel dans ses détails physiques. Mais une image qui raconte une histoire peut toujours réussir là où les mots et les photos échouent, elle peut rassembler nos fins éparses et nos pensées errantes, les placer dans un chapeau et en sortir un lapin.

Le secret pour créer une image qui s'incruste dans la mémoire est de faire abstraction de la raison. Raisonner avec des mots c'est disparaître dans les cercles de l'abstraction. Une image tend à rendre visible l'abstrait. Et ce qui est visible dans l'esprit est ce qui y subsiste quand la netteté d'une scène a disparu. Souvenirs de formes et de couleurs, sensations et pensées fugaces sont installés dans la mémoire comme une souche qui pourrit au milieu des feuilles mais qui brille dans le noir. Cette lueur de la mémoire est quelque chose que nous avons tous en commun mais qui constitue un outil spécial pour l'artiste. Elle permet de recréer vaguement le flash d'intuition qui s'évanouit avec la compréhension. Elle donne forme aux pensées. Elle permet de faire avec les images ce qu'il est impossible de faire avec les mots.

Les mots sont des outils parfaits pour disséquer l'expérience. Mais pour la disséquer, il faut d'abord la tuer et l'ouvrir. Écrire c'est donner des noms à des perceptions sans nom, puis les manipuler pour raconter une histoire, transmettre une émotion ou présenter des faits. Le langage est un outil très flexible. Mais pour qu'il fonctionne, vous devez alignez vos mots et les ranger dans un certain ordre. Avec le langage, tout est séquence. Essayez de raconter une histoire à l'envers et de voir si elle a encore un sens. Essayez de raconter une blague en commençant par sa chute. Combien en rient ?

Le temps est l'essence de l'art de celui qui écrit. Mais en rendant l'expérience abstraite en la transformant en symboles, et en faisant de même avec les symboles en les convertissant dans le flux du temps, votre conscience devient un produit de l'abstraction. Ce que cela vous fait gagner en compréhension profonde vous fait perdre en spontanéité. Une image bien faite peut recapturer la lueur d'une première impression. Elle peut restituer à l'entendement le sens de globalité que nous espérons toujours extraire d'une scène.

La plupart des illustrations peuvent-elle en dire autant ? Non. L'illustration n'a pas toujours eu les mêmes objectifs. A l'origine, les illustrateurs illustraient. Ils dessinaient des images pour aider les lecteurs à visualiser les scènes clé d'un récit, ou pour égayer des idées ternes. Les illustrations pouvaient colorer des statistiques ou animer la logique d'un débat ennuyeux. Aujourd'hui le mot illustration n'a plus rien d'exact. Il remonte à un temps où les éditeurs avaient besoin d'images pour intéresser les lecteurs à un livre inhabituel ou pour aérer des pages couvertes de caractères gris. Tout cela a changé au cours du demi-siècle écoulé.

Pour une grande part, l'art qui pousse désormais entre les fissures des médias électroniques réclame de nous une attention toute autre. Commentaire graphique est le nom donné par certains à cet art mais c'est à mon sens une expression trop lourde qui me rappelle le temps où les femmes de chambre à New York exigeaient de leurs employeurs qu'elles se fassent appeler « techniciennes domestiques ». Nul n'est besoin de donner une autre étiquette à cette nouvelle façon que nous avons d'utiliser les images mais saisir le changement d'attitude qui l'a provoquée aide à comprendre en quoi et pourquoi elle diffère de celle de Norman Rockwell.

Autrefois, pour illustrer, on lisait un texte et créait une image qui devait correspondre au point de vue de l'auteur. Mais un artiste doté d'un point de vue propre veut commencer là où commence l'auteur et répondre à l'attente par une image et non par la prose.

Ce type d'image est prélittéraire. Elle se forme dans le brouillard de l'esprit une seconde avant que le big bang de la conscience ne le dissipe et que les gaz se condensent en pensées et les pensées en mots. Dans une image, le brouillard se condense en lumières, en ombres, en couleurs et en formes concrètes. Ce type d'image provient de l'inconscient. Il se peut qu'il n'illustre pas au sens habituel du mot car l'artiste n'a pas à transmettre la sensibilité d'un auteur. Au lieu de cela, l'artiste peut contourner l'intelligence et puiser dans la mémoire et les associations. Ce type d'indépendance permet à l'image de recapturer, si elle le peut ,la lueur d'une première impression. Il s'agit d'une manière différente de donner une forme au fond et, à l'heure où les films peuvent faire beaucoup des choses que l'illustration pouvait faire, d'un nouvel aspect de l'art populaire.

Form und Inhalt

Worte brauchen Zeit, um eine Nachricht zu vermitteln. Bilder brauchen Raum. Der ganz spezielle Wert einer Illustration liegt bei seiner Fähigkeit, Zeit zu sparen und die unterschiedlichen Bewusstseinsebenen in einem „frozen moment" zu komprimieren.

Ein Bild zu Zeichnen ist nicht unbedingt die beste Lösung für eine Bestandsaufnahme unserer Gefühle. Prosa ist dafür geeigneter. Ausserdem hat sich die Kunst der Fotografie und ihre Exaktheit bei der Erfassung einer reelen Momentaufnahme bis ins kleinste Detail hin, ausgeliefert. Trotz allem wird ein Bild, das eine Geschichte zu erzählen weiss, stets unantastbar für Worte oder Fotografien bleiben; ein Bild kann unsere Zweifel und abschweifende Gedanken fesseln, sie in einen Hut stecken und einen Hasen herauszaubern.

Das Geheimnis, ein Bild zu schaffen, das in Erinnerung bleibt, liegt darin, die Vernunft zu umgehen. Der Versuch, mit Worten zu argumentieren, resultiert im Untergang kreisförmiger Abstraktion. Ein Bild versucht stets, das Abstrakte sichtbar zu machen. Und das, was in Gedanken sichtbar bleibt, ist das, was zurückbleibt, nachdem eine vorbeiziehende Szene ihre Lebendigkeit verliert. Die verblassenden Erinnerungen von Formen und Farben, Eindrücken und vorbeiziehenden Gedanken sind alle in unserem Gedächtnis verankert, gerade so wie ein Baumstumpf im Wald, der unter dem Laub der umherstehenden Bäume zerfällt, doch bei Nacht erstrahlt. Das Feuerwerk der Erinnerungen ist etwas, das wir alle gemeinsam haben, doch für den Künstler dient es als ganz besonderes Werkzeug. Es gibt ihm die Möglichkeit, den schwach aufzuckenden Blitz aus dem Inneren zu rekreieren, der, sobald der Verstand eingeschaltet wird, verblasst. Es gibt den Gedanken Form. Es erlaubt, mit Bildern das zu tun, was mit Worten unmöglich ist.

Worte sind das geeignete Werkzeug, Erfahrungswerte aufzugliedern. Um jedoch aufgliedern zu können, muss zuerst die Erfahrung gelöscht und alles offen gelegt werden. Schreiben besteht darin, begriffslosen Vorstellungen Namen zu geben und diese dann zu manipulieren, um eine Geschichte zu erzählen, Gefühle zu vermitteln oder ganz einfach Fakten aufzulisten. Sprache ist ein sehr flexibles Werkzeug. Um sie jedoch richtig anwenden zu können, muss man die Worte in eine Reihenfolge bringen und sie geordnet herauslassen; das Wichtigste bei der Sprache ist die Reihenfolge. Versucht man, eine Geschichte von hinten anzufangen, wird man merken, wie wenig Sinn das ergibt. Oder auch einen Witz — mal sehen, wieviele da noch lachen.

Die Essenz der Schreibkunst ist die Zeit. Aber durch die Abstraktion von Erfahrungswerten in Symbolik und durch die Wahrnehmung von Symbolik im Zeitfluss, verwandelt sich unser Bewusstsein zu einem Teil dieser Abstraktion. Was man dadurch an Tiefgründigkeit gewinnt, verliert man an Spontanität. Ein gutes Bild vermag es, den ersten Eindruck widerzuspiegeln. Es kann den Eindruck von Ganzheit, den wir bei vorüberziehenden Szenen festzuhalten versuchen, wiederherstellen.

Ist dies immer der Fall bei Illustration? Nein, über die Jahre hinweg hat die Illustration unterschiedliche Zwecke erfüllt. Traditionsgemäss haben Illustratoren illustriert. Sie zeichneten, um dem Leser die Hauptaussage einer Geschichte bildlich näher zu bringen oder auch, um eine weniger interessante Idee aufzuhellen. Illustrationen können Statistiken farblich untermalen oder die Logik eines langwierigen Disputs animieren. Tatsache ist, dass der Begriff Illustration heute nicht mehr korrekt ist. Er stammt noch aus der Zeit, als die Herausgeber Bildmaterial brauchten, um sowohl das Interesse der Leser für unbekannte Literatur zu wecken, als auch wenig ansprechende Zeitungsseiten aufzulockern. In den letzten fünfzig Jahren hat sich all dies verändert.

Viel Kunst, die sich heute durch die Ritzen der elektronischen Medien drängt, hat einen anderen Anspruch an unsere Wahrnehmung. Manche nennen diese Kunst „grafische Kommentierung", aber mir erscheint dieses Wort eher unpassend, es erinnert mich an die Zeit, als in New York die Hausgehilfen von ihren Arbeitgebern verlangten, sie als "Hausingenieure" zu bezeichnen. Es besteht kein Grund für eine Neu-Definierung unserer zeitgemässen Verwertung von Bildern, man muss nur verstehen, in welcher Form und warum diese sich von Norman Rockwell differenziert. Dann wird es uns auch leichter fallen, diese neue Haltung zu verstehen.

In der traditionellen Illustration studierte man ein Manuskript und erstellte dann ein Bild im Einklang mit der Sichtweise des Autors. Ein Künstler mit eigener Meinung allerdings möchte genau dort anfangen, wo auch der Schriftsteller beginnt und sein Werk in Form von Bildern, anstelle von Prosa, präsentieren.

Diese Art von Bild könnte man als "Prä-literarisch" bezeichnen. Dieses formt sich im Nebel der Gedanken, eine Sekunde bevor der grosse Knall des Bewusstseins den Nebel auseinanderzutreiben vermag und die Gase sich abkühlen, sich zu Gedanken formen und die Gedanken zu Worten werden. In diesem Bild jedoch kühlt sich der Nebel ab und verwandelt sich in Licht und Schatten, Farben und Formen. Diese Art von Bild ist ein Produkt des Unterbewusstseins. Es mag wohl sein, dass es keine Illustration im herkömmlichen Sinne ist, da der Künstler nicht die Sensibilität eines Schriftstellers einbringen muss. Im Gegenteil, er kann sich den intellektuellen Teil zurechtschneidern und Erinnerungen und Verbindungsstücke hinzusetzen. Diese Art von Unabhängigkeit verleiht einem Bild die Möglichkeit, nicht nur einem Inhalt Form zu geben, sondern den Zauber des ersten Eindruckes festzuhalten. Vor allem, wenn man bedenkt, dass heutzutage mit Filmen all das erreicht werden kann, was einst Aufgabe der Illustration war, ist das gezeichnete Wort ganz sicher eine neue Form von populärer Kunst.

The Changing State of the Art

I have been commissioning editorial illustration for more than three decades, and was an avid fan long before that. I watched trends and fashions come and go, come and stay, and come and die like grapes on the vine. As a kid I was as awed by Norman Rockwell's covers for the Saturday Evening Post as were virtually everyone in the United States. He was our Vermeer. His gritty though idyllic representations of America, his romantic panoramas of small towns and nostalgic places, void of irony and full of passion, triggered the pleasantest of emotions. I followed those lesser lights in his circle who observed and captured comical and poignant moments through realistic depictions, even though their art became increasingly musty. Back in the forties and fifties the dichotomy between art and illustration was as profound as black and white. Abstract Expressionism dominated the American art scene and influenced the world too. With few exceptions, abstraction was prohibited in American editorial and advertising art. At first, only a few "modern" pioneers, including Ben Shahn, Robert Weaver, Robert Andrew Parker, and Thomas B. Allen, injected a kind of raw impressionism and astute symbolism into their work. Push Pin Studios' Milton Glaser, Seymour Chwast, Paul Davis, Reynold Ruffins, and James McMullan introduced eclectic references, including the Art Nouveau, Art Deco, Cubism, and Surrealism. In fact, by the early Sixties Surrealism in spirit of Magritte and Dali emerged as a viable commercial style. In Europe, illustration and cartooning was always more sophisticated. The work of Andre Francois, Ronald Searle, Roland Topor, and Jean-Michel Folon was as heady as it was witty. Still, it was not until the late Sixties, in the wake of the historic youth culture revolution of that time, that American illustration became a more personal art form with all the weight of the purer arts.

By this time many of the most influential illustrators had established unique personas as graphic commentators. Ed Sorel, David Levine, Ralph Steadman, and Robert Grossman were among those who expressed social and political opinions with wit and irony through superb drawing and painting skills. They laid the groundwork for the acceptance of illustration as more than a mere replication or interpretation of another's texts. Sure, they were beholden to those manuscripts as a touchstone, but their ideas and concepts complimented rather than supplemented; they could expand upon rather than slavishly follow the word. The late Sixties gave rise to underground comics, psychedelic posters, and other timely stylistic manifestations, but it also reintroduced the history of graphic commentary as a resource for contemporary illustration. Brad Holland was among the pioneers nourished by this history – works by Kathe Kollowitz, Henrich Klee, Georg Grosz, and notably Francesco Goya – and produced illustration that was at once narrative and representational but also replete with a personal vocabulary of new vernacular symbols. Commonly accepted clichés were rejected in favor of mediated freedom. The venerable practice of an art director or editor underlining passages to be illustrated was no longer acceptable. Holland challenged editors not to interfere with his ideas. And once this notion of illustrator as "author" caught on, the floodgates opened for many others.

The above is obviously only a partial story of how illustration evolved into the state we find today – extremely eclectic, defiantly personal, intensely conceptual, astutely witty, and irrepressibly expressive. These are just a few of the viable descriptions of our current art. Once it was possible to see only a few dominant, highly crafted and usually painterly styles. Today, in this volume alone, there are countless ways to draw a cat (or anything else that is either familiar and unfamiliar). While every artist represented has antecedents — both artistry and technique — and some replicate the past and passé styles as though yesterday were today, a stunning number are original. It is possible to identify those artists who "own" their methods — Anita Kunz, Mirko Ilic, Christoph Neimann, Gary Baseman, Hanoch Piven — while others who borrow from history and peers do so by adding a personal touch that shows they are not just mimicking.

There is more actually startling — not just professional or slick — illustration that tests accepted perceptual norms today than ever before. There is more illustration that not only comes close to pure "art" (as in the muse made me do it) than in the past thirty years. And there is more so-called "pure" art that resembles illustration. Representation has come back to art (witness Damien Hirst's latest hyper-realist canvases), narrative is key, sequential progression is formative, and many illustrators have created a repertory of characters and forms that flow seamlessly from one illustration to the next. Realism may only be a fad — rebellion against the overly intellectualized art movements of the late Twentieth and early Twenty-first centuries — but it also may be what art is truly about. The purpose of illustration is to illuminate, to add light but also depth to a manuscript. That much illustration today is often separate from, indeed triggered by forces beyond the traditional manuscript, is testament to the need for illustrators to create. The role of muse-fed artists — to reflect and comment on human essences — are currently assumed by some commercially motivated illustrators. In an age when mass communication prevails, having work reproduced for millions of people to see is as honorable as the rarified art cloistered in a gallery or museum. Publications are museums of the streets, and illustrators provide the good, the bad, and the ugly for these venues.

Sadly, with such a wealth — perhaps even a renaissance — of commercial art, the markets for such are being ever constricted. The rise of photography, the increase of Photoshop and other digital manipulation tools, and the expediency of the stock house have each had a deleterious effect, not on the quality, but on the prolificacy of superior illustration. Perhaps this is merely a stage, but perhaps it is another evolutionary state that this book vividly documents.

Le monde de l'art en évolution

Cela fait maintenant plus de 30 ans que je commande des illustrations éditoriales. Je suis un fan depuis bien plus longtemps encore. J'ai vu des tendances et des modes aller et venir, naître et disparaître, comme le raisin sur la vigne. Enfant, tout comme presque tout le monde aux États-Unis, j'étais pantois d'admiration devant les images que dessinait Norman Rockwell en une du Saturday Evening Post. Il était notre Vermeer. Ses représentations tout à la fois réalistes et idylliques de l'Amérique, ses panoramas romantiques de petites villes et de lieux nostalgiques, dépourvus d'ironie et passionnés, suscitaient des émotions des plus délectables. J'ai suivi ceux de ses disciples qui observaient et capturaient des moments comiques et poignants à travers des représentations réalistes. Mais avec le temps, leur art est devenu de plus en plus dépassé. Dans les années 40 et 50, la dichotomie entre l'art et l'illustration était aussi profonde que celle entre le noir et le blanc. L'expression-

nisme abstrait dominait l'art américain et influençait le reste du monde. A quelques expressions près, l'abstraction était proscrite dans le monde de l'édition et de la publicité
américain. Au début, seule une poignée de pionniers « modernes » dont Ben Shahn, Robert
Weaver, Robert Andrew Parker et Thomas B. Allen injectèrent une espèce d'impressionnisme
brut et de symbolisme astucieux dans leur travail. Milton Glaser, Seymour Chwast, Paul Davis, Reynold Ruffins et James McMullan, des Push Pin Studios, introduisirent des références
éclectiques, dont celles de l'Art Nouveau, de l'Art Déco, du Cubisme et du Surréalisme. En
fait, déjà avant le début des années 60, le surréalisme dans l'esprit de Magritte et de Dali
émergea en tant que style commercial valable. En Europe, l'illustration et le dessin animé
ont toujours été plus sophistiqués. Le travail d'André François, de Ronald Searle, de Roland
Topor et de Jean-Michel Folon était aussi fascinant que spirituel. Mais ce n'est pas avant la
fin des années 60, dans le sillage de la révolution culturelle de la jeunesse de cette époque,
que l'illustration américaine devint une forme d'art plus personnelle dotée du même poids
que les arts les plus purs.

A cette époque, nombre des illustrateurs les plus influents s'étaient déjà établis comme commentateurs graphiques. Ed Sorel, David Levine, Ralph Steadman et Robert Grossman faisaient partie de ceux qui exprimaient des opinions sociales et politiques avec esprit
et ironie en usant de leurs extraordinaires talents de dessinateur et de peintre. C'est grâce
à eux que l'illustration commença à être acceptée comme davantage qu'une simple répli-
que ou interprétation du texte d'un autre. Pour eux, les textes jouaient bien sûr le rôle de
pierre de touche mais leurs idées et concepts étaient plus un complément qu'un supplément
et pouvaient prendre leur envol plutôt que suivre servilement les mots. La fin des années 60
vit naître les BD underground, les affiches psychédéliques et autres manifestations stylisti-
ques opportunes mais réintroduisit également l'histoire du commentaire graphique comme
ressource pour l'illustration contemporaine. Brad Holland était l'un des pionniers nourris
par cette histoire – voir les travaux de Kathe Kollowitz, Henrich Klee, Georg Grosz et tout
particulièrement de Francesco Goya – et créa des illustrations à la fois narratives, repré-
sentatives et pleines d'un vocabulaire personnel de nouveaux symboles vernaculaires. Des
clichés acceptés par le plus grand nombre furent rejetés en faveur d'une liberté négociée.
Le temps où les directeurs artistiques ou les éditeurs soulignaient les passages à illustrer
était révolu. Holland défia les éditeurs d'interférer avec ses idées. Et une fois que cette
notion de l'illustrateur vu comme « auteur » fut populaire, beaucoup d'autres s'engagèrent
dans la brèche.

Ceci n'est évidemment qu'un résumé de la manière dont l'illustration a évolué jusqu'à
l'état qu'on lui connaît aujourd'hui : extrêmement éclectique, insolemment personnelle,
intensément conceptuelle, astucieusement spirituelle et expressive de façon irrépressible.
Les descriptions de cet ouvrage ne sont que quelques-unes des descriptions de l'art tel que
nous le connaissons aujourd'hui. Autrefois, il était possible de ne discerner qu'une poignée
de styles dominants, très travaillés et généralement peints. Aujourd'hui, rien que dans ce
domaine, on dénombre mille et une façons de dessiner un chat (ou n'importe quoi d'autre,
que le sujet soit familier ou non). Si chaque artiste représenté ici a des antécédents, aussi
bien artistiques que techniques, et si certains reproduisent les styles d'autrefois comme
si hier était aujourd'hui, un très grand nombre d'entre eux sont tout à fait originaux. Il est
possible d'identifier les artistes « propriétaires » de leur méthode – Anita Kunz, Mirko Ilic,

Christoph Niemann, Gary Baseman, Hanoch Piven — tandis que ceux qui empruntent à l'histoire et à leurs pairs apportent une touche personnelle qui montrent bien qu'ils font bien plus qu'imiter.

Il y a aujourd'hui plus d'illustrations impressionnantes — et non pas seulement professionnelles et habiles — que jamais auparavant. Il y a davantage d'illustrations qui font plus que s'approcher de l'art pur que durant les trente dernières années réunies. Et il y a davantage d'œuvres d'« art pur » qui s'apparentent à l'illustration. Le figuratif a fait son retour (j'en veux pour preuve les derniers canevas hyper-réalistes de Damien Hirst), la narration est le maître mot, la progression séquentielle est formatrice et de nombreux illustrateurs ont créé un répertoire de personnages et de formes qui circulent sans problème d'une illustration à l'autre. Le réalisme n'est peut-être qu'un engouement — une rébellion contre les mouvements artistiques surintellectualisés de la fin du 20e siècle et du début du 21e siècle — mais peut-être est-il aussi ce qu'est véritablement l'art. Le but de l'illustration est d'illuminer, d'ajouter de la lumière mais aussi de la profondeur à un texte. Ce surcroît d'illustration aujourd'hui est souvent séparé, voire né des forces allant au-delà du texte traditionnel, il témoigne du besoin des illustrateurs de créer. Le rôle des artistes inspirés par des muses — pour refléter et commenter les essences humaines — est actuellement endossé par des illustrateurs motivés par l'aspect commercial. A une époque où la communication de masse prévaut, faire reproduire des travaux pour des millions de gens est aussi honorable que l'est l'art raréfié cloîtré dans une galerie ou un musée. Les publications sont les musées des rues et les illustrateurs en sont les fournisseurs de qualité, de médiocrité et de laideur.

Malheureusement, malgré la richesse — voire la renaissance — de l'art commercial, les marchés disponibles sont de plus en plus restreints. L'essor de la photographie, l'ascension de Photoshop et autres outils de manipulation numérique, et l'opportunisme du « stock house » ont tous un effet délétère, non sur la qualité mais sur la prolificité de l'illustration avec un grand I. Peut-être n'est-ce qu'une phase mais peut-être est-ce aussi un autre stade de l'évolution de l'illustration dont ce recueil se fait le fervent écho.

Kunst im Wandel

Seit mehr als drei Jahrzehnten nehme ich Auftragsarbeiten für Verlage an, und selbst vor dieser Zeit war ich ein begeisterter Fan. Ich habe miterlebt, wie bestimmte Trends und Modeerscheinungen gekommen und gegangen sind, gekommen und geblieben oder wie Eintagsfliegen gestorben sind. Bereits als Kind faszinierten mich Norman Rockwells Titelseiten der Saturday Evening Post, so wie viele andere Amerikaner. Er war unser Vermeer. Durch seine entschlossenen und doch idyllischen Darstellungen Amerikas, seine romantischen Panoramen von Kleinstädten und nostalgischen Orten, frei von jeglicher Ironie und voller Leidenschaft, löste er stets ein Gefühl des Wohlbefindens aus. Ich schloss mich den weniger Auffälligen seines Kreises an, deren Interesse darin bestand, die eher komischen und prägnanten Momente durch realistische Beschreibungen wiederzugeben, auch wenn ihre Arbeiten zunehmend abgedroschener wurden. In den 40er und 50er Jahren könnte man die Dichotomie zwischen Kunst und Illustration als einen Schwarz-Weiss-Kontrast beschreiben. Abstrakter Expressionismus dominierte die amerikanische Kunstszene und hatte ausserdem Einfluss auf die ganze Welt. Von wenigen Ausnahmen abgesehen, war abstrakte Kunst im amerikanischen Verlagswesen und der Werbebranche verboten. Anfangs waren es nur einige wenige "moderne" Pioniere, wie Ben Shahn, Robert Weaver, Robert Andrew Parker und Thomas B. Allen, die eine Art harten Impressionismus und intelligenten Symbolismus in ihre Arbeiten einfliessen liessen. Push Pin Studios' Milton Glaser, Seymour Chwast, Paul Davis, Reynold Ruffins sowie James McMullan brachten erstmals eklektische Referenzen mit ein, darunter Art Nouveau, Art Deco, Kubismus und Surrealismus. Tatsache ist, dass Anfang der 60er Jahre der Surrealismus im Sinne von Magritte und Dali als kommerzielle Stilrichtung grosse Anerkennung fand. In Europa bewegten sich Illustration und Comiczeichnung immer schon auf weitaus höherem Niveau. Die Arbeiten von Andre Francois, Ronald Searle, Roland Topor und Jean-Michel Folon waren sowohl intelligent als auch geistreich. Dennoch dauerte es bis in die späten 60er Jahre — ausgelöst durch die historische Revolution der Jugendkultur -, bis sich Illustration in Amerika als eigene Kunstform und mit dem vergleichbaren Ansehen eines reinen Kunsstils etablieren konnte.

Bis zu diesem Zeitpunkt hatten schon viele der einflussreichen Illustratoren ihre Funktion als grafische Meinungsbildner begonnen. Ed Sorel, David Levine, Ralph Steadman sowie Robert Grossmann zählten zu den Künstlern, die ihre politische Meinung und Sozialkritik durch faszinierende Mal- und Zeichentechniken mit Geist und Ironie an die Öffentlichkeit trugen. Sie waren diejenigen, die den Grundstein für die Akzeptanz der Illustration legten und dieser einen höheren Stellenwert als die reine Reproduktion oder Interpretation eines bereits existierenden Textes gaben. Sicherlich sahen sie diese Manuskripte als Prüfstein, doch darüberhinaus ergänzten sich ihre Ideen und Konzepte; darauf konnten sie aufbauen, anstatt nur stumpfsinnig dem Wortverlauf zu folgen. Die späten 60er brachten zum Einen die sogenannten Untergrund-Comics, Psychoposter sowie andere zeitgemässe Manifeste hervor, zum Anderen waren sie bezeichnend für das erneute Erscheinen von grafischen Stellungnahmen als Quelle zeitgeschichtlicher Illustration. Brad Holland war einer der Pioniere, beeinflusst durch die Geschichte und die Arbeiten von Käthe Kollwitz, Henrich Klee, Georg Grosz und vor allem Francesco Goya. Seine Illustrationen waren sowohl narrativ als auch repräsentativ und trotzdem fehlte es ihnen nicht an persönlichem Vokabular neuer mundartlicher Symbolik. Allgemein akzeptierte Klischees wurden abgewiesen und statt dessen fand vermittelbare Freiheit Anerkennung. Die herkömmliche Arbeitsweise eines Art Directors oder Verlegers, die darin bestand, Textabschnitte zu markieren und diese zu illustrieren, wurde nicht mehr akzeptiert. Holland provozierte ganz bewusst seine Verleger und verlangte, sich in seine Ideen nicht einzumischen. Nach und nach wurde nun der Illustrator in der Rolle des Autors anerkannt und ebnete den Weg für viele andere.

Offensichtlich ist das bisher Geschriebene nur ein kleiner Teil der Entwicklung der Illustration bis hin zum heutigen Stand - extrem eklektisch, unverschämt persönlich, stark konzeptual, geistreich, witzig und unschlagbar expressiv. Dies sind nur einige wenige der möglichen Beschreibungen unserer derzeitigen Kunst. Früher gab es nur ein paar dominante, kunstvolle und anerkannte Stilrichtungen. Heutzutage, alleine in dieser Ausgabe, werden unzählige Möglichkeiten aufgezeigt, um beispielsweise eine Katze zu zeichnen (oder sonst irgendetwas, bekannt oder unbekannt). Während jeder hier vorgestellte Künstler ein Wissen sowohl auf künstlerischer als auch technischer Ebene mit sich bringt, und einige sogar die Vergangenheit und vergangene Stilrichtungen gerade so behandeln, als seien sie wieder modern, gibt es dennoch eine Vielfalt an Ursprünglichem. Die Künstler mit einer ganz individuellen Arbeitsmethodik wie Anita Kunz, Mirko Ilic, Christoph Niemann, Gary Baseman und Hanoch Piven, sind klar zu identifizieren. Andere wiederum lehnen sich an historische Arbeiten und Künstler an und fügen ihre persönliche Note hinzu, woran zu erkennen ist, dass sie nicht nur Kopieren.

Es gibt eine Vielzahl geradezu alarmierender Illustration - und nicht nur rein professioneller Art -, die akzeptierte Wahrnehmungsformen mehr denn je auf die Waagschale legt. Es gibt heute weitaus mehr Illustration, die der reinen Kunstform gleichkommt als in den vergangenen 30 Jahren. Und es gibt mehr sogenannte "reine" Kunst, die den Anschein von Illustration hat. Die Repräsentation hat ihren Weg zurück zur Kunst gefunden (Beweis sind Damien Hirsts letzte hyperrealistische Leinwände), die Erzählung ist entscheidend, eine fortlaufende Weiterentwicklung formgebend und einige Illustratoren haben sogar ein Repertoire an Charakteren und Formen kreiert, das fliessend von einer Illustration zur nächsten übergeht. Realismus kann ganz einfach nur eine Modeerscheinung sein - eine Auflehnung gegen die extrem intellektuellen Kunstbewegungen des späten 20. und frühen 21. Jahrhunderts - es kann aber auch schlicht und einfach das verkörpern, was Kunst wirklich ist. Die Absicht von Illustration ist es, zu beleuchten, einem Manuskript sowohl Licht, als auch Tiefe hinzuzufügen. Die Tatsache, dass heutzutage Illustration oft getrennt, ja sogar mit aller Macht vom traditionellen Manuskript losgelöst ist, ist Beweis für das Bedürfnis der Illustratoren, zu kreieren. Reflektion und Stellungnahme zu menschlichen Bedürfnissen wird derzeit von einigen kommerziell orientierten Künstlern ausgeübt. Ein Kunstwerk für Millionen von Menschen zu reproduzieren in einem Zeitalter, in dem Massenkommunikation die Norm ist, ist ebenso ehrenvoll, wie die Kunst, die man in einer Galerie oder einem Museum wiederfindet. Publikationen sind die Museen der Strasse und die Illustratoren bieten die guten, die schlechten und die hässlichen Dinge dafür.

Trotz all diesen Reichtums an kommerzieller Kunst - vielleicht sollte man es sogar Renaissance nennen -, sind die Märkte dafür leider eher begrenzt. Die Popularität der Fotografie, die Zunahme von Photoshop und anderen digitalen Manipulationsmitteln sowie die Zweckdienlichkeit von Archiven haben alle einen schädlichen Einfluss, nicht auf die Qualität, aber auf die Lebensdauer hervorragender Illustration ausgeübt. Vielleicht handelt es sich hierbei nur um eine Phase, doch ist es vielleicht eine neue revolutionäre Phase, die besonders lebendig in diesem Buch dokumentiert wird.

Contents

Contents

Jorge Alderete

Pop illustration, which uses trash culture, 50's science fiction films, wrestling and surf music imagery in a psychotropic illustrations, animations and comics.

Illustrations, animations et BD pop et psychotropiques qui s'inspirent de la culture trash, des films de science-fiction des années 50, de l'imagerie musicale du surf et du catch.

Pop-Illustration, die sich der „trash culture" bedient, Science-Fiction-Filme aus den 50er Jahren, Kämpfer und Surfmusikbilder in psychotropischer Illustration, Animation und Comics.

www.jorgealderete.com

NAME: Jorge Alderete **LOCATION:** Mexico City, Mexico **CONTACT:** contacto@jorgealderete.com **TOOLS:** Paper & Pencil, Corel Draw, Adobe Photoshop. **AWARDS:** SND Society for News Design, International Prize a! Diseño (Mexico) **CLIENTS:** MTV, Once TV, El Pais, Clarín, Sitges Film Festival, T-26 digital type foundry, Union Fonts, Die Gestalten Verlag, Iconography 2, Place, Tiki Art Now.

Miki Amano

I like to draw. I like to draw sad things. I like to draw strong things. I like to draw fun and clever things too. In fact, my illustration oeuvre is full of cute, forlorn, and independent women. Usually this combination of qualities in a female goes unseen. That's why I find creating these images particularly satisfying. My hope is that others find comfort in girls like these too.

J'aime dessiner. J'aime dessiner des choses tristes. J'aime dessiner des choses fortes. J'aime aussi dessiner des choses amusantes et intelligentes. En fait, mon œuvre illustrative est remplie de femmes belles, tristes et indépendantes. Cette combinaison de qualités que peut avoir une femme passe généralement aperçue. C'est pourquoi je trouve particulièrement gratifiant de créer ces images. J'ai l'espoir que d'autres trouvent aussi du réconfort auprès de jeunes femmes comme les miennes.

Ich zeichne gerne. Ich zeichne gerne traurige Dinge. Ich zeichne gerne starke Dinge. Außerdem zeichne ich gerne lustige und intelligente Sachen. Tatsache ist, dass mein Illustrationswerk voller niedlicher, verlassener und unabhängiger Frauen ist. Eine solche Kombination weiblicher Qualitäten ist eher ungewöhnlich. Gerade deshalb befriedigt mich die Kreation solcher Bilder. Ich hoffe, dass auch andere Trost bei den von mir dargestellten Mädchen finden werden.

www.mikiamano.com

NAME: Miki Amano **LOCATION:** Tokyo, Japan **CONTACT:** mikiamano@mikiamano.com **TOOLS:** pen, ink, silk-screen, photography, collage, Adobe Photoshop, Adobe Illustrator. **AWARDS:** Design Fort Netdiver.com, Parsons School of Design NY, Stereotypography CD-R Design Competition. **AGENT:** Traffic <trafficnyc.com> **CLIENTS:** Jane Magazine, YM, Bust, Cosmo Girl, Journal Standard Japan, TAP, Calypso, New School University.

IMAGINATION

Creativity isn't about being a kook. It's about using the raw material inside you to become the amazing, independent woman you are. By Kierna Mayo

Long before I landed my dream job as a magazine editor, I'd look at fashion magazines and wonder how those pages came to be. I didn't know a thing about what it was like to be at a photo shoot or how editors shaped the stories I read. All I knew was that reading magazines made me fantasize about a world that seemed a lot more exciting than mine. When I was bored, I'd grab a magazine and get lost in dreams. I'm convinced that all that imagining I did back then led me to exactly where I am today. You may think using your imagination is for children, but it actually goes way beyond a little girl tying a blanket around her neck and running around proclaiming, "I am Supergirl!"

What the child in you knows *instinctively* is that imagination is about planting a seed of possibility in your own mind. When you fantasize, there are no boundaries; you can be or do whatever wild idea you create! That's why it's one of the most important things you can do to shape your future. After all, if you don't *see* it, how can you ever *be* it? Just think, the Wright brothers defied gravity and invented the airplane. And even before personal computers were must-haves, someone imagined a world where people would instantly receive electronic mail. Well, we can all thank the power of imagination for the airplanes and e-mail we love. I use Julia Cameron's best-selling book *The Artist's Way* (Tarcher/Putnam, 2002, $11, **amazon.com**) to boost my imagination. So fine-tune your own fantasies with these exercises and see how far you can go.

OPEN UP TO POSSIBILITIES

You know that saying "Free your mind"? Truth is, that's how ideas flow more readily—but it's not always easy. One thing that helps is freestyle writing. So set your alarm for a half-hour earlier, and every morning before you start your day, try to write one complete page of stream-of-consciousness thoughts before you roll out of bed. Write about *anything* without worrying about making sense. Just jot down what you think as it pops into your head. I've been doing this forever, and now I hardly miss a day because it really does help to open me up to all my thoughts and emotions. Like one time, I started writing about my 1-year-old niece dressed up as a Teletubby and somehow ended up scribbling about how I hate the way my house shakes when the bus goes by! See what I mean? It's not about correct spelling or penmanship. It's about letting your mind run wild. By exercising your imagination muscle every day, you're better able to tap into your imagination—whether it's to come up with a cool project topic, figure out a summer plan, whatever.

GO BACK TO THE FUTURE

One way to help you realize just how many possibilities are out there is by time traveling—zeroing in on where you've been and where you'd like to go. So when you have some private time, grab a photo of yourself from when you were about 6 and try to remember what you were like then. Sit quietly with your photo and gaze into that little girl's eyes. Then close your eyes and try to relive the sensation of being a child. What comes to mind? Do you remember your first roller-coaster ride? With your eyes still closed, add about 20 years to that girl's life. Now you are in your future! Is your future self living just down the road from where you live now—or have you ended up in a completely different part of the country, far from what you've known? Time travel reminds me that where I am now is not where I was or where I will be—and that's true for you too.

WEAR A DIFFERENT HAT

Sometimes it's hard to dream big because you're so used to all the confines of being who you are. So instead of trying to imagine a different version of yourself, try to imagine yourself as someone completely different. Who are you? What kind of style do you have? Maybe in real life, you're tone deaf, but in another life, you're an opera star, an FBI agent—or a stay-at-home mom with three kids. Think being a rancher would be cool, but you've never even ridden a horse? So what?! Pick your most exciting life and make that your theme for a day. Like, if you choose to be a real estate agent, walk around your neighborhood and try to guess how much each home is worth. If you just allow imagination to lead you to real fun, you'll get to try out all kinds of new things.

GO ON SOLO DATES

How else can you help yourself tap into your imagination? By taking yourself out on creative "dates." One weekend afternoon, go out without any money and just walk around, paying attention to the interesting sights and people who can inspire the creativity in you. If there's a museum or an art gallery in your neighborhood, stop by. If you take the time to notice, you'll find inspiration everywhere. I love to look at the architecture of old buildings, eavesdrop on interesting conversations, pay attention to the shapes of clouds, and window-shop. And if I do fall in love with an outfit in a window, instead of figuring out how I can get enough money to buy it, I ask myself how I might create something similar with a cool DIY touch.

Doing things like this will help you become the kind of person who truly enjoys her own company. With a good imagination, you're never bored—when you free yourself to fantasize, new worlds open up. And that kind of power will make you more independent than you thought possible. But like magic, imagination only works if you believe in it. So just *imagine* all that imagination can do for you! ▯

butterfly effect: It's just my new perfume.... Like it?

ILLUSTRATION BY MIKI AMANO

Jean-Marie Angles

Most of my inspiration comes from the cinema. I've been influenced by movies of Fellini, specially the most stylised like Casanova or Satyricon. I'm trying to evoke an atmosphere with few characters and few elements of settings and a coloured background, like the scene of the detective in Minnelli`s movie "Band Wagon". The visual aspect of my characters comes from the 60's "cine-bis" (like Mario Bava, Jesus Franco, Umberto Lenzi, etc) and the 60's Bollywood movies.

Le cinéma est ma principale source d'inspiration. Je suis influencé par les films de Fellini et particulièrement ceux les plus stylisés, Casanova et Satyricon par exemple. J'essaie de créer une atmosphère à l'aide de quelques personnages, de quelques éléments de décor et d'un fond coloré, tout comme dans la scène du détective dans le film « Band Wagon » de Minelli. L'aspect visuel de mes personnages vient du ciné-bis des années 60 (tel que celui de Mario Bava, de Jesus Franco ou d'Umberto Lenzi) et des films de Bollywood des années 60 également.

Ich lasse mich hauptsächlich im Kino inspirieren. Mich haben Filme von Fellini beeindruckt, vor allem herausragende Filme wie „Casanova" oder „Satyricon". Ich versuche, ein Ambiente mit wenigen Charakteren zu schaffen, einer einfachen Umgebungsbeschreibung und einem farbigen Hindergrund, wie z.B. die Szene des Detektivs aus Minellis Film "Band Wagon". Die visuellen Aspekte meiner Charaktere stammen aus den 60ern "cine-bis" (Mario Bava, Jesus Franco, Umberto Lenzi, etc.) und den 60er Bollywood-Filmen.

NAME: Jean-Marie Angles **LOCATION:** Lille, France **CONTACT:** j-m.angles@wanadoo.fr **TOOLS:** my characters are made with Plastibo (a synthetic material) shaped on a wire frame work. **AGENT:** Illustrissimo <www.illustrissimo.com> **CLIENTS:** Telecom (France), Femina, Danone, Albin Michel, Caisse D'epargne, etc.

Jorge Arévalo

The Macintosh is just a tool and not an illustration style. I am a graphic designer, so my works depend on format, printing, paper, text and spirit of the publications. That means that illustration should not be an isolated element.

Le Macintosh n'est qu'un outil, pas un style d'illustration. Étant graphiste, mes travaux dépendent du format, de l'impression, du papier, du texte et de l'esprit des publications. Ceci signifie que l'illustration ne doit pas constituer un élément isolé.

Der Macintosh ist ein reines Werkzeug, kein Illustrationsstil. Ich bin Grafikdesigner und demnach hängen meine Arbeiten von Format, Druck, Papier, Text und dem Geist der Veröffentlichungen ab. Das bedeutet, dass Illustration kein isoliertes Element darstellen sollte.

NAME: Jorge Arévalo **LOCATION:** Spain **CONTACT:** contacto@jorgearevalo.com **TOOLS:** Macromedia Freehand. **AWARDS:** Society for New Design Award (Gold/Silver), Special mention at Baseline magazine. **AGENT:** The Yellow Group (USA) <www.the-yellow-group.com> **CLIENTS:** Rolling Stone, Reporter, and magazines for Telefónica, BBVA, Leroy Merlín, FNAC, etc.

Ana **Bagayan**

I don't think style or concept can stand alone, one without the other. I like to use subtle humour, a dark twist, and a lot of detail in my artwork to pull the viewer in.

Je crois que style et concept ne vont pas l'un sans l'autre. Pour capturer l'attention de l'observateur, j'aime utiliser un humour subtil, un côté obscur et beaucoup de détails.

Ich denke, Stil und Konzept kann man nicht voneinander trennen. Ich verwende bei meiner Arbeit gerne versteckten Humor, einen dunklen Schatten und eine Menge an Details, um die Aufmerksamkeit des Beobachters zu erlangen.

www.anabagayan.com

NAME: Ana Bagayan **LOCATION:** California, USA **CONTACT:** anabagayan@aol.com **TOOLS:** Oil on panel. **CLIENTS:** Rolling Stone, Spin magazine, GQ, Portland Mercury Newspaper, Babe Films, Mighty Fine, Boston Magazine.

Istvan Banyai

An organic combination of turn-of-the-century Viennese retro, interjected with American pop, some European absurdity added for flavour, served on a cartoon-style colour palette... no social realism added.

Un mélange naturel de rétro viennois début de siècle, saupoudré de pop américain et d'absurdité européenne pour donner de la saveur, servi sur une palette de couleurs style dessin animé. Aucun réalisme social ajouté.

Eine organische Kombination aus Viennese Retro um die Jahrhundertwende, vermischt mit amerikanischem Pop, ein bisschen europäische Absurdität für den Geschmack und das Ganze serviert auf einer Farbpalette im Zeichentrickstil...ohne jegliche Zugabe von Sozialrealismus.

www.ist-one.com

NAME: Istvan Banyai **LOCATION:** New York, USA **CONTACT:** ibanyai@sbcglobal.net **TOOLS:** Pencil on paper, scan, Adobe Photoshop, or inked and painted on animation cell. **AWARDS:** Children's Choice Award, Print Magazine, New York Time bookreview, best book of the Year/Zoom. **CLIENTS:** New Yorker, Playboy, Esquire, Rolling Stone, Sony, Verve Records, Nickelodeon, MTV, Absolut Vodka, etc.

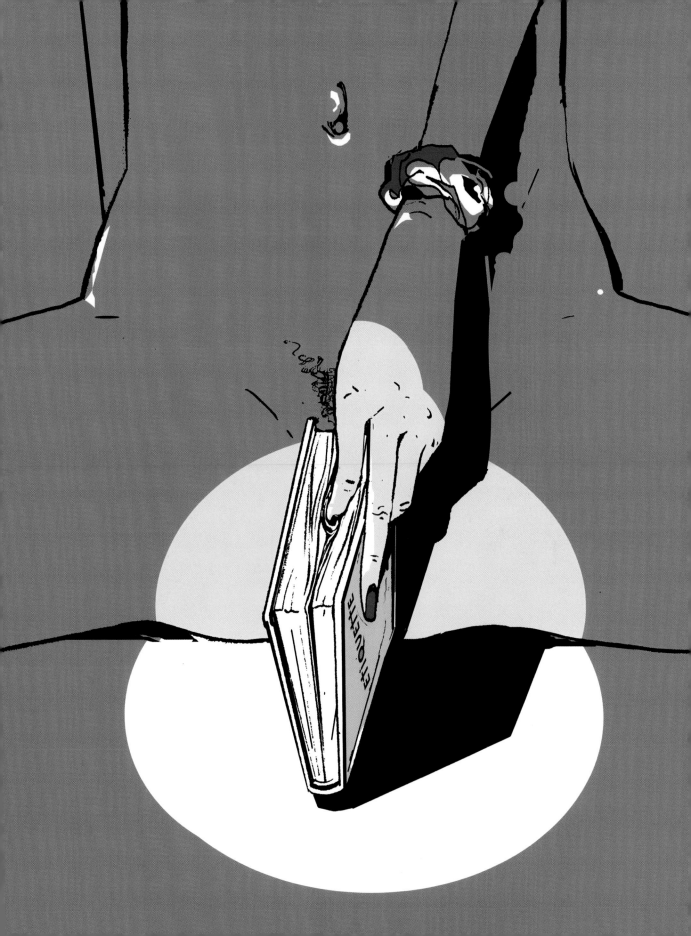

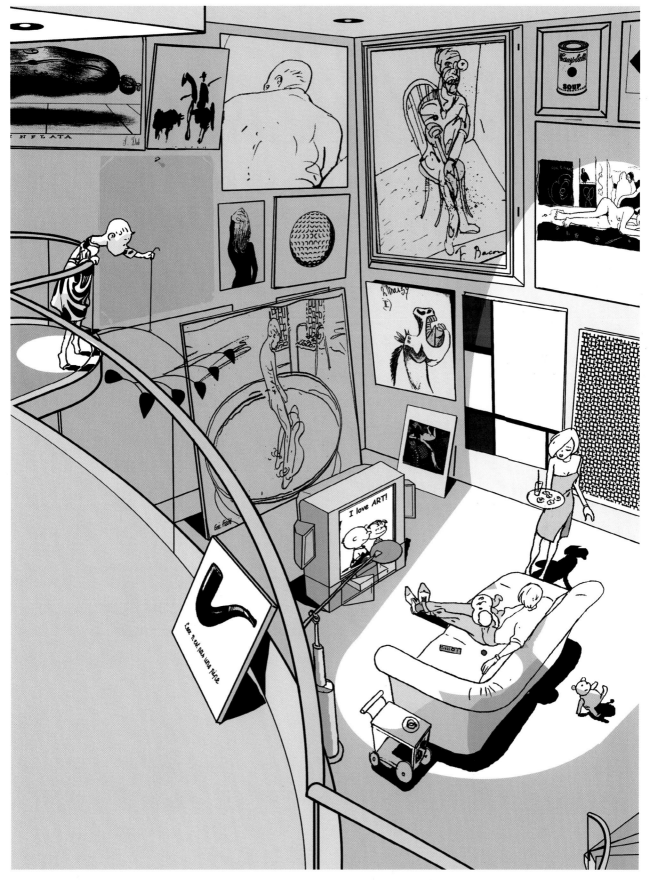

THE NEW YORKER

THE NEW YORKER

Shawn **Barber**

Every assignment is a new challenge. I really try to come up with the most appropriate image for each given assignment and don't try to force a specific style on the work. When I first started out, I was forcing a style- the past couple of years, I have been much more comfortable and confident with my work and process, and have allowed the working process to define the final outcome. The most exciting part of this business, for me, is not knowing what will come next.

Chaque commande est un nouveau défi. J'essaie vraiment de trouver l'image la plus appropriée à chaque commande et je ne tente pas d'imposer un style spécifique à mon travail. A mes débuts, j'essayais de m'imposer un style. Ces dernières années, je suis beaucoup plus à l'aise et plus sûr dans mon travail et dans ma méthodologie. Je laisse le processus de travail définir le résultat final. Pour moi, le plus fascinant dans ce métier est de ne pas savoir ce dont demain sera fait.

Jeder Auftrag ist eine neue Herausforderung. Ich versuche stets, das angemessene Image für jedes Produkt zu finden, anstatt diesem einen bestimmten Stil aufzuzwingen. Anfangs tat ich das, doch im Laufe der Jahre habe ich an Vertrauen gewonnen, fühle mich immer wohler im Prozess und gestatte es dem Arbeitsverlauf, das Endresultat zu bestimmen. Der aufregendste Teil in diesem Beruf ist es, nie zu wissen, was als Nächstes kommt.

www.sdbarber.com

NAME: Shawn Barber **LOCATION:** San Francisco, CA, USA **CONTACT:** seen970@hotmail.com **TOOLS:** oil paint, acrylic paint. **AWARDS:** RSVP Portraits, Communication Arts, American Illustration, Society of Illustrators, The Artist's Magazine. **AGENT:** Magnet Reps <www.magnetreps.com> **CLIENTS:** Atlantic Records, The New Yorker, The Grammy Awards, Rolling Stone, Converse, Scholastic Books, GQ, MTV Networks, The Source, Maxim, Elektra Records, Target, Hoffman Bikes, T.E.D. Conference, etc.

Urbanities

Getting the most out of life in the city.

CALENDAR

JULY 10 - AUG 10
Performance: Cirque du Soleil
The 1994 extravaganza from this Quebec-by-way-of-Las-Vegas troupe, "Alegría" features synchro trapeze, aerial high bars, Mongolian contortion, fire knife dancing, tumbling, catching and all sorts of athletic showmanship, all lightly dusted with cheese, but still thrilling. At the Grand Chapiteau, a "state of the art big top" (who knew?) at Cambie Bridge and Pacific Boulevard. 800-361-4595. Cirquedusoleil.com

JULY 18 - 20
Music: Vancouver Folk Music Festival
Not just for hippies and helicopter dancers.

CONTINUED ON PAGE 70

JULY 21
Elvis Costello
A.k.a. the Emotional Toothpaste, a.k.a. Little Napoleon, a.k.a. Mr. Diana Krall. In concert with Steve Nieve. (See page 70 for details.)

SHAWN BARBER

Christian Barthold

I use a big range of graphic design- and illustration-styles, and have always been interested in things I haven't done before. But what I'll always like is to combine different techniques, ranging from simple drawings to photorealistic imagery. My recent work is slightly surrealistic imagery ranging from an artist's sketchbook-look to fashion.

J'ai recours à un large éventail de styles de graphisme et d'illustration et ai toujours été intéressé par ce que je n'ai jamais fait auparavant. Mais ce que j'aime par dessus tout c'est combiner diverses techniques allant de simples dessins à l'imagerie photo-réaliste. Mon travail le plus récent est constitué d'images légèrement surréalistes inspirées aussi bien des carnets d'esquisses d'artistes que de la mode.

Ich wende viele verschiedene Stile des Grafikdesigns und der Illustration an, und war schon immer daran interessiert, neue Dinge auszuprobieren. Was mir stets gefallen wird, ist die Kombination von verschiedenen Techniken, von einfachen Zeichnungen bis hin zu fotorealistischen Bildern. Meine letzte Arbeit weist surrealistische Bildelemente auf, von dem Künstler-Sketchbook-Look bis hin zu Fashion.

http://christian-barthold.illustration.de

NAME: Christian Barthold **LOCATION:** Cologne, Germany **CONTACT:** weaverofyourdreams@gmx.de **TOOLS:** Adobe Photoshop, Collage (by hand), pencil, acrylics, photography. **CLIENTS:** Die Zeit, ZeitLeben, Wirtschaftswoche, Capital, Impulse, Stern, Psychologie Heute, SmartBooks (Switzerland), Hansol Education (Korea), ImageSource (UK).

Gary Baseman

I am a visual problem solver. I find the essence of what needs to be communicated and hit the viewer over the head and smash his or her brain all over the heart of my image.

Ma manière de résoudre les problèmes est visuelle. Au cœur de mon image, je trouve ce qui doit être communiqué et frapper le cerveau de l'observateur.

Ich löse Probleme auf visuellem Weg. Ich finde die Essenz dessen, was Kommuniziert werden soll, versetze dem Beobachter einen Schlag auf den Kopf und zerschlage sein oder ihr gesamtes Gehirn direkt über dem Herzen meines Bildes.

www.garybaseman.com

NAME: Gary Baseman **LOCATION:** Los Angeles, CA, USA **CONTACT:** basemanart@earthlink.net **TOOLS:** blood and guts. **AWARDS:** Emmys, BAFTA, American Illustration, Art Director's Club, 100 Show, D&AD. **CLIENTS:** Time, New Yorker, Cranium, Nike, Rolling Stone, Mercedes Benz.

David von Bassewitz

...to increase the speed of light by an idea...

... accélérer la vitesse de la lumière avec une idée...

...die Lichtgeschwindigkeit um einen Gedanken beschleunigen...

www.davidvonbassewitz.de

NAME: David von Bassewitz **LOCATION:** Hamburg, Germany **CONTACT:** mail@davidvonbassewitz.de **TOOLS:** mixed media. **AWARDS:** ADC, Grand Prix Européen de Bande **AGENT:** Contours <www.contours-art.de> **CLIENTS:** Die Zeit, Publicis, Brot für die Welt.

Melinda **Beck**

My work is ever changing because I don't want to become bored or complacent. When I develop a method to the point where I am satisfied I feel the need to alter it again so that I'm not making the same image over and over. I enjoy the process, trying new things, and the experience of discovery.

Ne voulant ni m'ennuyer ni devenir suffisante, je fais en sorte que mon travail soit en constante évolution. Lorsque je suis enfin satisfaite d'une méthode que j'ai élaborée, je ressens le besoin de la modifier afin de ne pas toujours répéter les mêmes images. J'aime les processus d'expérimentation et de découverte.

Meine Arbeiten unterliegen einem ständigen Wechsel, da ich mich weder langweilen noch träge werden möchte. Wenn ich eine neue Methode zu meiner Zufriedenheit entwickelt habe, verspüre ich den Drang, sie wieder zu ändern, um nicht die gleichen Bilder zu wiederholen. Mir gefällt der Prozess, neue Erfahrungen zu sammeln und stets neue Entdeckungen zu machen.

www.melindabeck.com

NAME: Melinda Beck **LOCATION:** New York, USA **CONTACT:** studio@melindabeck.com **TOOLS:** pen, ink, collage, mixed media, Adobe Photoshop. **AWARDS:** AIGA, American Illustration, The Art Directors Club, Communication Arts, ID Magazine, Print Magazine, The Society of Publication Designers, and The Society of Illustrators.
CLIENTS: Nickelodeon, Nike, MTV, Island Records, Entertainment Weekly, Rolling Stone, Newsweek, The New York Times, The Progressive, and Time Magazine.

THE LAST RIDE OF THE POLO SHIRT BANDIT

WILLIAM GUESS WAS HIS NAME—AND IT WAS PROPHETIC. WHEN HE SHOT HIMSELF WHILE SURROUNDED BY THE POLICE, HE LEFT UNANSWERED THE QUESTION THAT HAD STUMPED HIS PURSUERS: WHY DID AN ORDINARY MIDDLE-CLASS TEXAN TURN INTO THE MOST PROLIFIC BANK ROBBER IN THE STATE'S HISTORY? BY HELEN THORPE

Sarah Beetson

I work completely by hand, combining strong line drawings with an inexhaustive variety of mixed media. I am particularly inspired by fashion and vintage clothing and paraphernalia, the movies of John Waters, rock music, Bernard Willhelm, Gaultier and Galliano, old restaurant signs and logos from bars, cafes and fairgrounds across the globe.

Je travaille entièrement à la main et combine des dessins à base de traits épais avec une variété inépuisable de supports. Je m'inspire tout particulièrement de la mode et des vêtements et accessoires vintage, des films de John Waters, du rock, de Bernard Willhelm, de Gaultier et de Galliano, des enseignes anciennes de restaurant et des logos de bars, des cafés et des champs de foire du monde entier.

Ich arbeite nur frei Hand, eine Kombination aus starker Linienzeichnung und einer unerschöpflichen Vielfalt unterschiedlicher Medien. Vor allem inspiriert mich Mode und Vintage-Klamotten, Paraphernalia sowie Filme von John Waters, Rockmusik, Bernhard Willhelm, Gaultier und Galliano, alte Restaurantschilder sowie Logos von Bars, Cafes und Messeanlagen der ganzen Welt.

NAME: Sarah Beetson **LOCATION:** London, Uk **CONTACT:** sarahb@illustrationweb.com; sarahbeets@hotmail.com **TOOLS:** fluro gluepaint, stickie dots, canadian beer stickers, sweeties and sweetie wrappers, sequins, papers, australian apple labels. **AWARDS:** Pentland Prize for Fine Art, presented by Wayne Hemingway of Red or Dead. **AGENT:** i2iart (Canada) <www.i2iart.com>; Illustration ltd <www.illustrationweb.com> **CLIENTS:** Garden Life, Stella McCartney, Ford, Scholastic, etc.

Bildbad

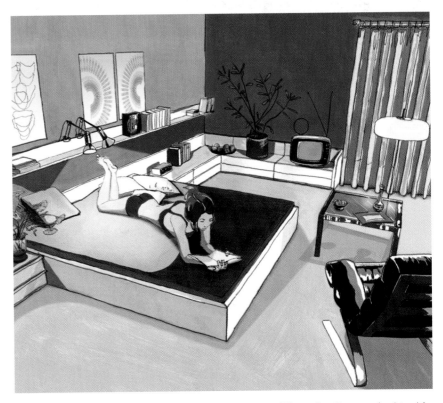

We are artists, who have specialised in 3D- design, animation and illustration. Our network exists within different design areas, finding extensive creative solutions on a high standard.

Nous sommes des artistes spécialisés dans le design, l'animation et les illustrations en 3D. Notre réseau s'étend sur différents domaines du design, ce qui nous permet d'établir de vastes solutions créatives de grande qualité.

Wir sind Künstler, spezialisiert auf 3D-Design, Animation und Illustration. Unser Netzwerk verläuft durch verschiedene Designbereiche, anhand derer wir umfassende und kreative Lösungen mit hohem Standard bieten können.

www.bildbad.de

NAME: Bildbad: Jutta Melsheimer & Kai Hofmann **LOCATION:** Berlin, Germany **CONTACT:** jutta@bildbad.de, kai@bildbad.de **TOOLS:** Adobe Photoshop, Discreet 3D Studio Max, pencil, gouache, etc. **AWARDS:** Miss Digital World, etc. **AGENT:** Schoenhals < www.schoenhals.de> **CLIENTS:** BBDO InterOne, Brigitte, Gruner & Jahr, GQ, Grey Worldwide, Ebay, McCann-Erickson, Ogilvy, Oral-B, Deutsche Telekom, Schering, expedia.de.

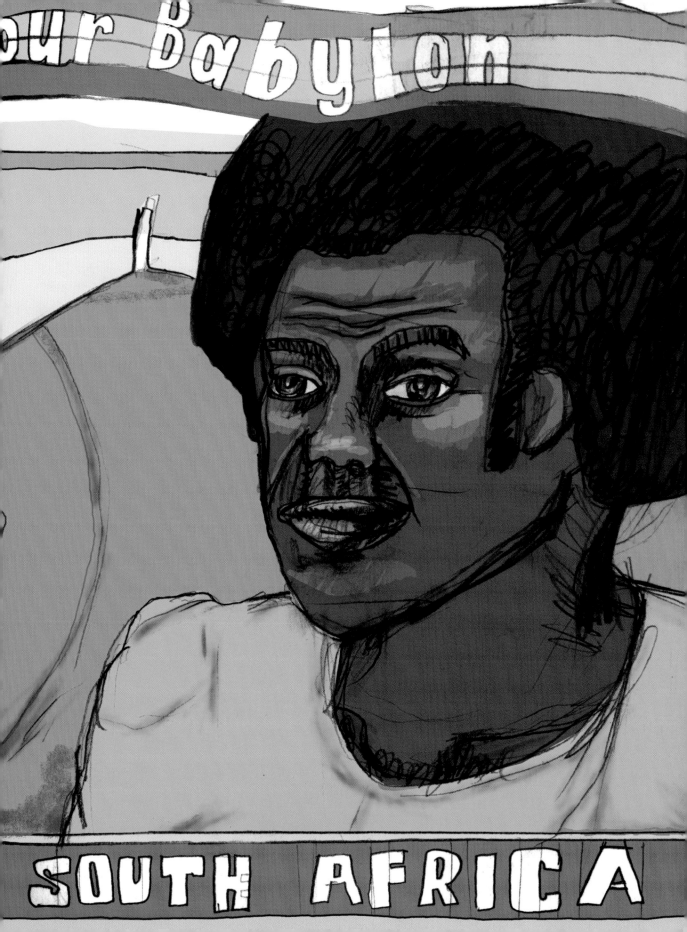

What I consider my best work, is mostly illustrations for which I am granted total freedom, like the series I do for the Atlantic Monthly, and for the stories I write and illustrate for children's books. Yet, I remain "addicted" to impossible deadlines, and stories deemed impossible to illustrate by art directors.

Mes meilleurs travaux sont selon moi les illustrations pour lesquelles je jouis de la liberté la plus totale, comme les séries que je fais pour l'Atlantic Monthly et les histoires que j'écris et illustre pour des livres pour enfants. Mais je reste « accro » à des délais impossibles et à des histoires considérées impossibles à illustrer par les directeurs artistiques.

Meine besten Arbeiten sind ohne Zweifel solche, bei denen ich absolute Freiheit hatte, wie zum Beispiel die Serie, die ich für Atlantic Monthly gestalte, und auch die Geschichten, die ich für Kinderbücher schreibe und illustriere. Trotz allem bin ich nach wie vor abhängig von unerreichbaren Deadlines und Geschichten, die von Art Directors schon als unmöglich zu Illustrieren abgetan wurden.

www.guybillout.com

NAME: Guy Billout **LOCATION:** Fairfield, CT, USA **CONTACT:** guy@guybillout.com **TOOLS:** watercolor and airbrush, Adobe Photoshop for corrections. **AWARDS:** Society of Illustrators NY (3 Gold/2 Silver), Hamilton King Award of the Society of Illustrators NY, 10 best illustrated children's book (New York Times List) **AGENT:** Margarethe Hubauer <www.margarethe.de> **CLIENTS:** Times, Fortune, The New Yorker, Playboy, Le Monde, Vogue, Glamour, Esquire, Mobil, JP Morgan, Met Life, Comcast, etc.

Jens Bonnke

As in other visual art forms like film, photography or painting, it's most crucial for an illustrator to come up with a good image. The final artwork should be exciting, surprising or somehow striking to the viewer - apart from being a witty visual translation of the content, of course. One of the biggest inspirations for my work is Goya's "El sueño de la razon produce monstruos" - "The sleep of reason brings forth monsters".

Comme dans d'autres formes d'art visuel comme le cinéma, la photographie ou la peinture, l'essentiel pour un illustrateur est de créer une bonne image. Le produit fini doit être excitant, surprenant ou même frappant, en plus bien sûr d'être une traduction visuelle spirituelle du contenu. L'une de mes plus grandes sources d'inspiration est l'œuvre de Goya intitulée "El sueño de la razon produce monstruos" (Le sommeil de la raison produit des monstres).

Genauso wie bei anderen visuellen Künsten wie Film, Fotografie oder Gemälden ist es auch bei der Illustration ganz entscheidend, ein gutes Bild zu schaffen. Das Kunstwerk sollte aufregend sein, eine überraschung bieten oder zumindest den Betrachter berühren - abgesehen von einer intelligenten Wiedergabe seines Inhaltes. Eine besondere Inspiration für meine Arbeiten ist für mich Goyas Werk "El sueño de la razon produce monstruos" - "Der Traum der Vernunft gebiert Ungeheuer".

www.jensbonnke.com

NAME: Jens Bonnke **LOCATION:** Berlin, Germany **CONTACT:** jb@jensbonnke.com **TOOLS:** Digital scratchboard. **CLIENTS:** ARD, Berliner Zeitung, Cornelsen, Geldidee, Haffmans, Junge Karriere, Jung von Matt, Das Magazin, MetaDesign, Petra, Piper, Playboy, Readers Digest, Rolling Stone, Römerturm, Scholz & Friends, Spiegel, Stern, Stiftung Warentest, Süddeutsche Zeitung Magazin, Taz, Tip, Verbraucherzentrale, Wagenbach, WDR Childrens Television, Woman, Die Zeit.

Dieter Braun

I paint and draw for as long as I can think back. Over time my pencil turned into a mouse, the lines became vectors, my piggy bank grew and my spare time shrunk. Apart from heavyweight box champion, Oscar-winning Hollywood-actor or Elvis Presley impersonator, being an illustrator is still my favourite profession. It must be love.

Autant qu'il m'en souvienne, j'ai toujours peint et dessiné. Avec le temps, mon crayon s'est mué en souris, les lignes sont devenues des vecteurs, ma tirelire a grossi et mon temps libre s'est amenuisé. A part champion de boxe poids lourd, acteur lauréat d'un Oscar et imitateur d'Elvis Presley, le métier d'illustrateur reste ma profession préférée. Ca tient de l'amour je crois.

Solange mein Erinnerungsvermögen reicht, male und zeichne ich. Im Laufe der Zeit ist aus meinem Bleistift eine Mouse geworden, aus Linien wurden Vektoren, mein Sparschwein wuchs und meine Freizeit wurde immer knapper. Abgesehen von einem Schwergewicht-Boxweltmeister, Schauspieler mit Oskarnominierung oder Imitator von Elvis Presley ist Illustrator immer noch mein Lieblingsberuf. Das muss wohl wahre Liebe sein.

www.brauntown.com

NAME: Dieter Braun **LOCATION:** Hamburg, Germany **CONTACT:** dieter@brauntown.com **TOOLS:** Macromedia Freehand, Adobe Photoshop. **AGENT:** Germany, Austria and Switzerland by myself; Kate Larkworthy <www.larkworthy.com> **CLIENTS:** Allegra, Continental Airlines, Cosmopolitan, Delta Airlines, Elle, Jung Von Matt, LA Magazine, Lufthansa Magazine, Petra, Spex, Springer & Jacoby, The Wall Street Journal, Time Magazine, Torrani, New York Times, Playboy, Greenpeace Magazine.

Jason Brooks

Every day thousands of images compete for our attention and it is the difficult job of an illustrator to stand out and communicate from this staccato background. The fact that most of these images are photographs, TV-lens based images, can work to the advantage of an illustrator because a drawing or digital painting can show something different, a more personal view of the world in a different media which can really capture attention in a more original way. That is what I try to do with my work. To present an alternative, idealised, more glossy reality, admittedly filled with beautiful people and great design but inspired and fuelled by the things I see and experience. For me, the key elements of creativity and design are memory, technique and imagination so I try to keep these things alive in my work and to keep improving.

Tous les jours, des milliers d'images se disputent notre attention et c'est le difficile métier de l'illustrateur que de sortir du lot. Le fait qu'une large part de ces images soient des photos et des images télévisées peut jouer à l'avantage des illustrateurs puisque un dessin ou une peinture numérisée peut montrer quelque chose de différent, une vision plus personnelle du monde avec un support différent véritablement à même de capter l'attention de façon bien plus originale. C'est ce que j'essaie de faire avec mon travail. Présenter une réalité alternative, idéalisée et plus brillante remplie certes de « beautiful people » et de superbes design mais inspirée et nourrie par les choses que je vois et que je vis. Pour moi, les éléments clés de la créativité et du design sont la mémoire, la technique et l'imagination. J'essaie donc de maintenir ces éléments vivants dans mon travail et de m'améliorer sans cesse.

Täglich kämpfen tausende von Bildern um unsere Aufmerksamkeit und es ist die schwierige Aufgabe eines Illustrators, hervorzustechen und sich vor diesem wirren Hintergrund mitzuteilen. Die Tatsache, dass es sich hauptsächlich um Fotografien, oder Fernsehkamera-Bilder handelt, kann sich zum Vorteil für den Illustrator herausstellen, da eine Zeichnung oder ein digital angefertigtes Gemälde etwas ganz Anderes ausdrücken kann - eine persönlichere Sichtweise der Welt in einem anderen Medienformat, das es ermöglicht, Aufmerksamkeit auf eine viel originellere Weise zu gewinnen. Und genau das versuche ich, mit meiner Arbeit zu erreichen. Eine Alternative anzubieten, eine idealisierte, viel strahlendere Realität zu bieten, voll von wunderschönen Menschen und perfektem Design, jedoch inspiriert und angespornt durch reale Dinge, die ich sehe und erlebe. Die Hauptelemente für Kreativität und Design sind für mich Erinnerungsvermögen, Technik und Fantasie und von daher versuche ich, diese Elemente bei meinen Arbeiten lebendig werden zu lassen und mich täglich zu verbessern.

www.jason-brooks.com

NAME: Jason Brooks **LOCATION:** London, UK **CONTACT:** brooks.design@virgin.net **TOOLS:** Adobe Photoshop. Adobe Illustrator, Apple Computer, pen and ink, gouache, pencil, collage. **AWARDS:** Vogue Sotheby's Cecil Beaton (Fashion Illustration). **AGENT:** Folio (London) <www.folioart.co.uk> **CLIENTS:** Elle, Vogue, The Times London, Veuve Clicquot, L'Oreal, British Airways, Perrier, Coty, Ritz Hotels, Ellesse, Martini, Mercedes-Benz, Finlandia Vodka, Nike.

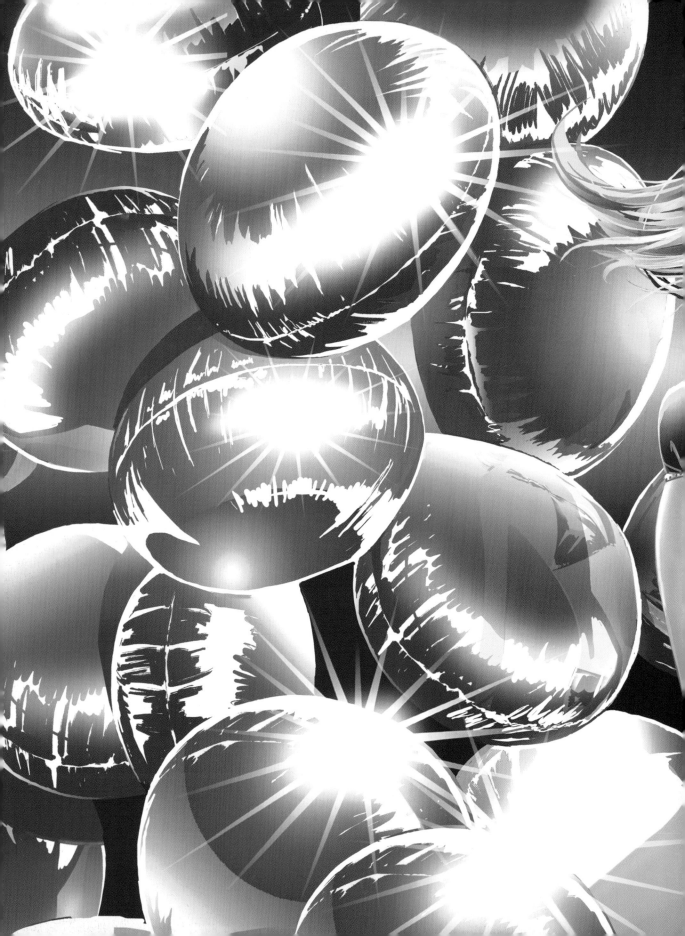

Mick Brownfield

I love the movies, comics and popular culture, and I try to reflect this as much as possible in my work. I believe in working constantly and hope that among the humdrum jobs, there will be projects where I can indulge myself. I am famous for pastiche and variety and that suits me fine.

J'aime le cinéma, la BD et la culture populaire et tente de refléter cela autant que possible dans mon travail. Je crois au travail acharné et espère toujours que dans la monotonie des commandes qu'on me confie il y aura des projets qui me permettront de me faire plaisir. Je suis connu pour le pastiche et la variété et ça me convient bien.

Ich liebe den Film, Comics und Traditionskultur, und versuche, dies stets in meinen Arbeiten widerzuspiegeln. Ich bin davon überzeugt, pausenlos zu arbeiten und hoffe stets, zwischen den eher eintönigen Arbeiten Projekte zu finden, die mich voll und ganz einnehmen. Ich bin bekannt für Pastiche und Abwechslung, und das ist mir gerade recht so.

www.www.mickbrownfield.com

NAME: Mick Brownfield **LOCATION:** Richmond, Surrey, England **CONTACT:** mickbrownfield@hotmail.com **TOOLS:** anything and everything but never the computer.
CLIENTS: The Times, BBC, Disney, Heineken, Guinness, Shell, Coca-Cola.

Charles Burns

I think the best comics are created by a single author; one that writes, draws, letters, and inks everything. Being a single author you have complete control over the entire process and you can be as self indulgent as you want...

Je pense que les meilleures BD sont celles qui ont un auteur unique qui se charge de tout le processus, du scénario au dessin en passant par le lettrage et l'encrage. En étant seul à la barre, on a un contrôle total de l'ensemble du processus et on peut être aussi indulgent avec soi-même qu'on le souhaite...

Ich denke, die besten Comics werden von einem Autoren alleine kreiert; jemand, der schreibt, vorzeichnet, die Sprechblasen formuliert und dann alles in Tinte zeichnet. Der Vorteil, alleiniger Autor zu sein, ist die Kontrolle über den gesamten Prozess zu haben, ausserdem entscheidet man selbst, wie tiefgründig man sein möchte.

NAME: Charles Burns **LOCATION:** USA **CONTACT:** burningstudio@earthlink.net **TOOLS:** Traditional painting **AWARDS:** Harvey Award, Will Eisner Award, Comics Journal "Top 100 English-Language Comics of the Century", etc. **CLIENTS:** Esquire, Time Magazine, Iggy Pop, NY Times, etc.

Paula Sanz Caballero

I began to experiment with fabric and embroidery, and my technique evolves from the figurative pictorial concept to the sewn finish, drawing on topics full of irony, tortuous relationships, crime and scornful feminine revenge. Since then, my artwork, as well as my graphic design illustrations have been based on this stylistic pattern.

J'ai commencé à expérimenter avec du tissu et des broderies et ma technique va du concept illustré figuratif à la finition cousue, puisant dans des thèmes pleins d'ironie, de relations tortueuses, de crimes et de revanche féminine méprisante. Depuis lors, mes œuvres d'art ainsi que mes illustrations graphiques sont basées sur ce modèle stylistique.

Ich begann, mit Stoffen und Stickerei zu experimentieren; meine Techniken reichen von figurativ bildlichen Konzepten bis hin zum fertig genähten Stoff, ich zeichne Themenbereiche voller Ironie, qualvolle Beziehungen, Kriminalität sowie weibliche Rachezüge. Von jeher basieren sowohl meine Kunstwerke als auch meine Grafikdesign - Illustrationen auf diesen Stilrichtungen.

www.paulasanzcaballero.iespana.es

NAME: Paula Sanz Caballero **LOCATION:** Spain **CONTACT:** nairobiflat@teleline.es **TOOLS:** needle, threads, scisors, fabrics. **AGENT:** Agent 002 <www.agent002.com>; UNIT.nl <www.unit.nl>; Taiko & Associates <www.ua-net.com> **CLIENTS:** Vogue, ELLE, Marie Claire, Neo2, Telva, El Mundo, El Pais, El Mueble, Casa Ideal, Cosmopolitan, Red, Avantgarde, Link, Linda, Flair Living, Harper Collins, Coredo, and Roger la Borde.

Finn Campbell-Notman

I bring evething out there into my illustration. Film, Literature, Cultural Theory, Architecture, Autobiography, Fine Art, Sculpture etc, all the things which one encounters and filters through ones personal artistic lens All of this meets at the point of my pencil. Each commission is an application of my singular artistic synthesis, each image draws upon the brief and upon my experience resulting in an image which is informed, authored, directed: an illustration.

Mes illustrations sont inspirées par tout ce qui m'entoure. Cinéma, littérature, théorie culturelle, architecture, autobiographie, beaux-arts, sculpture, etc., tout ce que l'on peut rencontrer et filtrer avec sa lentille artistique, tout cela est rassemblé à la pointe de mon crayon. Chaque commande est une application de ma synthèse artistique particulière, chaque image va au-delà des instructions que l'on me donne et de mon expérience, et résulte en une image informée, ciblée et portant l'empreinte de son auteur : une illustration.

Ich lasse so ziemlich alles in meine Illustrationen einfliessen. Film, Literatur, kulturelle Theorien, Architektur, Autobiografien, Kunst, Skulpturen etc., all das, was man findet und durch seine ganz persönliche Künstlerbrille filtert. All das trifft auf der Spitze meines Stiftes zusammen. Jeder Auftrag ist die Anwendung meiner künstlerischen Synthese, jede meiner Zeichnungen basiert auf Briefing und Erfahrung und wird schliesslich zu einem Bild, das sowohl durchdacht, kreiert als auch bestimmt ist: eine Illustration.

NAME: Finn Campbell-Notman **LOCATION:** London, UK **CONTACT:** all@folioart.co.uk **TOOLS:** Adobe Photoshop, Sennelier Acid Free Paper, Berol Venus Pencils, Apple Computer. **AWARDS:** A.O.I Images 26 Silver, 27 Silver , 28 Bronze. D&AD LAB **AGENT:** Folio <www.folioart.co.uk> **CLIENTS:** Adidas, Audi, Coca Cola, The Times, The Financial Times, The Independent, The Sunday Times Magazine, Random House, Hodder & Staughton, etc.

Maria **Cardelli**

I started painting with oils when I was very young and it has always been my preferred medium. As a commercial illustrator, though, I have had to reinvent myself. Focusing primarily on fashion subjects, I create my work from collages, combining media that might include fabric, feathers, beads, even shells, which are digitized and manipulated. I am particularly inspired by modernist architecture, bold shapes, sinewy forms, subtle textures, and colour in all things.

J'ai commencé la peinture à l'huile lorsque j'étais très jeune et elle reste ma technique préférée. Cependant, en tant qu'illustratrice commerciale, j'ai dû me réinventer. Je me consacre principalement au thème de la mode et travaille à partir de collages, en combinant des supports tels que du tissu, des plumes, des perles et même des coquillages. Je traite ces collages en les numérisant et les manipulant. Je m'inspire particulièrement de l'architecture moderniste, de formes audacieuses, de silhouettes élancées, de textures subtiles et des couleurs de tout ce qui m'entoure.

Als ich noch sehr jung war, begann ich schon mit Öl zu malen und bis heute ist es mein bevorzugtes Medium. Als kommerzieller Illustrator jedoch, musste ich mich wieder neu definieren. Mit dem Schwerpunkt auf Modeobjekten, kreiere ich meine Arbeiten anhand von Kollagen und der Kombination von Materialien, die sowohl Stoffe, Federn, Perlen als auch Muscheln beinhalten können, welche ich dann digitalisiere und manipuliere. Besonders inspiriert mich Jugendstilarchitektur, grosszügige und kraftvolle Formen, subtile Muster und vor allem Farben.

www.mywholeportfolio.com/mariacardelli

NAME: Maria Cardelli **LOCATION:** New York, USA **CONTACT:** maria@illustrationweb.com **TOOLS:** Mixed Media, Adobe Photoshop, Adobe Illustrator. **AGENT:** Illustration LTD <www.illustrationweb.com> **CLIENTS:** Cosmopolitan, Vogue, The Times, Nordstrom Department Stores, Time Out, New York Magazine, PC Magazine, Architectural Digest, BET Network, Telecom, Wellfit Magazine, The Wall Street Journal, Elle Decoration, Penguin Putnam USA, The Boston Globe, and more.

Alison Casson

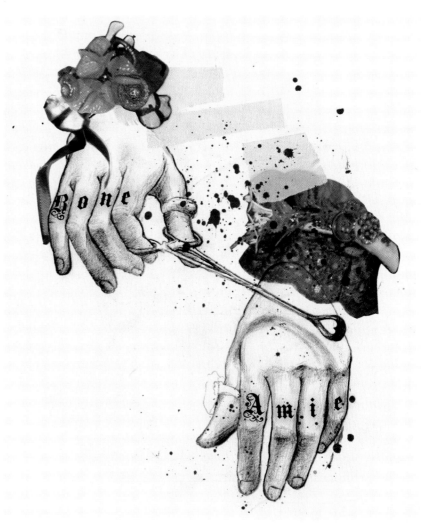

I am fundamentally devoted to my many forms of art. I'm motivated and seduced by the process and the product. My work is diverse, drawing on inspiration from Victorian, 20's, 40's, and 80's styles, sailor tales, tattoo art, graffiti, and an overwhelming drive to create. Working with a large range of materials, from graphite, paint, sewing and digital media, my work is sentimental, romantic, aggressive and sexual.

Je suis entièrement dévouée aux nombreuses formes d'art que je pratique. Je suis motivée et séduite par le processus et le produit. Mon travail est très varié, il s'inspire du style victorien et de celui des années 20, 40 et 80, des histoires de marins, de l'art du tatouage, des graffitis et d'une volonté acharnée de créer. Je me sers d'un large éventail de matériaux allant du graphite à la peinture et de la couture au support numérique. Mon travail est sentimental, romantique, agressif et sexuel.

Meine ganze Hingabe gilt den vielen unterschiedlichen Formen meiner Kunst. Mich motiviert und verführt sowohl der Arbeitsprozess als auch das Produkt. Meine Arbeiten sind sehr breit gefächert, inspiriert vom viktorianischen Stil, den 20er, 40er und 80er Jahren, von Seemannsgeschichten, Tatookunst, Graffiti und darüber hinaus verspüre ich ständig einen Drang zur Kreation. Ich arbeite mit einer Vielzahl von unterschiedlichen Materialien, angefangen von Graphit über Farbe, Nähmaterial und bis hin zu den digitalen Medien. Ich würde meine Arbeiten als sentimental, romantisch, aggressiv und sexuell bezeichnen.

www.alisoncasson.com

NAME: Alison Casson **LOCATION:** Los Angeles, California, USA **CONTACT:** alice@alisoncasson.com **TOOLS:** Acrylic, oil, spray-paint, collage, Apple G4, Husqvarna Designer One, laze cutter, my hands. **AWARDS:** SILA Illustration West (Merit), AIAP AI20. **CLIENTS:** This is my Method, Siamese Hooker, Shogun Studios, Funky Monkey, Bone Amie, Jean Schmidt, Chantal Menard, Los Angeles Children's Hospital, Fishwrap Magazine.

Daniel Chang

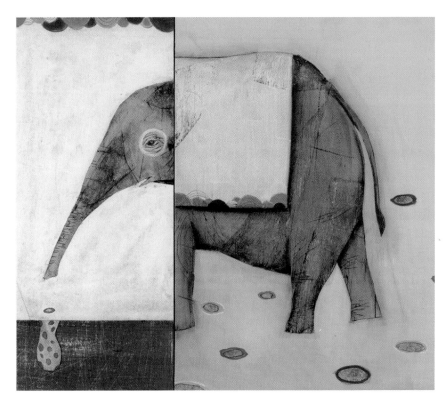

My work is concept and process driven. I begin most pieces by digesting ideas through juxtaposing words and phrases until I find an interesting place to begin. From that point I start assembling the work from paintings and drawings which piece together into an evolving narrative. Despite the description this process is not linear but rather organic and ever changing.

Concepts et processus sont les moteurs de mon travail. Je commence souvent mes illustrations en digérant des idées par la juxtaposition de mots et de phrases jusqu'à ce que j'aie trouvé par où commencer. A partir de là je commence à assembler mon travail à partir de peintures et de dessins qui s'associent dans une histoire évolutive. Contrairement à ce que cette description laisse croire, ce processus n'est pas linéaire mais plutôt naturel et en constante évolution.

Meine Arbeit wird durch Konzept und Prozess bestimmt. Meist beginne ich mit der Verarbeitung einiger Ideen, indem ich Wörter und Sätze so lange gegenüberstelle, bis ich einen geeigneten Ausgangspunkt finde. Dann fange ich an, Gemälde und Zeichnungen so zu komponieren, bis sich eine Erzählung ergibt. Trotz der Beschreibung handelt es sich hierbei nicht um eine lineare Entwicklung, sondern vielmehr um einen organischen, sich ständig verändernden Prozess.

www.danielchang.net

NAME: Daniel Chang **LOCATION:** Orange County, California, USA **CONTACT:** mail@danielchang.net **TOOLS:** acrylic, graphite. **AWARDS:** American Illustration, Society of Illustrators, Illustration West. **AGENT:** Frank Sturges <www.sturgesreps.com> **CLIENTS:** Sony, Billabong, Von Zipper, Hewlett-Packard, IBM, UCLA, Oligvy & Mather, Motion Theory, Random House, Harper Collins, St. Supery Winery, Entertainment Weekly, Bloomberg, Harvard Business Review, Independent, etc.

Technology Report: WORM Tape

WORM tape offers many benefits over other archiving media such as low price and portability. Additionally, most WORM tape cartridges fit into existing tape libraries

BY JEROME M. WENDT

keep it all. That's increasingly the company line handed down by management to storage administrators. With sometimes conflicting and overlapping government regulations about retaining sensitive data within organizations, no longer can any data be viewed as disposable. More often than not, storage administrators end up storing everything, with a growing number examining write once, read many (WORM) tape as a method for satisfy long-term data retention requirements.

ARCHIVE
with
WORM
tape

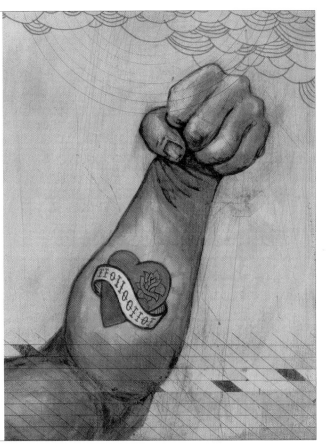

ILLUSTRATION BY DANIEL CHANG

Marcos Chin

Illustration, I think, is about problem solving. With commercial assignments especially, I think the illustrator who alongside with the art director, has to jointly realize an image to compliment text or to communicate an existing idea. Personally, my own interests and experiences oftentimes manifest themselves visually in my work, as do my influences from other artists and designers from the past and present.

A mon sens, illustrer c'est résoudre des problèmes. Particulièrement dans le domaine commercial, où l'illustrateur, avec le directeur artistique, doit réaliser une image qui doit compléter un texte ou communiquer une idée. Dans mon cas, mes centres d'intérêt et mes expériences se manifestent souvent visuellement dans mon travail, à l'instar de mes influences, qui me viennent d'autres artistes et illustrateurs d'aujourd'hui et d'hier.

Meiner Meinung nach dient Illustration zur Lösung von Problemen. Besonders bei kommerziellen Aufträgen muss der Illustrator gemeinsam mit dem Art Director ein textbegleitendes Bild erstellen oder einen bereits vorhandenen Gedankenvorgang kommunizieren. Bei mir persönlich spiegeln sich sowohl meine eigenen Interessen und Erfahrungswerte visuell in meinen Arbeiten wider als auch die Beeinflussung durch andere Künstler und Designer aus Vergangenheit und Gegenwart.

www.marcoschin.com

NAME: Marcos Chin **LOCATION:** Toronto, Canada **CONTACT:** marcos@marcoschin.com **TOOLS:** pencil, Adobe Illustrator, Adobe Photoshop. **AWARDS:** American Illustration, Society of Illustrators NY, Applied Arts. **CLIENTS:** Lavalife, Hers, Rolling Stone, Sports Illustrated, Time; System Recordings, The New Yorker, The New York Times, and Esquire.

Joe Ciardiello

Ben "Frog" Webster

It's all about the drawing. The most important thing is to find something in an assignment that will be interesting for me to draw. Everything else is secondary. I prefer to draw directly with pen whenever possible. It is the most honest, direct and spontaneous way for me to achieve the expressiveness that I'm after.

Tout est une question de dessin. Le plus important pour moi dans une commande est que je repère quelque chose que je trouve intéressant à dessiner. Tout le reste est secondaire. Je préfère dessiner directement au crayon quand c'est possible. C'est la façon la plus honnête, la plus directe et la plus spontanée pour moi d'obtenir l'expressivité que je recherche.

Bei mir dreht sich alles nur um die Zeichnung. Mir geht es haupsächlich darum, bei einem Auftrag den Aspekt zu finden, der interessant zum Zeichnen ist. Alles andere ist zweitrangig. Wann immer ich die Möglichkeit habe, versuche ich direkt mit dem Stift zu zeichnen. Das ist für mich die ehrlichste, direkteste und spontanste Art und Weise, Ausdruckstärke - die ich stets zu vermitteln versuche -, weiterzugeben.

www.joeciardiello.com

NAME: Joe Ciardiello **LOCATION:** Milford, New Jersey, USA **CONTACT:** joe@joeciardiello.com **TOOLS:** Pen, Ink and Watercolor on Paper. **AWARDS:** American Illustration, SPD, Society of Illustrators (2 Silver). **CLIENTS:** Capitol Records, Jazziz, The New Yorker, Playboy, Rolling Stone, Sports Illustrated, Time Magazine, US News & World Report.

ciardiello

Greg Clarke

I try to infuse everything I do with what I hope is a singular sensibility...not so much a style as a point of view.

J'essaie d'insuffler à tout ce que je fais ce que j'espère être une sensibilité singulière... Pas tant un style qu'un point de vue.

Ich versuche, all das, was ich tue, mit dem, was ich mir als einzige Sensibilität erhoffe, zu vermischen... nicht unbedingt ein Stil, vielmehr eine Art Blickwinkel.

www.gregclarke.com

NAME: Greg Clarke **LOCATION:** California, USA **CONTACT:** greg@gregclarke.com **TOOLS:** pencil, acrylic, watercolor, pastels. **AWARDS:** Numerous from American Illustration and Communication Arts; Society of Illustrators NY (2 Silver). **AGENT:** <www.heflinreps.com>; <www.theartworks.com> **CLIENTS:** The New Yorker, Time Magazine, The Atlantic Monthly, Rolling Stone, New York Times, Volkswagen, Einstein Bros., Bagels, Purina.

Tavis Coburn

As an Illustrator my job is to solve problems visually, and to inject a "cool" factor into my clients product, service, or campaign. I feel like I'm an architect sometimes, building a visual structure out of individual elements, each having their own distinct voice yet combined together these elements create new meaning for themselves and their relationships to each other.

En tant qu'illustrateur, mon travail est de résoudre visuellement des problèmes et d'injecter un facteur « cool » dans le produit, le service ou la campagne de mes clients. J'ai parfois le sentiment d'être un architecte qui construit une structure visuelle à partir d'éléments individuels ayant chacun leur propre voix. Mais combinés, ces éléments créent de nouvelles significations pour eux-mêmes et dans leur inter-relation.

Als Illustrator ist es meine Aufgabe, Probleme visuell zu lösen und den Produkten, dem Service oder den Werbekampagnen meiner Klienten einen Schuss "cool" beizufügen. Manchmal habe ich das Gefühl, ein Architekt zu sein, der eine visuelle Struktur aus individuellen Elementen erschafft. Jedes mit seiner eigenen Stimme, die zusammengestellt, jedoch einen neuen Sinn für sich selbst und in ihrer Beziehung untereinander geben.

www.taviscoburn.com

NAME: Tavis Coburn **LOCATION:** Toronto, Canada; Los Angeles, USA **CONTACT:** tc@taviscoburn.com **TOOLS:** 255 mesh silkscreens, Nazdar oil based screen inks, stiff squeegee, Off white paper, Adobe CS, Gouache, #1,2,3 Windsor Newton Series 7 brushes, photocopier, scanner, and my Apple G5. **AWARDS:** Society of Publication Designers, American Illustration, Society of Illustrators, and more. **CLIENTS:** Time Magazine, GQ, Rolling Stone, Universal, Ford, United Airlines, etc.

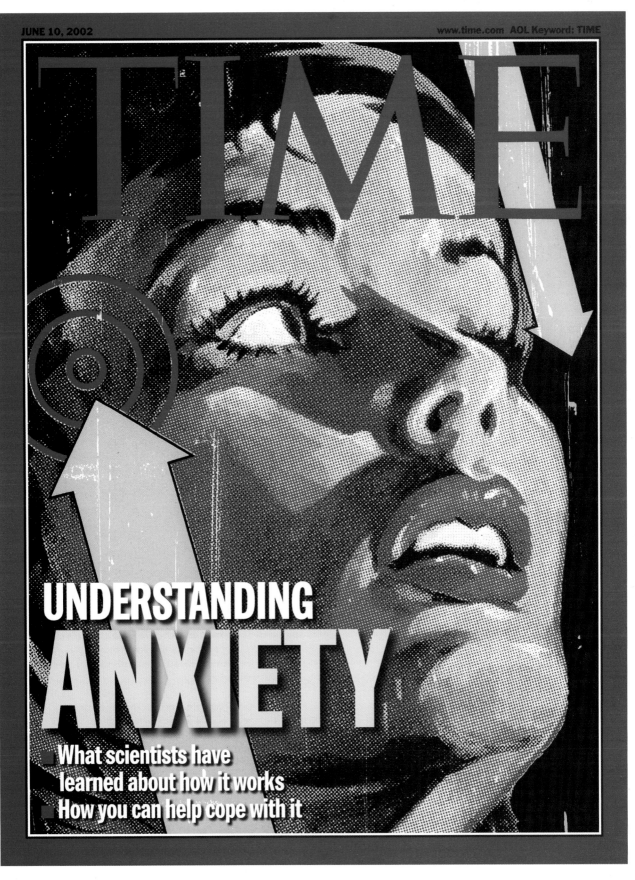

UNDERSTANDING
ANXIETY

What scientists have
learned about how it works
How you can help cope with it

Fernanda Cohen

Illustration should always complement both words and imagination blocking neither one of them. As an illustrator, my major challenge is to capture the bare message of a subject, and deliver it in a clear and visually captivating container. I personally enjoy subtlety, naïveté and humour in all visual arts.

Une illustration devrait toujours venir en complément des mots et de l'imagination et ne bloquer ni l'un ni l'autre. En tant qu'illustratrice, mon plus grand défi est de capturer le message brut d'un sujet et de le restituer dans un contenant clair et visuellement captivant. Personnellement, j'aime la subtilité, la naïveté et l'humour dans toutes les formes d'art visuel.

Bei der Illustration sollten sich Wort und Vorstellungsvermögen stets komplementieren und sich niemals gegenseitig blockieren. Als Illustrator sehe ich es als meine grösste Herausforderung an, die Basisaussage einer Sache zu erfassen und sie auf klare und visuell anziehende Art und Weise wiederzugeben. Mir persönlich gefällt Spitzfindigkeit, Naivität und Humor bei allen visuellen Künsten.

www.fernandacohen.com

NAME: Fernanda Cohen **LOCATION:** New York,USA **CONTACT:** taschen@fernandacohen.com **TOOLS:** Pen & Ink. **AWARDS:** Society of Illustrators, ALT Pick Awards, Communication Arts, American Illustration, Graphis. **CLIENTS:** The New York Times, Harvard University, The New York Times Magazine, Continental Airlines, Dwell Magazine, The New York Times Magazine, New York Magazine, Travel & Leisure, Flaunt Magazine, Garden Life London, BIGnews Magazine, Ikram, etc.

The New York Times Magazine

JANUARY 16, 2005 / SECTION 6

The Second Term

His Calculations

Does the Social Security Crisis Add Up?
An actuarial history of a program under assault since it began.
By Roger Lowenstein

The Slow-Motion Tax Revolution
How Bush could do what Reagan couldn't.
By Nicholas Confessore

When a Desperate Housewife Marries Again, and Again, and Again . . . (See Style, Page 49)

Brian Cronin

My approach to each illustration that i am commissioned to do is basically to make it personal. I try and make the story I'm illustrating a personal reaction as much as I can within the confines of the medium. In other words it's about my personal reaction to the piece rather than trying to explain it in a literal way or making a parallel image. Sometimes the images are quite literal others a bit abstract but this is my reaction and I like to keep it loose so I am open to what ever interpretation I feel is right for this particular assignment.

Ma façon de travailler est essentiellement de rendre personnelles toutes les illustrations que l'on me commande. Autant que possible et dans le cadre du support, j'essaie de donner une réaction personnelle à l'histoire que j'illustre. En d'autres termes, je préfère une réaction personnelle à une explication littérale ou à la création d'une image parallèle. Parfois les images sont assez littérales ou un peu abstraites mais c'est ma réaction et j'aime la laisser libre afin de rester ouvert à toutes les interprétations qui me semblent appropriées pour une commande en particulier.

Jede Illustration, die mir in Auftrag gegeben wird, gehe ich grundsätzlich mit dem Vorsatz an, sie vor allem persönlich zu gestalten. Soweit es mir das jeweilige Medium erlaubt, versuche ich die Geschichte, die ich illustriere, als eine persönliche Reaktion erkenntlich werden zu lassen. Mit anderen Worten, es ist vielmehr meine persönliche Reaktion auf die Arbeit als der Versuch, mich wortwörtlich auszudrücken oder gar ein paralleles Bild zu schaffen. Manchmal sind die Bilder in sich schon prosaisch, andere hingegen eher abstrakt, aber mir geht es um meine eigene Reaktion und ich bin stets darauf bedacht, mir alle Wege offen zu halten und jeden Auftrag ganz nach meinem eigenen Gefühl anzugehen.

www.briancronin.com

NAME: Brian Cronin **LOCATION:** New York, USA **CONTACT:** brian@briancronin.com **TOOLS:** Brush and Pencil. **AWARDS:** The Society of Illustrators NY (Gold/Silver), The Art Directors Club NY (Gold/Silver), The Society of Publication Designers (Gold/Silver), D&DA (Yellow Pencil). **CLIENTS:** The New Yorker, The New York Times, The Washington Post, Newsweek, Time, Outside, GQ, Details, LA Times, Microsoft, Vibe, Details, Penguin, Rolling Stone, IBM, and more.

GRAHAM GREENE CENTENNIAL 1904-2004

Travels with My Aunt

PENGUIN CLASSICS DELUXE EDITION

GRAHAM GREENE

Introduction by Gloria Emerson

Thomas Dannenberg

Illustration is something of a ménage à trois involving the artist, his muse and the client. When it clicks, it's absolutely wonderful. However, there is always the possibility of jealousy, conflicts, negotiations and compromises. As in love, experience can be helpful in handling such situations. I love illustrations that have an idea or concept behind them. I try to persuade my clients to take some chances, to be more lyrical and less literal.

L'illustration est une sorte de ménage à trois impliquant l'artiste, sa muse et le client. Lorsqu'il y a coup de foudre, c'est formidable. Mais cela n'empêche pas qu'il y ait toujours la possibilité de jalousies, de conflits, de négociations et de compromis. Comme en amour, l'expérience peut aider à gérer ce genre de situations. J'aime les illustrations qui reposent sur une idée ou un concept. J'essaie de persuader mes clients de prendre des risques pour être plus lyriques et moins littéraux.

Illustration ist für mich so etwas wie eine "ménage à trois" zwischen dem Künstler, seiner Muse und dem Kunden. Wenn sie zusammenpassen, ist das einfach genial. Trotz allem besteht immer die Gefahr von Eifersucht, Konflikten, Verhandlungen und Kompromissen. Genauso wie in der Liebe kann Erfahrung dazu beitragen, solche Situationen richtig zu bewerten. Ich liebe Illustrationen, die eine Idee oder ein Konzept beinhalten. Ich versuche stets, meine Kunden davon zu überzeugen, auch mal ein Risiko einzugehen, nicht alles nur wörtlich sondern auch lyrisch zu sehen.

www.dannenbergdesign.com

NAME: Thomas Dannenberg **LOCATION:** Ontario, Canada **CONTACT:** thomas@dannenbergdesign.com **TOOLS:** Adobe Photoshop is king! **AWARDS:** Berliner Kindl Poster Contest (Gold/2 Silver), CAPIC National Annual Awards (Gold/Silver/3 Bronze), Studio Magazine Annual Awards (Gold), Applied Arts Magazine Annual Awards. **CLIENTS:** Cosmopolitan, Fortune, Lufthansa, IBM, Coca-Cola, Nestlé, Schering, Universal Studios, Hewlett Packard, American Express, Bank of Montreal, and more.

Delicatessen

We love the fifties! Our work is a tribute to the style of the mid 50`s (called also Exotica or Lounge) and also artists like Jim Flora and Shag. We try to evoke the taste of that era with an ironic and light touch.

Nous adorons les années 50 ! Notre travail est un hommage au style du milieu des années 50 (également appelé Exotica ou Lounge) ainsi qu'à des artistes tels que Jim Flora et Shag. Nous tentons d'évoquer l'atmosphère de cette époque avec une pointe d'ironie et de légèreté.

Wir lieben die fünfziger Jahre! Unsere Arbeit ist ein Tribut an den Stil der 50er (auch Exotica oder Lounge genannt) und an Künstler wie Jim Flora und Shag. Wir versuchen, den Geschmack dieser Zeit mit einem ironischen und unaufdringlichen Touch wiederaufleben zu lassen.

www.delicatessen.it

NAME: Delicatessen (Gabriele Fantuzzi) **LOCATION:** Reggio Emilia, Italy **CONTACT:** gabriele@delica.it **TOOLS:** Adobe Illustrator, Adobe Photoshop. **AGENT:** Kate Larkworthy <www.larkworthy.com>, Illustrissimo (France) <www.illustrissimo.com> **CLIENTS:** Conde Nast, MTV, SKY, Los Angeles Times, Random House, Sperling & Kupfer, etc...

LOVE, MARRIAGE,

BY PAMELA STOCK
ILLUSTRATIONS
BY DELICATESSEN

No money, no sex, and no time. This isn't how you pictured parenthood with the man you love. Here's how to get your relationship back on track.

AND BABY

INNER GODDESS SEEKS HIDDEN KING

artner locked in a passionless rut? If so, says relationships you should start nurturing your differences, and respect his regal power

Vanessa Dell

My style has developed from the way I draw. I quite like imperfection so the people I paint whether they are for straight portraits or imagined tend to be a little awkward looking — I suppose this gives them vulnerability. I enjoy painting both traditionally and on the computer and thrive on a narrative.

Mon style s'est développé à partir de la façon dont je dessine. J'aime les imperfections et les gens que je peins d'après nature ou à partir de ma propre imagination ont tendance à avoir une apparence un peu bizarre. Je suppose que ça leur donne une certaine vulnérabilité. J'adore peindre, que ce soit à l'ancienne ou sur un ordinateur et j'aime me nourrir d'une histoire.

Meiner Art zu Zeichnen ist mein ganz persönlicher Stil. Mir gefällt die Unvollkommenheit, daher sehen die Menschen, die ich zeichne - seien es Porträts oder frei aus dem Kopf -, meist etwas seltsam aus und ich denke, das gibt ihnen eine gewisse Verletzbarkeit. Ich zeichne gerne nach traditioneller Art, aber auch am Computer und versuche stets, Geschichten zu vermitteln.

www.vanessadell.com

NAME: Vanessa Dell **LOCATION:** UK **CONTACT:** vanessadell@hotmail.com **TOOLS:** Oils, Painter. **AGENT:** Illustration LTD <www.illustrationweb.com> **CLIENTS:** BBC, Oxford University Press, National Geographic Traveller Mag. Rolling Stone, Good Housekeeping, Scholastic, Saatchi and Saatchi, Proximity London.

an origin

Pengui

BY

Munsingwear

I ♥ HONKY

Vanessa Dell

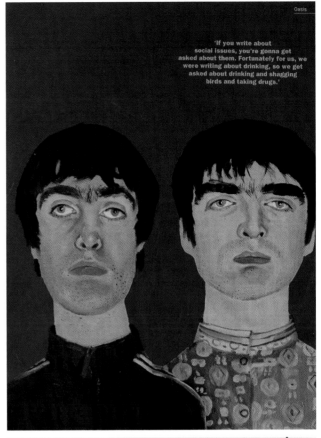

'If you write about social issues, you're gonna get asked about them. Fortunately for us, we were writing about drinking, so we get asked about drinking and shagging birds and taking drugs.'

Time for you

Just when you thought you had the sofa back to yourselves...

Grown-up children are boomeranging back to their parents at an alarming rate. And whether the cause is student debt or sky-high mortgages, says Libby Purves, these home-againers are seriously eroding their parents' financial futures – and clogging up the bathroom during the morning rush

In the opening pages of Bridget Jones's Diary there's a scene in which our heroine is sitting in her flat just before New Year, dreading the idea of going home to her parents because it will make her feel like a teenager again. It's a feeling many will identify with. Once you've established your independence and moved your possessions out, it's good to go home from time to time, but you're never quite a grown-up in your parents' house. At least not until you produce a few babies and grey hairs of your own.

But times are changing. Homes are impossibly expensive to buy and jobs are often insecure or based on short contracts. Graduates have debts too. And debt breeds debt. As well as having student loans storing up possible future problems, young people are spending increasing amounts of money they don't have, building up huge sums they can't pay off. This, it seems, is a generation heading for disaster. 'When these young people get older, they'll be in real trouble,' explains Martin Hayward, Chairman at The Henley Centre, which predicts social trends. 'Many will find they aren't able CONTINUED ON PAGE

eBoy

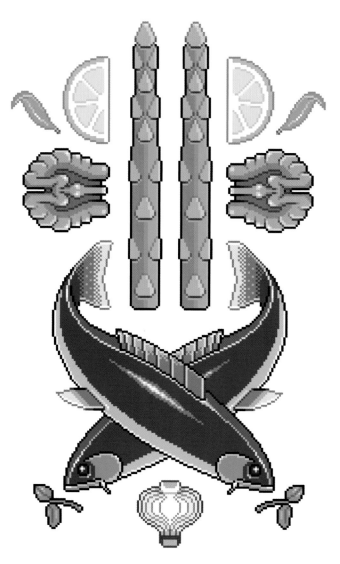

The basic idea driving eBoy is the embracement of the new possibilities of emerging digital world. Pictures could be copied as many times as necessary if they were digital -- no printing and low production costs. Data could be sent to the most distant placed of the globe in seconds. The work had to be designed specifically for the screen and so eBoy went the pixel way.

L'idée de base de eBoy est d'embrasser les nouvelles possibilités du monde numérique émergeant. Les images peuvent être copiées autant de fois que nécessaire si elles sont numériques, il n'y a pas de coûts d'impression et les coûts de production sont bas. Les données peuvent être envoyées aux endroits les plus éloignés du globe en quelques secondes. Le travail doit alors être conçu spécifiquement

Die Hauptidee, die eboy auszeichnet, ist das Zusammenführen von neuen Möglichkeiten, die sich aus der digitalen Welt ergeben. Bilder könnten so oft wie nötig kopiert werden, wären sie digital — kein Druck und niedrige Produktionskosten. Dateien könnten in Sekundenschnelle ans andere Ende der Welt geschickt werden. Die Arbeit muss speziell für den Bildschirm designed werden und so hat sich eboy dazu entschieden, den Pixelweg zu gehen.

www.eboy.com

NAME: eBoy **LOCATION:** Berlin, Germany and New York, USA **CONTACT:** eboy@eboy.com **TOOLS:** Adobe Photoshop, Adobe Illustrator. **CLIENTS:** Wired Magazine, IDN, Paul Smith, Coca-Cola, The Face, Diesel, Levi's, ESPN Magazine, FontShop, Nestlé, MTV, Fortune Magazine, Boston Magazine, Pentagram, VH-1, The Guardian, Renault, DaimlerChrysler, Adidas, Nike, Kellog's, The New York Times Magazine, The New Yorker, Honda, Spin Magazine, and many more…

Jan Feindt

I am combining old school and new school techniques. I am drawing with a pen and Indian ink and then finish the piece in Photoshop. I like the exactness of the pen and ink technique, the high level of detail that you can achieve with it. My colours must be modern and flat. So Photoshop gives me the flashiness that my work requires.

J'ai recours à des techniques de l'ancienne et de la nouvelle école. Je dessine avec une plume et de l'encre indienne et effectue les finitions avec Photoshop. J'aime la précision de la technique de la plume et de l'encre, le degré de détails qu'elle autorise. Mes couleurs doivent être modernes et mates. Photoshop me donne donc le tape-à-l'œil dont mes travaux ont besoin.

Ich kombiniere Techniken der alten und neuen Schule. Ich zeichne mit Stift und indischer Tinte und stelle die Arbeit dann mit Photoshop fertig. Mir gefällt die Exaktheit von Stift- und Federtechnik, vor allem die Detailtreue, die man erreichen kann. Meine Farben müssen modern und auffällig sein. Photoshop gibt mir die Möglichkeit, diese Auffälligkeit zu erzielen.

www.janfeindt.de

NAME: Jan Feindt LOCATION: Berlin, Germany CONTACT: janfeindt@gmx.de TOOLS: pen, indian ink, Adobe Photoshop. CLIENTS: Rolling Stone, Men's Health, Men's Health Best Life, Amico, Musik Express, Die Zeit, Süddeutsche Zeitung, Das Magazin, Mare, Word, PC Plus, Maariv, TV Today, Strawberry Frog, Aare/Sauerländer, Carhartt.

Joseph Daniel *Fiedler*

My work is essentially a simple celebration of Painting, especially Nineteenth Century Narrative meets Mid-Twentieth Whatever. Think Puvis on Acid. Ingres meets Jasper Johns or Jack the Dripper meets Son of Flipper. Or as Terry Brown, Director of the New York Society of Illustrators claims, "…like John Collier with broken glasses."! Mostly, I try to create a simulacrum of something that I've seen somewhere before or imagined. Something reproduced, dreamed or buried under layers of yellowed varnish, grit and partially torn.

Mon travail est essentiellement une fête de la peinture où se rencontrent en particulier la peinture narrative du 19e siècle et celle du milieu du 20e siècle. Imaginez Puvis sous acide. Ingres rencontre Jasper Johns ou Jack l'éventreur rencontre le fils de Flipper le dauphin. Ou, tout comme le dit Terry Brown, le président de la société new-yorkaise des illustrateurs : « c'est du John Collier avec des lunettes cassées » ! J'essaie la plupart du temps de créer un simulacre de quelque chose que j'ai déjà vu quelque part ou que j'ai imaginé. Quelque chose reproduit, rêvé ou enfoui sous des couches de vernis jauni partiellement écaillé.

Meine Arbeit würde ich hauptsächlich als eine Zelebrierung von Gemälden bezeichnen, vor allem „Erzählung aus dem 19. Jahrhundert trifft auf Mit-Zwanziger", na ja, was auch immer. Stelle dir Puvis auf Acid vor. Ingres trifft auf Jasper Johns oder Jack the Dripper trifft auf den Sohn Flippers. Oder so wie Terry Brown, Direktor der Gesellschaft der New Yorker Illustratoren, es beschreibt "…wie John Collier mit kaputter Brille"! Meist versuche ich, ein Abbild von bereits Gesehenem oder zumindest Vorgestelltem zu kreieren. Etwas Reproduziertes, Geträumtes oder unter Schichten gelben Lackes Vergrabenes, mit Sprüngen und teils zerissen.

www.scaryjoey.com

NAME: Joseph Daniel Fiedler **LOCATION:** Detroit, MI, USA **CONTACT:** fiedler@scaryjoey.com **TOOLS:** Mixed Medium on Paper or Panel, Windsor & Newton Griffin Alkyd.
AWARDS: Communication Arts, The Society of Illustrators, Society of Newspaper Design, etc. **CLIENTS:** Time, Business Week, Playboy, Travel & Leisure, Health, The Wall Street Journal, The New York Times, The Chicago Tribune, Sony Music and Advertising, McCann Healthcare, Pfizer, Japan Airlines, All Nippon Airways, etc.

Fernando Figowy

My work allows me to unite my two passions: fine art and graphic design. In my illustrations I can express my self visually and communicate an idea or a sensation. It gives me great placer when people that are viewing my illustrations can reproduce the emotion that I have put in to it.

Mon travail me permet de concilier mes deux passions : les beaux-arts et le graphisme. Avec mes illustrations, je peux m'exprimer visuellement et communiquer une idée ou une sensation. Constater que les gens qui ont vu mes illustrations peuvent reproduire l'émotion que j'y ai mis me procure un plaisir immense.

Meine Arbeit erlaubt es mir, meine zwei Leidenschaften zu vereinen: Kunst und Grafikdesign. Meine Illustrationen ermöglichen es mir, mich selbst visuell auszudrücken und Ideen und Eindrücke zu vermitteln. Es freut mich, dass Menschen, die meine Illustrationen sehen, dazu fähig sind, die Gefühle nachzuempfinden, die ich in die Arbeit reingesteckt habe.

NAME: Fernando Figowy **LOCATION:** Barcelona, Spain **CONTACT:** fernandofigowy@menta.net **TOOLS:** Adobe photoshop, Macromedia Flash, pencil, ink. **AGENT:** Agent 002 <www.agent002.com> **CLIENTS:** Casals, Woman, Clara, Mia, Hymsa, Fundación Expoitiner, Madame Figaro, JW Thompson, La Distillerie, CBM Media, Clarín Digital, Grijalbo, Luna, Noticias, El Porteño, Hogar Hoy, Internet Surf, Tres Puntos, El Espectador, El Planeta Urbano, Sección Aurea, Disney Explora, La Prensa, Perfil.

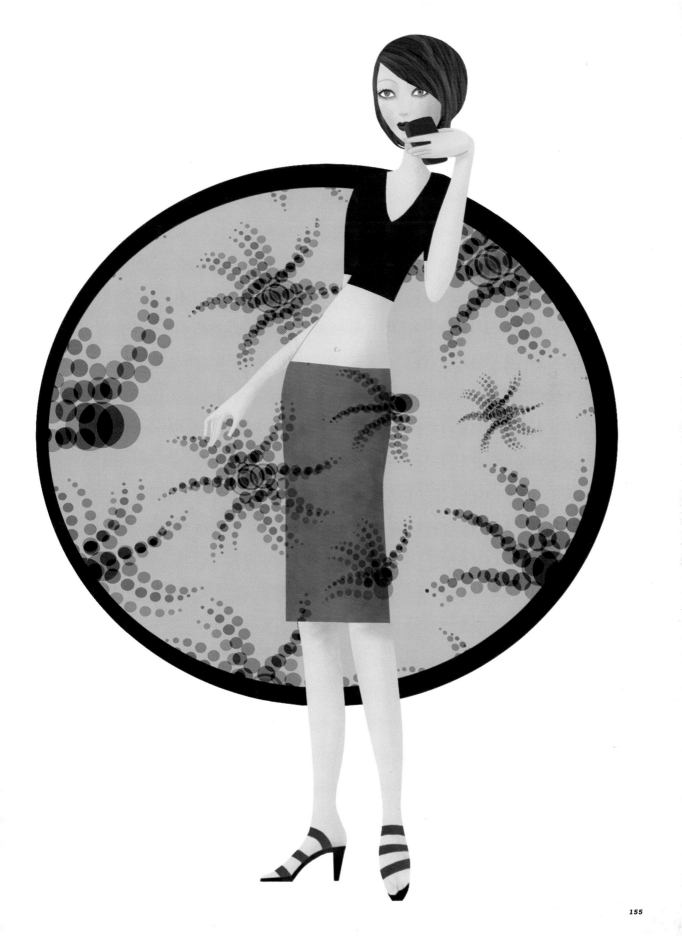

Forever Young

Forever Young explores an rich, dreamlike universe, populated with colourful impressions, day dreams, furtive visions and selective memories.

Forever Young explore un univers riche et onirique peuplé d'impressions colorées, de rêves éveillés, de visions furtives et de souvenirs sélectifs.

Forever Young erkundet ein komplexes, traumhaftes Universum, bewohnt von farbenfrohen Eindrücken, Tagträumen, heimlichen Visionen und ausgewählten Erinnerungen.

NAME: Forever Young: Olivier Leprivier and Leslie Clerc **LOCATION:** Paris, France **CONTACT:** contact@creative-syndicate **TOOLS:** Pencil, ink, photographs, Adobe Photoshop, Adobe Illustrator. **AGENT:** Creative Syndicate <www.creative-syndicate.com> **CLIENTS:** Coca-Cola, Galeries Lafayette, Sampling Agency, BP Architecture.

Douglas Fraser

As a graphic artist, having my work printed is the final goal. A variety of printed material, newspapers, magazines, comics, posters, etc. have all been a source of inspiration since childhood. The look of my work, which I define as comic-book-social-realism, developed by combining a reductive, generic quality with a specific, figurative presentation. I describe or communicate with line and black shadows laid over colour.

En tant que graphiste, mon objectif final consiste à ce que mon travail soit imprimé. Journaux, magazines, bandes dessinées, posters, etc., des supports imprimés en tous genres sont mes sources d'inspiration depuis l'enfance. J'ai développé le style de mon travail, que je définis comme du réalisme social de bande dessinée, en combinant une qualité générique réductive avec une présentation figurative spécifique. Je décris ou communique avec des ombres hachurées ou noires sur de la couleur.

Als grafischer Künstler ist es mein Hauptziel, dass meine Arbeiten gedruckt werden. Eine Vielzahl von Medien, wie Zeitungen, Zeitschriften, Comics, Poster, etc. dienten mir seit meiner Kindheit als Quellen der Inspiration. Meine Arbeiten würde ich als sozialrealistische Comicbücher beschreiben, eine Kombination aus reduzierter, generischer Qualität mit einer ganz speziellen bildlichen Präsentation. Ich beschreibe und kommuniziere mit Linien sowie schwarzen Schatten, die ich über die Farbschichten auftrage.

www.fraserart.com

NAME: Douglas Fraser **LOCATION:** Victoria, British Columbia, Canada **CONTACT:** doug@fraserart.com **TOOLS:** Alkyds (oil based), brush & ink, Adobe Illustrator.
AGENT: Lindgren & Smith (USA) <www.lindgrensmith.com>; Catherine Collins (UK) <catherinecollins.co.uk> **CLIENTS:** New York Times, Los Angeles Times, Chicago Tribune, Washington Post, TIME magazine, Los Angeles Magazine, Rolling Stone, The Progressive, NIKE, LEVI'S, Suzuki, Samsung, SONY, etc...

Craig Frazier

Ideas are an essential ingredient in creating an illustrated voice. Without them, we have little foundation in telling a story that will arrest anyone's attention for more than a second. It's the idea that draws the viewer beyond the surface of the page. It's the idea that establishes the premise for the conversation. It's the idea that rescues us from our tendency to think along dangerously straight and ordinary lines. It's the idea that moves us. If an illustration has a central idea, it offers more to assess than simply its subjective features. It doesn't mean it will be accepted just because it has one, but with an intellectual basis, our work becomes much more receptive to objective evaluation. Working in ideas gives us a meter to judge the merit of our solutions. We begin to look for answers inside the heart of our drawings.

Les idées contribuent de façon essentielle à la création d'une voix illustrée. Sans elle, nous n'avons presque pas de base pour raconter une histoire qui retiendra l'attention de qui que ce soit pendant plus d'une seconde. C'est l'idée qui attire l'observateur au-delà de la surface de la page. C'est l'idée qui établit la prémisse de la conversation. C'est l'idée qui nous sauve de notre tendance à penser selon des lignes dangereusement droites et ordinaires. C'est l'idée qui nous meut. Lorsqu'une illustration comporte une idée centrale, elle offre plus à juger que ses seuls traits subjectifs. Cela ne veut pas dire que l'illustration sera acceptée par le simple fait qu'elle comporte une idée mais, avec une base intellectuelle, notre travail devient bien plus réceptif à l'évaluation objective. Travailler avec des idées nous donne un moyen de juger les mérites de nos solutions. Nous commençons à chercher des réponses au cœur de nos dessins.

Ideen sind der wichtigste Bestandteil bei der Kreation einer illustrativen Stimme. Ohne diese Stimme haben wir wenig Möglichkeiten, Gehör zu finden. Die Idee lässt den Besucher unter die Oberfläche der Seite schauen. Die Idee gibt Anlass für weiteres Interesse. Die Idee rettet uns davor, nur in geraden und gewöhnlichen Linien zu denken. Es ist die Idee, die uns bewegt. Hat die Illustration eine zentrale Idee, bietet sie uns, ausser den offensichtlichen Merkmalen, eine Vielzahl von Bewertungsmöglichkeiten. Das heisst natürlich noch lange nicht, dass dies aufgrund der Idee akzeptiert wird, doch mit einer intellektuellen Basis besteht weitaus mehr Möglichkeit, unsere Arbeit unter einem objektiven Gesichtspunkt zu betrachten. Wenn wir mit Ideen arbeiten, geben wir uns selbst einen Masstab an die Hand, mit dem wir den Erfolg unserer Lösungsvorschläge beurteilen können. Wir beginnen, in dem Herzen unserer Zeichnungen nach Antworten zu suchen.

www.craigfrazier.com

NAME: Craig Frazier **LOCATION:** Mill Valley, CA, USA **CONTACT:** craig@craigfrazier.com **TOOLS:** Micron 01 pen, tissue pad, Exacto knife and amberlith, Adobe Photoshop. **AWARDS:** American Illustration, Communication Arts, Graphis, Society of Illustrators. **AGENT:** Joni Pon, Craig Frazier Studio <joni@craigfrazier.com>
CLIENTS: NY Times, Time Magazine, Fortune, Forbes, Newsweek, Wall Street Journal, Adobe, American Express, Chevrolet, MasterCard, United Airlines, and more.

Colour is the most important feature of my illustration works. I prefer using simple lines and colours showing diverse subjects, especially interesting scenes combined, old scenery and high-tech of the future. There are often some giant robots, weapons or spacecrafts shuttling or creating enormous smoke or explosion around the traditional Taiwanese architecture in my illustrations. I hope every image of my works could leave infinite space for viewers` imagination and that they could also feel the interaction between the characters and stories of my works.

La couleur est la caractéristique la plus importante de mes travaux d'illustration. Je privilégie des lignes et des couleurs simples montrant divers sujets et notamment des scènes intéressantes dans lesquelles sont combinés des paysages anciens et des éléments high-tech futuristes. Dans mes illustrations, au milieu de l'architecture taiwanaise traditionnelle, on trouve souvent des robots géants, des armes ou des vaisseaux spatiaux laissant derrière eux un énorme nuage de fumée. J'espère que chacune de mes images laisse le champ libre à l'imagination des observateurs et que ces derniers peuvent également ressentir les interactions entre les personnages et les histoires de mes travaux.

Farbe ist für mich das wichtigste Element meiner Illustrationen. Ich bevorzuge, unterschiedliche Themen mit einfachen Linien und Farben darzustellen, die Kombination interessanter Gegebenheiten, Altbekanntes sowie High Tech der Zukunft. In meinen Illustrationen stelle ich oft riesige Roboter, Waffen oder fliegende Raumschiffe dar, kreiere Rauch und Explosionen im Stil taiwanesischer Architektur. Ich hoffe, die Bilder meiner Arbeiten lassen genügend Freiraum für die Fantasie der Zuschauer und die Interaktion zwischen den Charakteren und den Geschichten meiner Arbeiten ist ersichtlich.

www.fu-design.com

NAME: Chu Keng FU **LOCATION:** Taipei, Taiwan **CONTACT:** fudesign@mail2000.com.tw **TOOLS:** Macromedia Flash, Adobe Photoshop. **AWARDS:** Netdiver Best of the Year, FWA Site Of The Day, Two star plasticpilot, Internet tiny awards, Graphics.com Team, Coolhomepage.com, etc

Carmen G. Huerta

Basically I try to achieve an harmonious mix between machine and handmade work; though working mostly with a computer, which normally makes figures look too correct and cold, my challenge is to give some kind of warmth and human touch to the expressions. In addition to this, I think the point is about being able to reconcile newness and hottest trends with the classical concept of charm and elegance, which to me defines fashion illustration through the ages.

J'essaie en fait de créer un mélange harmonieux entre le dessin à l'ordinateur et celui à la main. Travaillant essentiellement avec un ordinateur, ce qui donne des formes trop correctes et trop froides, mon défi est d'apporter de la chaleur et une touche humaine aux expressions. En plus de cela, je pense que l'enjeu est d'être capable de concilier la nouveauté et les tendances les plus en vogue avec le concept classique de charme et d'élégance, qui définit à mon avis l'illustration à travers les âges.

Grundsätzlich versuche ich, eine gute Mischung zwischen Maschinenleistung und manuellen Arbeiten zu erreichen; da meist mit dem Computer gearbeitet wird, sehen die Figuren oft zu perfekt und unpersönlich aus. Ich sehe es als Herausforderung an, ihnen einen etwas wärmeren und menschlicheren Ausdruck zu verleihen. Ausserdem halte ich es für wichtig, Neuheiten und die heissesten Modetrends mit dem klassischen Konzept von Charme und Eleganz zu versöhnen, denn genau das definiert für mich zeitlose moderne Illustration.

www.cghuerta.com

NAME: Carmen García Huerta **LOCATION:** Madrid, Spain **CONTACT:** carmen@cghuerta.com **TOOLS:** Pencil, Adobe Illustrator, Adobe Photoshop. **AGENT:** Agent002 <www.agent002.com> **CLIENTS:** Vogue, Elle (Spain); Glamour, Madame (Germany); L'Officiel (Russia), Monsieur (France), Hint Magazine (NY), Woman, Vanidad, Ragazza, El País Semanal, Custo Barcelona, Kellogg's, Loewe, Eric Bompard, Carrera & Carrera, Jean Louis David, Unipapel, and more.

Andreas Gefe

For an illustration I need the following: 1. confidence, 2. sufficient time for a good idea in which at least one person occurs, 3. sufficient time for the realisation, 4. music. When these conditions are met, I try to paint a picture that I'd like to hang on my own wall at home. The decisive moment for me was the experience that it is worth following my own heart and persuing what I like. Only then I find a motive that agrees with a livingroom-wall.

Pour réaliser un travail d'illustration, j'ai besoin des éléments suivants : 1. de la confiance, 2. suffisamment de temps pour une bonne idée dans laquelle au moins une personne intervient, 3. suffisamment de temps pour la réalisation, 4. de la musique. Lorsque toutes ces conditions sont remplies, j'essaie de peindre une image que j'aimerais accrocher dans mon propre appartement. Le jour où j'ai constaté qu'il valait mieux que j'écoute mon cœur et que je continue à faire ce que j'aime a été décisif pour moi. Ce n'est que dans ces conditions que je peux trouver un motif qui puisse être digne du mur de mon salon.

Für eine Illustration brauche ich: 1.Vertrauen, 2. genügend Zeit für eine gute Idee in der mindestens ein Mensch vorkommt, 3. genügend Zeit zur Ausführung, 4. Musik. Wenn diese Bedingungen gegeben sind, versuche ich ein Bild zu malen, das ich zuhause aufhängen möchte. Für mich war der entscheidende Moment die Erfahrung, dass es sich lohnt der eigenen Nase, den eigenen Vorlieben nachzugehen. Nur so find ich ein Motiv, das sich mit einer Wohnzimmerwand verträgt.

NAME: Andreas Gefe **LOCATION:** Zürich, Switzerland **CONTACT:** gefe@bluemail.ch **TOOLS:** Acryl auf Karton, Monotypie, Adobe Photoshop. **AWARDS:** Eidgenössischen Wettbewerb für Gestaltung, Atelierstipendium des SchweizerischenBundesamtes für Kultur, Stiftung A.Wirz, Atelierstipendium des Kanton Schwyz, Comicwerkjahr der Stadt Zürich **CLIENTS:** Weltwoche, Das Magazin, NZZ am Sonntag,NZZ Folio,Strapazin, TagesAnzeiger, Handelszeitung, Vibrations.

Gomes

Marcio

No matter how or what my work is, it is always rooted on the firm belief that the style of an image is very important… but never as much as its concept.

Quel que soit mon travail, il est toujours dicté par la ferme conviction que le style d'une image est très important mais jamais autant que son concept.

Ganz egal, wie oder was meine Arbeiten darstellen, sie basieren stets auf der Überzeugung, dass der Stil eines Bildes ausserordentlich wichtig ist,…aber niemals so wichtig, wie sein Konzept.

www.magopaco.com

NAME: Marcio Gomes **LOCATION:** Rio de Janeiro, Brazil **CONTACT:** marciogomes@magopaco.com **TOOLS:** Adobe Photoshop, CorelDraw, pencil, technical pen.

Ben GOSS

I take every illustration project on it's own merits. In Editorial I like to do something that is be parallel to the story or subject matter. I don't like to be too literal or obvious. This way I can add something to the project. The illustration has to do the thing the words can't. I think illustration should be clever, intelligent and beautiful all at once. This can be the simplest thing or it can be close to bloody impossible.

Je traite chaque projet d'illustration qui m'est confié selon son mérite. Dans le domaine de la publication, j'aime établir un parallèle avec l'histoire ou le sujet. Je n'aime pas être trop littéral ou trop prévisible. Je peux ainsi apporter ma touche personnelle au projet. L'illustration doit faire le travail dont les mots sont incapables. Je pense qu'une illustration doit être intelligente et belle à la fois. Cela peut être extrêmement simple ou frôler l'impossible.

Jedes Illustrationsprojekt hat für mich seinen eigenen Wert. Im Redaktionsbereich verhalte ich mich gerne parallel zur Geschichte bzw. deren Kernaussage. Ich versuche, nicht unbedingt zu wörtlich oder offensichtlich zu sein. So bleibt mir immer die Möglichkeit, etwas dem Projekt hinzuzufügen. Illustration hat die Aufgabe, das auszudrücken, wo uns die Worte fehlen. Illustration sollte stets clever, intelligent und schön zugleich sein. Dies kann ganz einfach oder schier unmöglich erscheinen.

www.bengoss.com

NAME: Ben Goss **LOCATION:** Sydney, Australia **CONTACT:** bengoss@optusnet.com.au **TOOLS:** Acrylic, oils, medium, pencil, stretched print making paper, canvas. **AWARDS:** Communication Arts, AD&D (UK), Design Down Under (Australia), Sydney Award **AGENT:** Kate Larkworthy <www.larkworthy.com> **CLIENTS:** The New York Times, L.A. Times, Bloomberg Financial, Red Herring, Mckinsey, Ray Gun magazine, Yahoo, Chronicle Books, London Financial Review, Readers Digest, Elle, and more.

Ulli Grötz

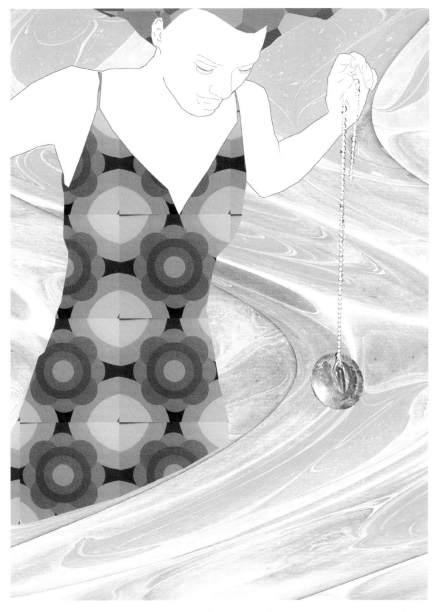

To give some colourful pleasure to the mind at the prepared table, inspiration takes a seat and consumes a biscuit.

Pour donner du plaisir coloré à l'esprit attablé, l'inspiration s'assoit et mange un biscuit.

Dem Verstand ein buntes Vergnügen bereiten an den vorbereiteten Tisch nimmt die Inspiration Platz um den Keks zu verspeisen.

www.subita.de

NAME: Ulli Grötz *LOCATION:* Kassel, Germany *CONTACT:* illustration@subita.de *TOOLS:* Adobe Photoshop. *CLIENTS:* Young Miss, Amica, HLZ Magazine.

Martin Haake

Telephone doodles, bad paintings, art brut and folk art - all that inspires me. I love the imperfect. I love every drawing that went wrong.

Gribouillages au téléphone, mauvaises peintures, art brut et art populaire, tout cela m'inspire. J'aime l'imperfection. J'aime les dessins non réussis.

Gekritzel beim Telefonieren, schlechte Gemälde, Kunst in Rohform und Traditionskunst - all das inspiriert mich. Ich liebe alles, das nicht perfekt ist. Ich liebe jede Zeichnung, die man als misslungen bezeichnen würde.

www.martinhaake.de

NAME: Martin Haake **LOCATION:** Berlin, Germany **CONTACT:** mail@martinhaake.de **TOOLS:** brush, acrylic, Adobe Photoshop. **AWARDS:** ADC Germany (Silver), D&AD UK (Silver), American Illustration, images-best of british illustration. **AGENT:** Lindgren & Smith (USA) < www.lindgrensmith.com>; CIA (UK) <www.centralillustration.com> **CLIENTS:** Barnes & Noble, Penguin Books, Washington Post, Bloomberg Wealth Manager, Playboy, GQ, Elle, Daimler Chrysler, Bacardi, JD Edwards, SZ Magazin, etc.

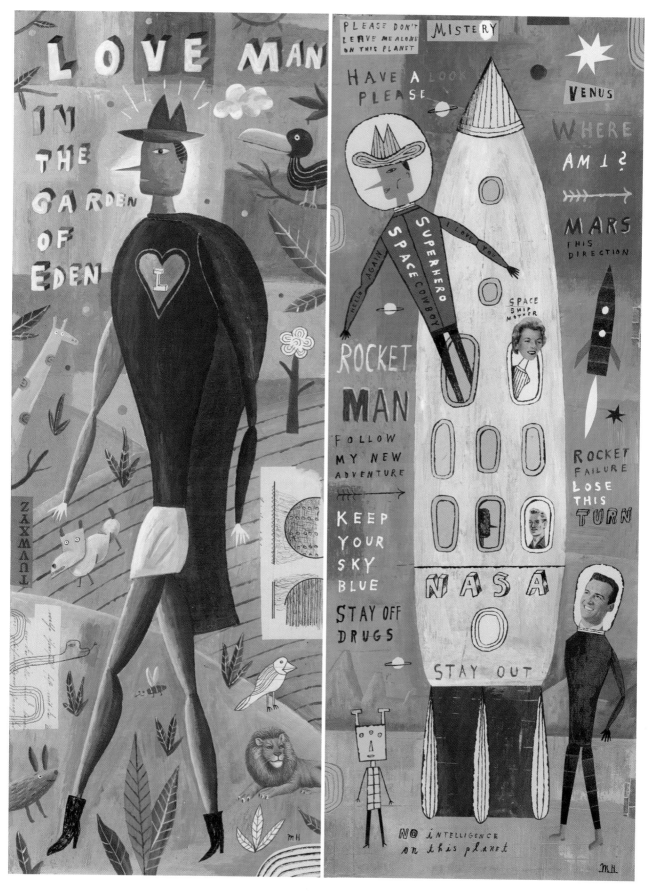

Olaf Hajek

My works are created with brush and colour only. I paint with acrylic on cardboard. The texture and surface feel of the material is very important and gives me a feeling of satisfaction while working. Stylistically I work with a certain naivety, combined with realistic ideas. Proportions and perspectives become neutralized. Influences from American Folkart, African art or Indian miniatures are worked into my realisation of modern subjects such as fashion, industry or psychology.

Dans mes travaux, je n'utilise que le pinceau et de la couleur. Je peins à l'acrylique sur du carton. La texture et la surface du matériau sont très importants et me donnent un sentiment de satisfaction pendant que je travaille. Mon style est assez naïf et est combiné avec des idées réalistes. Les proportions et les perspectives sont neutralisées. Je m'inspire de l'art populaire américain, de l'art africain ou de miniatures indiennes pour traiter des thèmes modernes tels que la mode, l'industrie ou la psychologie.

Meine Arbeiten entstehen ausschließlich mit Pinsel und Farbe. Ich male mit Acryl auf Karton. Die Textur und Haptik des Materials ist sehr wichtig und gibt mir das befriedigende Gefühl bei der Arbeit. Stilistisch arbeite ich mit einer gewissen Naivität, kombiniert mit realistischen Versatzstücken. Proportionen und Perspektiven werden aufgehoben. Meine Einflüsse von American Folkart, Afrikanischer Kunst oder indischen Miniaturen lasse ich in die Umsetzung moderner Themen, wie Mode, Wirtschaft oder Psychologie einfließen.

www.olafhajek.com

NAME: Olaf Hajek **LOCATION:** Berlin, Germany **CONTACT:** olafhajek@yahoo.com **TOOLS:** Acrylic on Cardboard **AWARDS:** ADC Europe (Gold), ADC Germany (Silver), D&AD London (Silver), Lead Award (Gold/Silver). **AGENT:** (Germany, Switzerland, Austria) <www.jutta-fricke.de>; (UK) <www.centralillustration.com>; (USA/Japan) <www.larkworthy.com>; (France) <www.agent002.com> **CLIENTS:** Bacardi, DaimlerChrysler, Nike, Rolling Stone, Playboy, GQ, The NewYork Times, etc.

HELMUT LANG

Asaf Hanuka

As kid I used to read a lot of comics, and as an adult I still do, and even got to publish few comic books, among them Bipolar, an experimental collaboration with my twin brother Tomer Hanuka. As an illustrator I sometime feel I am an undercover agent of comics, drawing frames of stories that never started and will never end, but will let the viewer, for a brief moment, meet few of those lost heroes.

Lorsque j'étais enfant, je lisais beaucoup de bandes dessinées. C'est toujours vrai aujourd'hui. J'ai même publié quelques BD, dont Bipolar, fruit d'une collaboration expérimentale avec mon frère jumeau Tomer Hanuka. En tant qu'illustrateur, j'ai parfois l'impression que je suis un agent secret de la BD, qui dessine des vignettes racontant des histoires qui n'ont jamais commencé et ne finiront jamais, mais qui permettront au lecteur, pour un court instant, de rencontrer quelques-uns de ces héros perdus.

Als Kind las ich viele Comics und als Erwachsener ebenso. Ich habe sogar ein paar Comicbücher veröffentlicht, unter anderem Bipolar, ein Experiment, das ich in Kollaboration mit meinem Bruder, Tomer Hanuka, durchführte. Als Illustrator habe ich manchmal das Gefühl, ich sei ein Comic-Geheimagent, der unzählige Bilder einer Geschichte zeichnet, die niemals begonnen und auch kein Ende hat, aber sie gibt dem Leser das Gefühl, für einen kurzen Moment einige dieser verlorenen Helden treffen zu können.

www.asafhanuka.com

NAME: Asaf Hanuka **LOCATION:** Tel Aviv, Israel **CONTACT:** asaf@asafhanuka.com **TOOLS:** Pen and Ink. **AGENT:** Gerald & Cullen Rapp <www.rappart.com> **CLIENTS:** Rolling Stone, Fortune Small Business, Spin, New York Times, Time, The Source Magazine, The Wall Street. Journal, The New TNN, Forbes, L.A. Times, U.S. News and World Report, Bloomberg, Scholastic, Men's Journal, PC World and Nintendo Power Magazine.

STEADY MOBBIN'

Radio promotion has more hustle than a Vegas card shark, meaning it takes much more than a good record to get airplay. We investigate these cloudy waters to find out whether this corrupt business practice is killing hip-hop.

Words by Lamar Maddox
Illustration by Assaf Hanuka

Know this: The cold politics of radio bite. "They said the record was wack," recalls veteran music man Jay Ones with a tone of bewilderment. "This group's hometown wasn't even playing the record at all because they thought it was not a hit." Speaking from the midtown Manhattan offices that house music consultant firm RPM Promotions and Marketing, the independent record promoter is in the middle of giving a Record Marketing 101 crash course. It was in December 2001 that RPM first got the call to promote a new single called "Grindin'" by little-known Norfolk, Va., hip-hop duo the Clipse.

"We were getting fronted on by some of the radio-station programmers, but in the clubs you could see a reaction," Ones says. "So me, their producer Pharrell [of the Neptunes] and the Clipse went on the road in a Winnebago and rode around the whole East Coast. We even went to Wilmington, N.C., where we did a free radio show. There were, like, 50 kids at this station early and when ['Grindin''] came on, all you heard were these kids going crazy. That's when we knew we had something."

As the Clipse story shows, getting your record to be taken seriously by any major market radio station, even in your hometown, is not as simple as making a great record. Even with the type of grassroots promotional efforts implemented on behalf of the Clipse, for most artists, getting songs placed on commercial radio has become an exercise in futility. Whereas in the past record label promoters and fresh-faced music acts barnstormed college campuses, local clubs and radio stations across the country in hopes of creating the next Jay-Z or Nelly, independent promoters, also known as indies, have become the new tastemakers for *Billboard* Top 40 glory. These brokers are now the underlining gatekeeper between underground infamy and SoundScan success. In this clandestine world, payola—an illegal practice in which a station employee accepts payments for playing a song—has become a legitimate practice.

"Today, getting your song on the radio more often is not about your local fan base, the quality of your music, or how hard you are working," says Michael Bracey, co-founder and chairman of the Future of Music Coalition, a nonprofit Washington, D.C., think tank that addresses pressing music-industry issues. "It's about what resources you are able to muster to put the machinery in place that can get your song pushed through."

Within payola's intricate system, record labels pay hefty sums to indies to push their records. Indies, in turn, pay stations yearly "promotion" fees at rates reported to run as high as $300,000. In exchange, indies become the exclusive brokers of broadcast companies, receiving weekly report cards that keep scores on new songs. As one radio insider explains it, "The indies are the middleman. It's like, instead of killing your wife, you hire somebody to do it. Instead of giving the payola directly to the DJ, you are giving it to the indie, who funnels the money to the radio station."

HOW WIDESPREAD IS THIS labol? Radio station conglomerates such as Emmis Communications Corp., Radio One and broadcasting giant Clear Channel Communications Inc. have all operated within the questionable yet legal practice of indie radio promo. San Antonio-based Clear Channel, whose vast empire of 1,225 radio stations includes New York's Power 105 and Los Angeles' Hot 92 Jams, is by far the nation's largest radio broadcast company. But recently, the conglomerate has been the target of media and political criticism for its dealings with indie promotion. Last September, Clear Channel made headlines when it granted three independent music promoters, Ted Astin, Wes Johnson and Reuben Rodriguez, exclusive rights to pitch records to its urban music program directors.

Record executives balked at the deal as promotional prices rose from a reported 20 percent to 100 percent at 42 Clear Channel urban stations—skyrocketing fees and charg-

Tomer Hanuka

I like drama. I feel it's the main engine of what I strive for in illustration. Sometimes it tips into horror, which is a developed dramatic language with certain rules that can be played off. The type of horror you see in B-Movies with a sense of self-awareness and humour. I am trying to go over the top and make it flamboyant. It could be a reactionary response, putting the drama back in horror where everything matters just a little too much.

J'aime le tragique. Je crois que c'est le principal moteur de mon travail d'illustration. Parfois, cela verse dans l'horreur, un langage dramatique développé doté de certaines règles qui peuvent être mises en contradiction. Le type d'horreur que l'on trouve dans les films de série B, avec une conscience de soi et un sens de l'humour. J'essaie de repousser les limites et de donner du flamboyant à mon travail. Une réponse réactionnaire pourrait consister à remettre le tragique dans l'horreur où tout a un petit peu trop d'importance.

Mir gefällt alles Dramatische. Für mich ist es der Hauptantrieb für das, was ich mit meinen Illustrationen erreichen möchte. Manchmal schlägt es in Horror über, der sich als dramatische Sprache mit ihren eigenen Regeln ausdrückt, die allerdings jederzeit überspielt werden können. Diese Art von Horror, die man aus den B-Movies kennt, mit Sinn für Selbstbewusstsein und Humor. Ich versuche, über die Grenzen zu schlagen und es extravagant erscheinen zu lassen. Beispielsweise die Verbindung von Drama mit Horror, so dass jegliche Begebenheit etwas zuviel an Bedeutung gewinnt.

www.thanuka.com

NAME: Tomer Hanuka **LOCATION:** London, UK **CONTACT:** tomer@thanuka.com **TOOLS:** Ink, Brush, Adobe Photoshop. **AWARDS:** Society of illustrators (Gold), Society of Illustrators (Silver), Society of publications Designers (Silver), American Illustration. **AGENT:** Gerald & Cullen Rapp <www.rappart.com> **CLIENTS:** Rolling Stone, The New York Times, The New Yorker, GQ, ESPN Magazine, Forbes Magazine, New York Magazine, Fast Company, Thompson Financial Media, Fortune Magazine, etc.

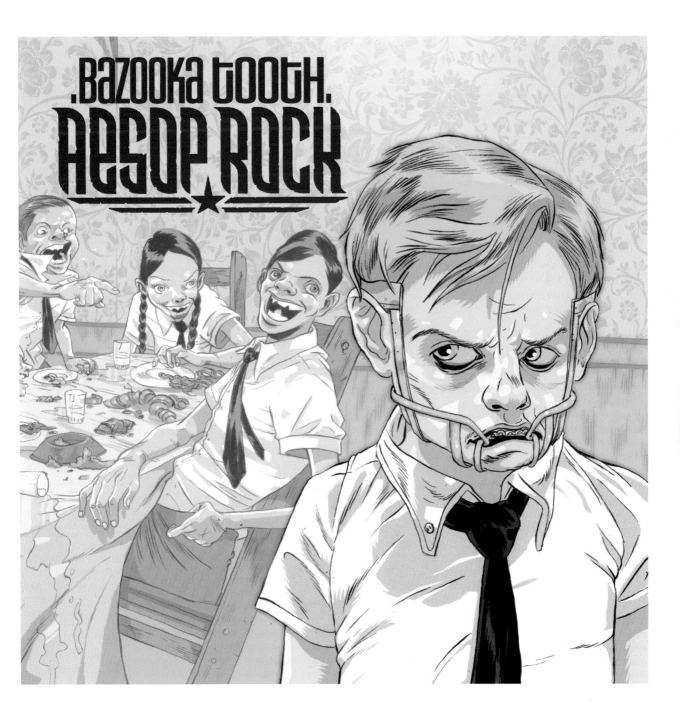

Warren Heise

I see illustration as a way for me to communicate with the world around me. By combining symbols that exist in our collective consciousness with those from my imagination, I have created a visual language that is uniquely my own. Along with the conceptual aspect of illustrating, the creative process is equally important. I often experiment by trying new techniques or by working in different mediums. This causes my work to vary stylistically and keeps the process fresh and exciting.

L'illustration est pour moi un moyen de communiquer avec le monde qui m'entoure. En mêlant des symboles existants dans notre inconscient collectif à ceux issus de mon imagination, je crée un langage visuel personnel. Le processus créatif est tout aussi important que l'aspect conceptuel. J'expérimente souvent en essayant de nouvelles techniques ou en travaillant avec des supports différents. Ainsi le style de mon travail varie en permanence et le processus de création reste inédit et excitant.

Illustration gibt mir die Möglichkeit, mit der Welt, die mich umgibt, zu kommunizieren. Durch Kombination von Symbolik – die, die bereits in unserem Bewusstsein existiert und die, die mein Vorstellungsvermögen erfasst–, habe ich meine eigene visuelle Sprache entwickelt. Gemeinsam mit dem konzeptuellen Aspekt von Illustration ist auch der kreative Prozess von grosser Wichtigkeit. Ich experimentiere stets mit neuen Techniken und unterschiedlichen Medien. Dadurch ändert sich oft der Stil meiner Arbeiten und der Prozess bleibt somit frisch und aufregend.

www.warrenheise.com

NAME: Warren Heise **LOCATION:** Edmonton, Alberta, Canada **CONTACT:** info@warrenheise.com **TOOLS:** Pencil, pen and ink, acrylics, silkscreen, stencils, Adobe Photoshop, Adobe Illustrator. **AWARDS:** American Illustration, Applied Arts, Graphics Canada Digital Art Competition. **CLIENTS:** Alphabet City, Pictoplasma, Wear It With Pride, MTV, Target, Bioware, LTD Snowboards, Apocalypse Snowboards, Greenpeace International, Highlights for Children Magazine, etc.

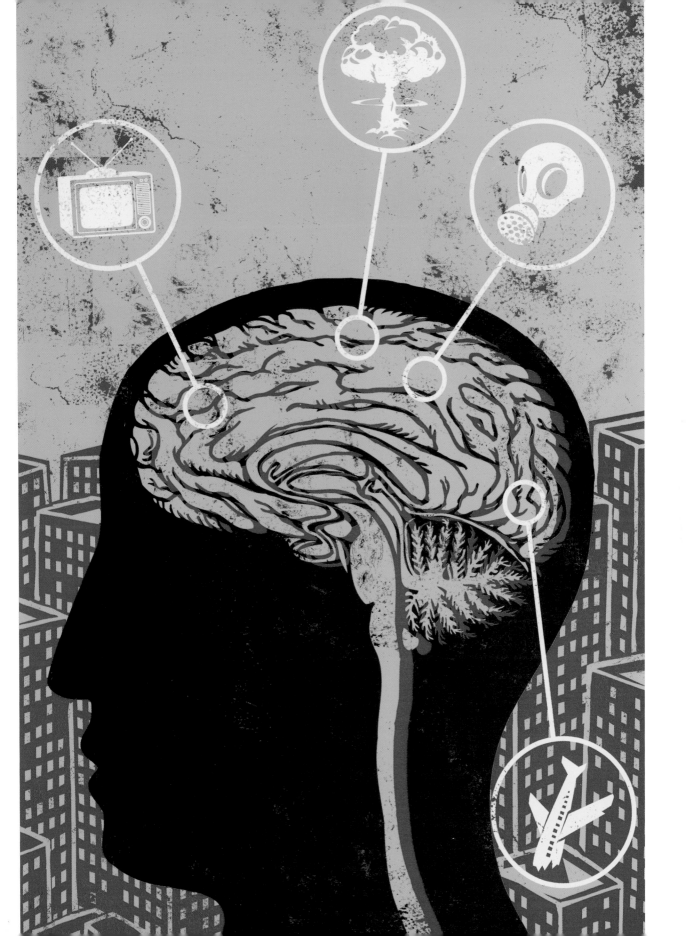

John Hendrix

I love to draw. My work is completely about drawing. There is something beautiful about the solitude of pen, paper, and a voice. The joy of making images, to me, is telling a small story. Not a lofty goal, nor a unique one to be sure. So, I don't consider drawing a mystical process, but merely a socially acceptable addiction. It is so important to be grateful and to admire the work of my elders and peers.

J'adore dessiner. Mon travail n'est rien d'autre que dessiner. La solitude du crayon, du papier et d'une voix a quelque chose de beau. Pour moi, la joie de créer des images raconte une petite histoire. Cet objectif n'est ni inatteignable ni unique. En bref, pour moi, le dessin n'est pas un processus mystique mais simplement une drogue socialement acceptable. Il est tellement important d'être reconnaissant et d'admirer le travail des ses aînés et de ses pairs.

Ich liebe es, zu zeichnen. In meiner Arbeit dreht sich alles ums Zeichnen. Die Einsamkeit eines Stiftes, eines Blattes und einer Stimme hat für mich etwas besonders Schönes. Bilder zu entwerfen, bedeutet für mich, eine kleine Geschichte zu erzählen. Sicherlich kein erhabenes oder aussergewöhnliches Ziel. Von daher bewerte ich Zeichnen nicht als einen mystischen Prozess, es ist für mich schlicht und einfach eine Sucht, die von der Gesellschaft anerkannt wird. Das Wichtigste ist, dankbar zu sein sowie die Arbeiten meiner Vorfahren und meinesgleichen wertzuschätzen.

www.johnhendrix.com

NAME: John Hendrix **LOCATION:** New York, USA **CONTACT:** mail@johnhendrix.com **TOOLS:** Pen & Ink, Acrylic. **AWARDS:** American Illustration, Society of Illustrators, SPD SPOT Competition, Communication Arts. **CLIENTS:** Sports Illustrated, Rolling Stone, The New Yorker, The Wall Street Journal, The New York Times, Scholastic Books, Harvard Business Review, Fast Company, New York Magazine, The Village Voice, PASTE Magazine, Random House and others.

The Rolling Stone Review

◀ *Beastie Boys as illustrated by*
John Hendrix

213

Jody Hewgill

I approach each assignment with the intent of capturing the essence of my subject, whether it is a portrait of someone or the driving theme of a play. My solutions may be conceptual, expressive, or merely decorative and I use stylization, colour and textures to help express the mood. I don't confine myself to literal depiction for I like to employ a little magic realism in some of my pieces. The art of Frida Kahlo and Pablo Picasso have been great sources of inspiration.

A chaque commande, mon intention est de capturer l'essence de mon sujet, qu'il s'agisse d'un portrait ou du thème principal d'une pièce de théâtre. Mes solutions peuvent être conceptuelles, expressives ou simplement décoratives et j'utilise la stylisation, la couleur et les textures pour créer une atmosphère. Je ne me limite pas à une illustration littérale car j'aime employer un peu de réalisme magique dans certains de mes travaux. Les œuvres de Frida Kahlo et de Pablo Picasso sont de grandes sources d'inspiration pour moi.

Ich gehe jeden Auftrag mit der Absicht an, die Essenz der Materie zu erfassen, ganz gleich ob es sich dabei um ein Portrait oder die Hauptaussage eines Theaterstückes handelt. Meine Lösungsvorschläge können konzeptionell, ausdrucksstark oder ganz einfach dekorativ sein und ich verwende Stilisierung, Farben sowie Oberflächen, um eine gewisse Stimmung auszudrücken. Ich begrenze mich nicht auf literarische Beschreibungen, oft gefällt mir ein wenig magischer Realismus für meine Arbeiten. Die Kunst von Frida Kahlo und Pablo Picasso sind meine Quellen der Inspiration.

www.jodyhewgill.com

NAME: Jody Hewgill **LOCATION:** Toronto, Ontario, Canada **CONTACT:** jody@jodyhewgill.com **TOOLS:** Acrylic paint on gessoed board or wood. **AWARDS:** The Society of Illustrators NY, Society of Illustrators LA, Advertising Design Club of Canada, Society of Publication Designers, American Illustration, Communication Arts. **CLIENTS:** Time Magazine, Entertainment Weekly, Los Angeles Magazine, Arena Stage, Holland America Cruises, Rolling Stone magazine, United Airlines, etc.

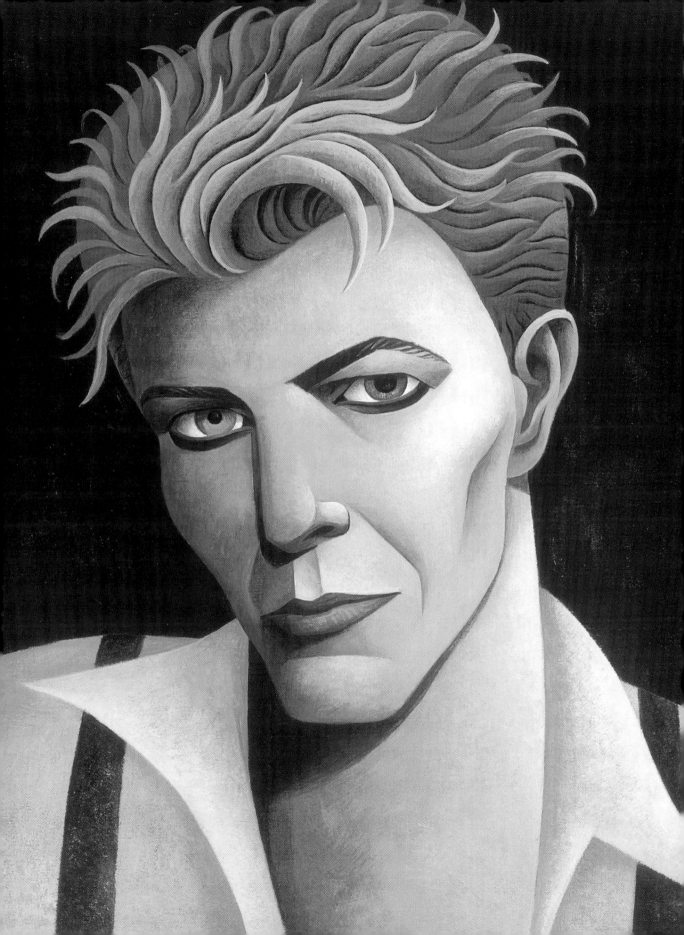

OCTOBER 25, 2004
TIME
IRAQ'S POWER BROKER
PIXAR'S INCREDIBLE NEW MOVIE
Does our DNA compel us to seek a higher power? Believe it or not, some scientists say yes
PLUS: A quiz—How spiritual are you?
THE GOD GENE
$3.95US
AOL Keyword: TIME

Brad Holland

My pictures are like book jackets for stories I haven't written and couldn't write because they're not stories that can be told in words. When a picture tells a story as a picture, it's self-sufficient. When it tries to capture a text, it becomes a hostage. I don't try to illustrate. I try to marry a picture to words and hope it's a successful marriage.

Mes images sont en quelque sorte des jaquettes de livres racontant des histoires que je n'ai pas écrites et que je ne pourrai jamais écrire car ce ne sont pas des histoires qui se racontent avec des mots. Lorsqu'une image raconte une histoire comme une image, elle est autosuffisante. Lorsqu'elle tente de capturer un texte, elle devient otage. Je n'essaie pas d'illustrer, j'essaie de marier une image à des mots en espérant que ce sera un mariage heureux.

Meine Bilder sind vergleichbar mit Bucheinbänden für Geschichten, die ich nicht geschrieben habe und auch niemals schreiben könnte, da es Geschichten sind, die unmöglich in Worte zu fassen sind. Wenn ein Bild als Bild eine Geschichte erzählt, ist es in sich komplett. Wenn es jedoch versucht, einen Text mit einzuschliessen, wird es zu einer Geisel. Ich versuche nicht, zu illustrieren. Ich versuche vielmehr, ein Bild mit Worten zu verheiraten und hoffe, es wird eine erfolgreiche Ehe.

www.bradholland.net

NAME: Brad Holland **LOCATION:** New York, USA **CONTACT:** brad-holland@verizon.net **TOOLS:** Ink, pastel, acrylic, oil. **AWARDS:** 27 gold medals from the Art Director's Club NY, The Society of Illustrators and The Society of Publication Designers; Playboy Editorial Award, Biennial of Illustration in Tokyo, and more. **AGENT:** Margarethe Hubauer <www.margarethe-hubauer.de> **CLIENTS:** The New York Times, The New Yorker, Time, Life, General Electric, AT&T, Toshiba, SONY, etc.

Thriving or Dying?

Is the Bicycle Industry Better
Off Today Than It Was
10 Years Ago?

By Marc Sani

Illustration by Brad Holland

Sterling Hundley

I've always found inspiration in the work of artists who are able to abandon their academic education and to take themselves "out of drawing". They force naivety back into their artwork, but they do so with an understanding of why things. Though the drawings of these artists are naïve, the sense of design, colour, composition and concept are still applied masterfully. As I mature as an artist, I wonder, "if I only knew then what I know now". This idea drives me as I seek to find a way to reintroduce innocence into my work.

J'ai toujours puisé mon inspiration dans le travail d'artistes capables d'abandonner leur éducation académique et de s'extirper du dessin. Ils réintègrent de force la naïveté dans leur art mais en comprenant le pourquoi du comment. Bien que les dessins de ces artistes soient naïfs, le sens du design, de la couleur, de la composition et du concept reste appliqué avec maestria. A mesure que je mûris en tant qu'artiste, je me dis souvent : « Ah ! Si seulement je savais à l'époque ce que je sais maintenant ! ». Cette idée me guide alors que je cherche à trouver le moyen de réintroduire l'innocence dans mon travail.

Meine Inspiration finde ich ausschliesslich bei den Künstlern, die die Fähigkeit besitzen, sich von ihrer akademischen Ausbildung zu lösen und sich selbst "ausserhalb ihrer Zeichnungen" anzusiedeln. Sie bringen eine gewisse Naivität in ihre Bilder zurück, und das mit einem Verständnis für Fragestellungen. Trotz dieser Naivität weisen ihre Werke weiterhin einen absoluten Sinn für Design, Farbe, Komposition und Konzept auf. In meinem Reifeprozess als Künstler frage ich mich, was wohl passiert wäre, "hätte ich all dies schon vorher gewusst". Dieses Konzept animiert mich, um meiner ständigen Suche nach der Möglichkeit, eine gewisse Unschuldigkeit in meine Arbeiten einfliessen zu lassen, gerecht zu werden.

www.sterlinghundley.com

NAME: Sterling Hundley **LOCATION:** Midlothian, VA **CONTACT:** sterling404@earthlink.net **TOOLS:** Oils, Pen and Ink, Acrylics, Collage, Pencil, Pastels, anything that will make a mark, or stick to a support. **AGENT:** Richard Solomon Artists Representative <www.richardsolomon.com> **CLIENTS:** Atlantic Monthly, Rolling Stone, Vibe, Texas Monthly, the Village Voice, New York Times, LA Times, GQ, New Yorker, Utne, the Progressive, Red Bull, the Martin Agency, Mullen, Random House, Scholastic, etc.

Hungry Dog

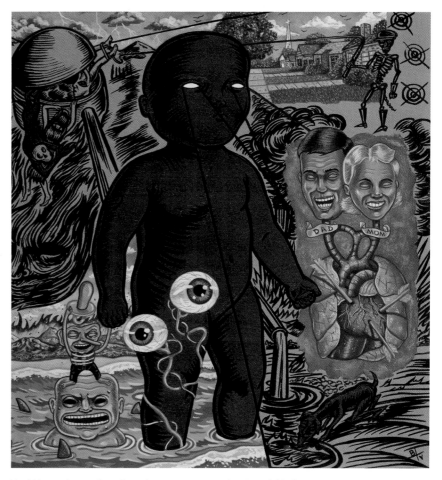

Would it surprise you if we chose the same reasons today as we did in Houston, Texas, in 1984? Have fun while making art, and find people who will pay you to have fun. How surprising to us that life and art integrated immediately, naturally and covertly. Hungry Dog Studio has evolved into who we are now, still challenging ourselves with image making and collaborating together.

Seriez-vous surpris si nous choisissions les mêmes raisons aujourd'hui qu'à Houston, Texas, en 1984 : s'amuser en faisant de l'art et trouver des gens qui vous paient pour que vous vous amusiez ? Nous avions été très étonnés de constater que la vie et l'art s'intégraient immédiatement, naturellement et secrètement. Hungry Dog Studio a évolué pour donner ce que nous sommes maintenant, nous qui nous mettons encore et toujours à l'épreuve avec la création d'images et par notre collaboration.

Wäre es verwunderlich, würden wir heute die gleichen Gründe angeben, wie damals 1984 in Houston, Texas? Habe Spass bei der Erschaffung von Kunst und suche dir Menschen, die dafür zahlen, dass du Spass hasst. Es hat uns sehr verwundert, wie Kunst und Leben sich sofort intergriert haben, ganz natürlich und doch versteckt. Hungry Dog Studio hat sich zu dem entwickelt, was wir heute verkörpern: Bildentwurf und Zusammenarbeit sind stets eine Herausforderung.

www.hungrydogstudio.com

NAME: Hungry Dog Studio **LOCATION:** Nashville, TN, USA **CONTACT:** bosco@hungrydogstudio.com **TOOLS:** mixed media. **AWARDS:** American Illustration; Art Directors Club NY (Silver), Communication Arts, Society of Publication Design, among others. **CLIENTS:** Time Magazine, Rolling Stone, Entertainment Weekly, Texas Monthly, Vibe Magazine, Murphy Design, Sagmeister Design, The Rock and Roll Hall of Fame Foundation, among others.

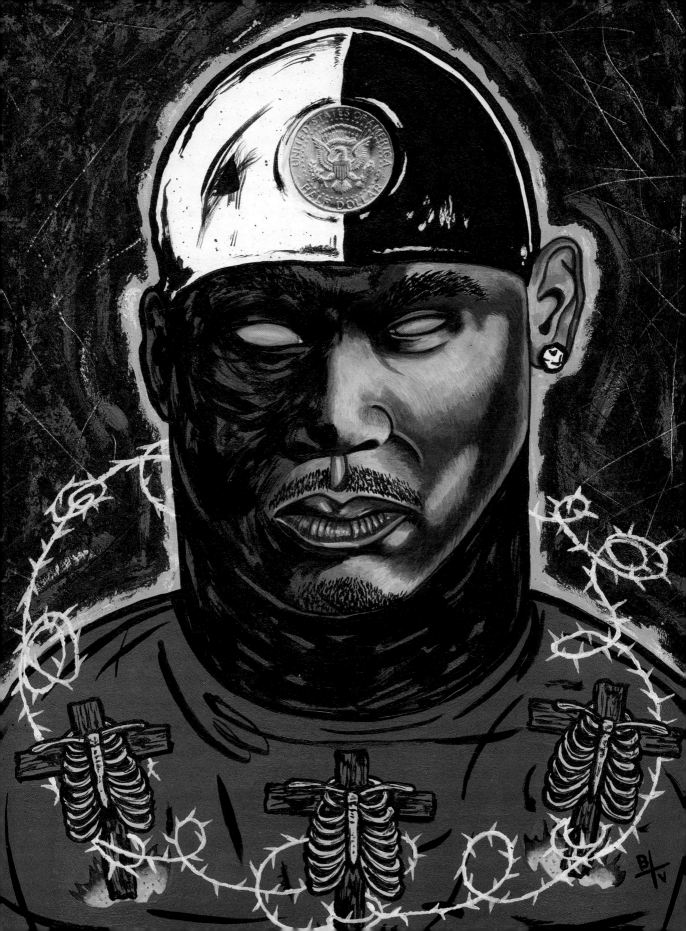

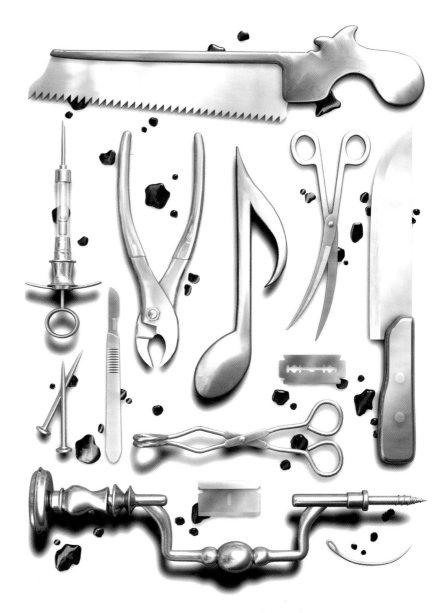

Work Philosophy: There must be either one of three things (if not all):
1) Lots of money
2) Lots of freedom
3) Lots of time

Philosophie de travail : l'une de ces trois conditions doit être remplie (si ce n'est toutes) :
1) Beaucoup d'argent
2) Beaucoup de liberté
3) Beaucoup de temps

Arbeitsphilosophie: Eines dieser drei Dinge muss vorhanden sein (wenn nicht alle drei):
1) Eine Menge Geld
2) Eine Menge Freiheit
3) Eine Menge Zeit

www.mirkoilic.com

NAME: Mirko Ilić **LOCATION:** New York, USA **CONTACT:** studio@mirkoilic.com **TOOLS:** Stick and dirt; Adobe Photoshop, Maya. **AWARDS:** Society of Illustrators, Society of Publication Designers, Art Directors Club, I.D. Magazine, Society of Newspaper Design, and others. **CLIENTS:** New York Times, L.A. Times, Wall Street Journal, Die Zeit, Time Magazine, Newsweek, National Geographic, Sports Illustrated, Nikon, Sony, Rizzoli, etc.

Jordin Isip

By using imagery, symbols, and metaphors from a personal visual vocabulary that is influenced by my history, culture, education, environment and instincts I create images that are a reflection of the way I think and interpret the world. It isn't always necessary for someone to "get it". Art doesn't always have to be easily deciphered. Success for me is sometimes just compelling someone to stop in their tracks, to engage them, and make them think. I like to make pieces that are iconic and universal, that can be read on many different levels and is open to interpretation by the viewer.

En me servant d'images, de symboles et de métaphores issus d'un vocabulaire visuel personnel marqué par mon histoire, ma culture, mon éducation, mon environnement et mes instincts, je crée des images qui sont le reflet de ma manière de penser et d'interpréter le monde. Il n'est pas toujours nécessaire que tout le monde comprenne mes illustrations. L'art ne doit pas toujours être déchiffrable facilement. Je peux parfois atteindre mon but en contraignant quelqu'un à s'arrêter, à retenir son attention et à le faire réfléchir. J'aime créer des illustrations ironiques et universelles, qui peuvent être lues à divers niveaux et sont ouvertes à l'interprétation de l'observateur.

Durch den Gebrauch von Bildern, Symbolik und Metaphern meines persönlichen visuellen Vokabulars, beeinflusst durch meine Vergangenheit, Kultur, Bildung, Umwelt und Instinkte, kreiere ich Bilder, die eine Reflektion meines Denkens und meiner Weltanschauung sind. Mir geht es nicht darum, dass mich jeder versteht. Kunst muss nicht unbedingt leicht zu entziffern sein. Erfolg bedeutet für mich der Zwang, jemanden in seimem Rhythmus stoppen zu können, ihn für sich zu gewinnen und zum Denken anzuregen. Ich kreiere gerne Kunstwerke mit ikonischem und universellem Charakter, die auf ganz unterschiedlichen Leveln verstanden werden können und deren Interpretation dem Betrachter freigestellt wird.

www.jordinisip.com

NAME: Jordin Isip **LOCATION:** New York **CONTACT:** jordin@jordinisip.com **TOOLS:** mixed-media. **AWARDS:** American Illustration, The Art Directors Club, Communication Arts, Print Magazine, The Society of Illustrators, The Society of Newspaper Designers, The Society of Publication Designers. **CLIENTS:** Adbusters, The Atlantic Monthly, The Los Angeles Times, The New York Times, Newsweek, The Progressive, Rolling Stone, Southern Records, Time Magazine, Verve Records.

Jason Cook **Jacey**

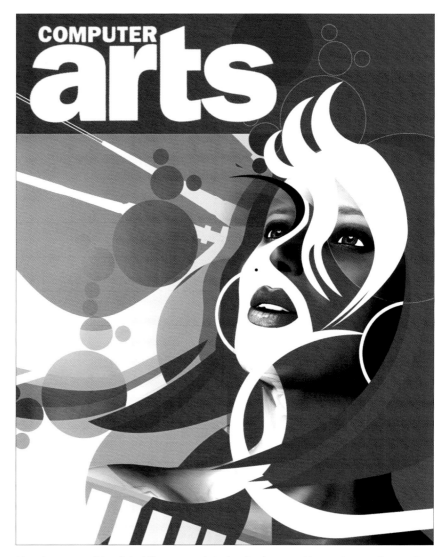

I have been a practicing digital illustrator and pixel pusher for around 8 years, I originally came from a photographic background and the progression to digital arts was a natural one. As a commercial illustrator I have divided my portfolio in to 4 varying styles and have given them their own name and entity.

Je travaille en tant qu'illustrateur numérique et « pixel pusher » depuis 8 ans environ. Ayant une formation de photographe, le passage aux arts numériques s'est fait naturellement. J'ai divisé mon portfolio d'illustrateur commercial en quatre styles différents auxquels j'ai donné un nom et une identité propre.

Die letzten acht Jahre habe ich als Illustrator im digitalen Bereich gearbeitet, ursprünglich war ich im Bereich der Fotografie tätig und von daher war der Wechsel in die Welt der digitalen Kunst ein natürlicher Prozess. Als kommerzieller Illustrator habe ich mein Portfolio in vier unterschiedliche Stilrichtungen unterteilt, jeweils mit eigenem Namen und eigener Identität.

www.jasoncook.co.uk

NAME: Jacey (Jason Cook) **LOCATION:** London, England **CONTACT:** jc@jacey.com **TOOLS:** Adobe Photoshop, Macromedia Freehand, Adobe AfterEffects, Cinema 4D, poser. **CLIENTS:** Lego, Honda, Vh1, IBM, The Times, Sky.

precious

Aaron Jasinski

Jasinski's work is most obviously marked by his vivid hues and engaging characters, but the unique appeal of his paintings is much more subtle: each face he paints is composed not only of exquisite detail, but of human emotion. Jasinski's carefully composed characters evoke feelings of familiarity and empathy within the viewer.

L'œuvre de Jasinski est surtout marquée par des nuances éclatantes et des personnages attachants. Le charme unique de ses peintures est toutefois bien plus subtil : chaque visage qu'il peint est chargé non seulement de détails mais aussi d'émotion humaine. Les personnages composés avec minutie par Jasinski éveillent des sentiments de familiarité et d'empathie chez l'observateur.

Jasinskis Arbeiten sind ganz offensichtlich durch seine lebendigen Farben und einnehmenden Charaktere geprägt, doch die besondere Anziehungskraft seiner Gemälde ist weitaus subtiler: Seine Gesichter überzeugen durch menschliche Echtheit und hervorragende Detailtreue. Jasinskis behutsam geschaffene Charaktere erwecken Vertrautheit und Symphatie beim Betrachter.

www.aaronjasinski.com

NAME: Aaron Jasinski **LOCATION:** Renton, WA, USA **CONTACT:** aaronjasinski@hotmail.com **TOOLS:** acrylic paints. **AGENT:** Shannon Associates <www.shannonassociates.com> **CLIENTS:** Hyperion Publishing, Rookie Reader, Read Magazine, DezArt Gallery, Arthouse 60, Deviant Art, Rasterized.org.

James Jean

I am hired to illuminate text, stories, and ideas. Often, this process starts from a few scribbles, and through steady erasing and redrawing is slowly refined and honed like a block of marble into something beautiful in the end. However, nothing is more beautiful and terrifying than an empty field of white paper, as the expanse of ideas and shapes stretches infinite and free until the first speck of graphite crosses the page.

On me demande d'illuminer des textes, des histoires et des idées. Souvent, ce processus commence par quelques gribouillages qui, après avoir été maintes fois effacés et recommencés, se transforment lentement en quelque chose de beau. Mais rien n'est plus beau ni plus terrifiant que le vide d'une page blanche quand les idées et les formes affluent à l'infini jusqu'à ce que le premier point de graphite rencontre la page.

Man nimmt mich unter Vertrag, um Texte, Geschichten und Ideen zu illuminieren. Oft beginnt dieser Prozess mit ein paar schnellen Skizzen und durch ständiges Ausradieren und neu Zeichnen beginnt sich langsam ein Bild zu formen, so wie man einen Marmorblock nach und nach zu etwas Wunderschönem bearbeitet. Trotz allem gibt es nichts Schöneres und gleichzeitig Erschreckenderes als ein Stück weisses Papier, auf Ideen und endlos freie Formgebung wartend, bis sich der erste Klecks Grafit schliesslich über die Seite zieht.

www.jamesjean.com

NAME: James Jean **LOCATION:** Santa Monica, CA, USA **CONTACT:** mail@jamesjean.com **TOOLS:** pencil, charcoal, watercolor, oils, acrylic, Adobe Photoshop. **AWARDS:** Will Eisner - Best Cover Artist, American Illustration, Society of Illustrators, Alan M. Goffman (Gold Medal), Society of Illustrators LA, etc. **CLIENTS:** DC Comics, the New York Times, the Washinton Post, Simon & Schuster, Scholastic, Atlantic Records, Elektra Records, Interscope Records, NYLON, Playboy, SPIN, ESPN the Magazine, etc.

Ben Kirchner

I like to create spaces - a building or a street - and then fill them with people and funny situations. I enjoy imagining the personalities of my characters, the clothes they would wear and the expressions on their faces. It feels like I am creating a miniature world.

J'aime créer des espaces — des édifices ou des rues — et les remplir avec des personnages ou des situations cocasses. Je m'amuse à imaginer la personnalité de mes personnages, les vêtements qu'ils porteraient et les expressions de leur visage. C'est comme si je créais un monde miniature.

Mir macht es Spass, Räume zu schaffen — ein Gebäude oder eine Strasse, und diese dann mit Menschen und ansprechenden Situationen zu bereichern. Ich stelle mir dann gerne die Persönlichkeiten meiner Charaktere vor, die Kleider, die sie tragen würden und ihre Gesichtsausdrücke. Gerade so, als ob ich eine Miniaturwelt kreieren würde.

NAME: Ben Kirchner **LOCATION:** England **CONTACT:** <info@heartagency.com> **TOOLS:** Pencils (normal and graphite ones), Adobe Illustrator, Adobe Photoshop.
AGENT: Heart <www.heartagency.com> **CLIENTS:** Adobe, The Guardian, The Observer, The Boston Globe, Interbrand, Atelierworks, McCann Erickson, Doner Cardwell Hawkins, The Sunday Times Travel Magazine, Management Today, Nickelodeon, People, Time Asia, Cargo, John Brown Publishing, Redwood, Future Publishing.

Kumiko Kitaoka

Live Happily

I want a lot of people to have a happy time.

Mon but est de faire passer de bons moments à beaucoup de gens.

Ich möchte möglichst viele Menschen glücklich machen.

www.linkclub.or.jp/~heel-toe

NAME: Kumiko Kitaoka   **LOCATION:** Japan   **CONTACT:** kitaoka@air.linkclub.or.jp   **TOOLS:** Corel Painter, Macromedia Flash, Adobe Photoshop, Adobe Illustrator.

Joachim Knappe

For me, the contents of the painting are only there to help the colours and forms appear. A simple idea that is staged in a good way leads to a good illustration, but not the other way round.

Pour moi, le thème d'une peinture ne sert qu'à aider les couleurs et les formes à apparaître. Une idée simple mise en scène correctement donne une bonne illustration. L'inverse n'est pas vrai.

Ein Gemälde hat für mich lediglich die Aufgabe, Form und Farben zur Geltung zu bringen. Eine einfache Idee, gut präsentiert, wird zu einer guten Illustration, aber umgekehrt funktioniert es nicht.

www.illustrationen-joachim-knappe.de

NAME: Joachim Knappe **LOCATION:** Hamburg, Germany **CONTACT:** mail@joachimknappe.com **TOOLS:** Apple Computer. **AWARDS:** Nomination for the German Jugendliteraturpreis für das Sachbuch "Das Internet" / Tessloff. **CLIENTS:** DTV, Ravensburger, Carlsen, und viele andere Kinder- und Jugendbuchverlage, Tessloff, Brockhaus.

Olivier Kugler

I love to do portraits or visual essays of people and places. I learned to draw by sketching on location and love to go back to this whenever I get the chance. I have found that there is something about the spontaneity and rawness in this process that is not usually found in drawings that are done from photographs. Despite this fact, I have learned to appreciate the advantages of using a digital camera as a means of getting reference.

J'aime faire des portraits ou des essais visuels de personnes et de lieux. J'ai appris à dessiner en extérieurs et adore revenir à cela lorsque j'en ai la possibilité. Je trouve que ce processus a quelque chose de spontané et d'âpre que l'on ne retrouve pas dans les dessins faits d'après photographies. Malgré tout, j'ai appris à apprécier les avantages que comporte la prise de vues de référence avec un appareil photo numérique.

Ich liebe es, Portraits und visuelle Interpretationen von Menschen und Orten zu machen. Ich habe es gelernt, Skizzen vor Ort zu zeichnen und praktiziere dies, wann immer ich die Möglichkeit dazu habe. Ich bin der Meinung, dieser Prozess beinhaltet eine gewisse Spontanität und Empfindlichkeit, die ich bei Zeichnungen, die anhand von Fotografien erstellt werden, nicht feststellen kann. Trotz allem habe ich es zu schätzen gelernt, eine digitale Kamera als Referenzmittel zu nutzen.

www.olivierkugler.com

NAME: Olivier Kugler **LOCATION:** London, UK; New York, USA **CONTACT:** ol_kugler@hotmail.com **TOOLS:** FABER-CASTELL HB pencils and the computer. **AWARDS:** The Association of Illustrators Editorial (Gold). **AGENT:** The Artworks <www.theartworksinc.com> **CLIENTS:** The Guardian, Conran Design, Harper Collins, Reader's Digest, Harper's, New York Times, New York Magazine, The New Yorker, Outside, Harper's, etc.

Thomas Kuhlenbeck

I maximise my satisfaction by incorporating as many hidden messages as possible into the pictures. These messages can only be decoded by playing the illustration backwards.

Je maximise ma satisfaction en intégrant autant de messages cachés que possible dans mes images. Ces messages ne peuvent être décodés que si on lit l'illustration à l'envers.

Ich maximiere meine Befriedigung, indem ich möglichst viele abseitige Botschaften in die Bilder einbaue, die nur dechiffriert werden können, indem man die Illustration rückwärts abspielt.

NAME: Thomas Kuhlenbeck **LOCATION:** Hannover, Germany **CONTACT:** kuhlenbeck@gmx.de **TOOLS:** Adobe Photoshop. **AWARDS:** ADC Germany (Bronze).
AGENT: Jutta Fricke <www.jutta-fricke.de> **CLIENTS:** Stern, Focus, Playboy, Zeit, SZ Magazin, Capital, Max, ReadersDigest, Scholz & Friends Berlin, Publicis Direct, DMB + B, McCann Euroadvertising, Serviceplan.

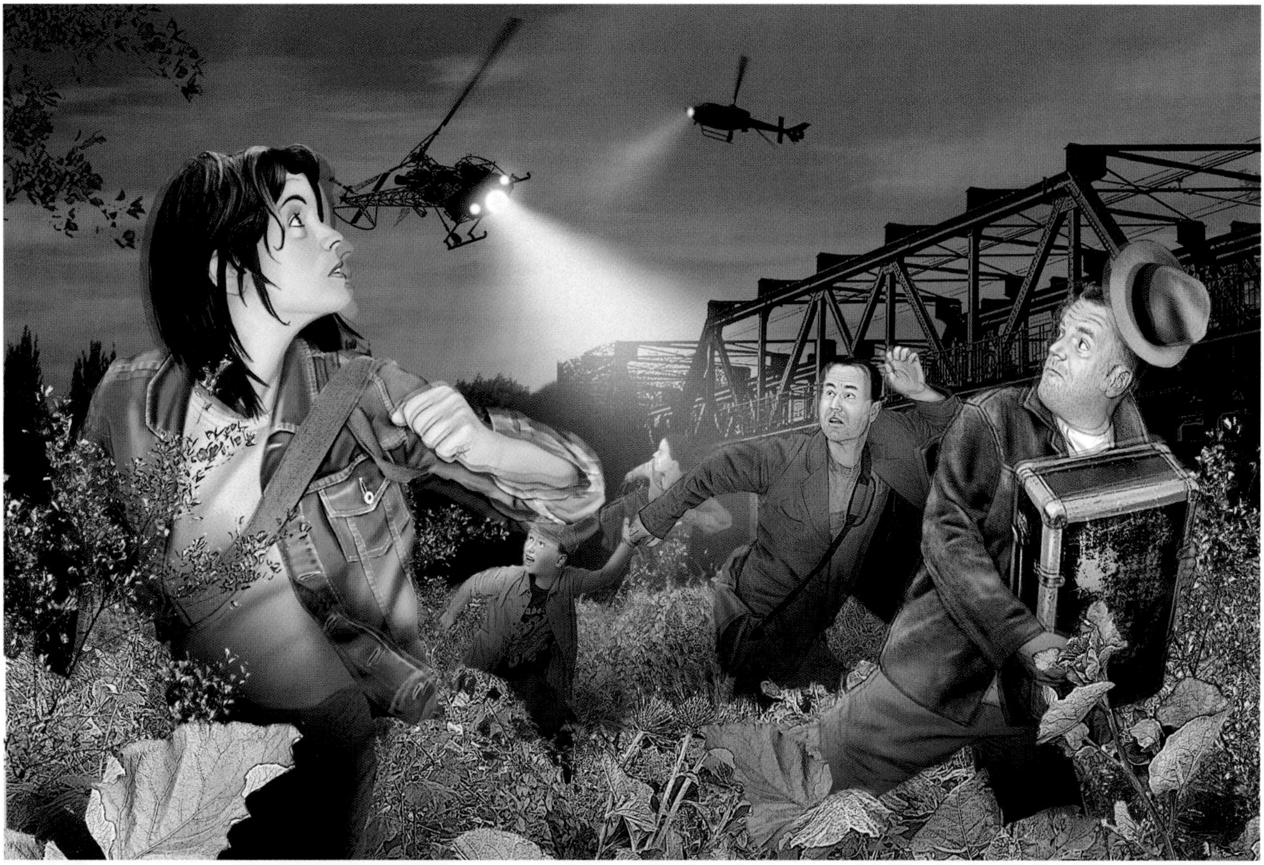

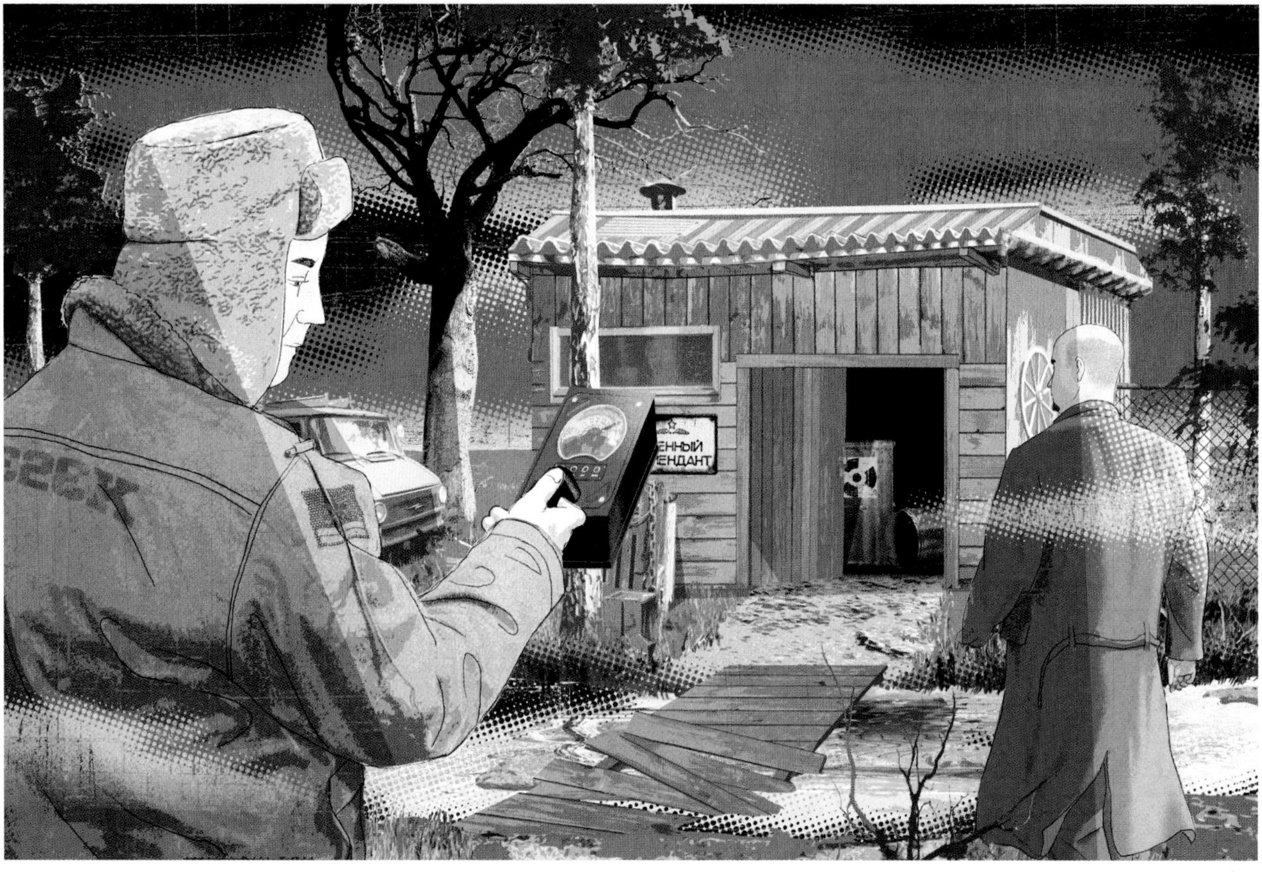

Anita Kunz

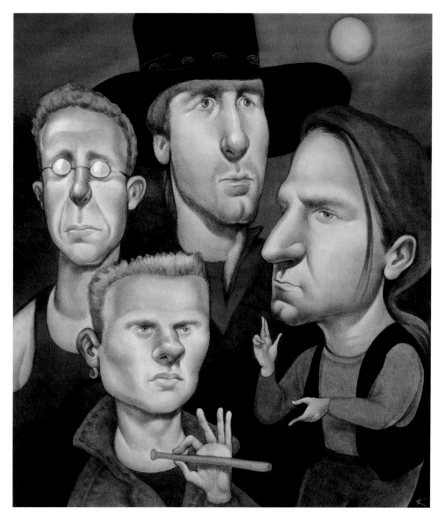

In my work, commenting on personal issues is far less interesting to me than participating in a larger dialogue, whether the subject is medical advances such as cloning or the cultural influences of celebrities like Madonna. I am a witness to the world around me, and my visual comments are reactions to these events. In every case, there is a fluidity, a desired response, though of course I cannot control that response; in some ways, what I really do is try and encourage thoughtful participation in the cultural moment.

Dans mon travail, commenter des questions personnelles est bien moins intéressant à mon sens que participer à un dialogue plus large, qu'il porte sur des avancées médicales telles que le clonage ou sur les influences culturelles de célébrités telles que Madonna. Je suis témoin du monde qui m'entoure et mes commentaires visuels sont des réactions aux événements que j'observe. Dans tous les cas il y a une fluidité, une réponse désirée, bien que je ne puisse pas bien sûr contrôler cette réponse. En un sens, ce que je fais véritablement c'est essayer d'encourager une participation réfléchie dans le moment culturel.

Bei meiner Arbeit ist mir ein ausführlicher Dialog wichtiger als jegliche persönliche Problemstellungen - sei es über den medizinischen Fortschritt im Klonbereich oder die kulturelle Beeinflussung durch Berühmtheiten wie Madonna. Ich bin Zeuge meiner Umwelt und meine visuellen Kommentare sind eine Reaktion auf das, was sich um mich herum abspielt. Informationsfluss gibt es stets und überall, für mich eine wünschenswerte Antwort, wobei ich diese Antwort natürlich nicht beeinflussen kann; in gewisser Weise bemühe ich mich um die Teilnahme am Denkprozess in unserem kulturellen Bezugskreis.

www.anitakunz.com

NAME: Anita Kunz **LOCATION:** Toronto, Ontario, Canada **CONTACT:** akunz@anitakunz.com **TOOLS:** watercolor, gouache, pencil. **AWARDS:** les Usherwood Lifetime Achievment, medals from the Society of Illustrators, The Hamilton King - Society of Illustrators, Society of Illustrators LA, American Illustration, Communication Arts, and others. **CLIENTS:** GQ magazine, Time Magazine, The New Yorker, The New York Times, etc.

The New York Times Magazine

JANUARY 18, 2003   SECTION 6

Athletes' use of
performance-enhancing drugs
will not be policed away.
Genetic manipulation may be next.
It's the game.

In Pursuit of
Doped
Excellence

By Michael Sokolove

Spring Fashion **So Many Pretty Things** (See Page 40)

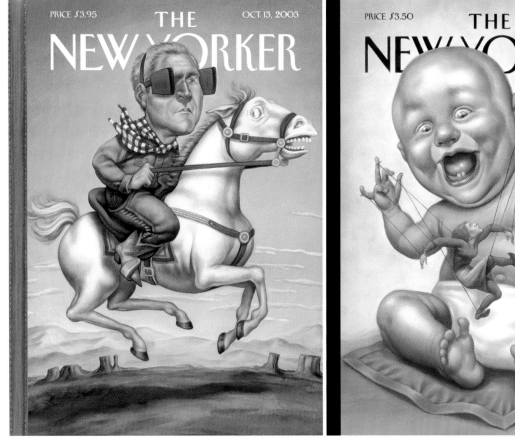

Yunmee Kyong

I hope to have dialogues with people, many living things, and non-living things in the world and would like to share smiles, oddness, thoughts and dreams through my illustrations.

Avec mes illustrations, j'espère instaurer un dialogue avec les gens, avec de nombreux êtres vivants et non vivants dans le monde et souhaite partager des sourires, des bizarreries, des pensées et des rêves.

Ich möchte mich mit Menschen verständigen, mit lebenden und nicht lebenden Dingen dieser Welt Kontakt aufnehmen, ich möchte Freude, Besonderheiten, Gedanken und Träume durch meine Illustrationen mit anderen teilen.

NAME: Yunmee Kyong **LOCATION:** New York, USA **CONTACT:** yunyum@hotmail.com **TOOLS:** Acrylics, ink, Adobe Photoshop. **AWARDS:** American illustration, Figure Futur, Children's book competetion, RSVP Dream competition. **AGENT:** Lindgren and Smith <www.lindrensmith.com> **CLIENTS:** Penguin Viking, New York Times, Boston Globe, World of Interior, Waitrose Food Magazine, Hong Design, Vegetarian Times, etc.

Joel Lardner

I use self-initiated projects to reinvent and regenerate my artwork. Keeping it fresh and retaining my initial enthusiasm. I enjoy a brief which gives scope for an innovative and expressive response. I have always been more concerned with showing my work in reproduction rather in any gallery context. I think we should challenge restrictive ideas of what illustration can be.

J'utilise les projets que j'entreprends moi-même pour réinventer et régénérer mon travail. Ainsi il garde sa fraîcheur et mon enthousiasme initial reste intact. J'aime les commandes qui donnent la possibilité d'une réponse innovante et expressive. J'ai toujours préféré montrer mon travail sur un support reproduit que dans une galerie. Je pense que l'on devrait contester les idées restrictives sur ce que peut être l'illustration.

Projekte, die ich aus eigener Initiative heraus angehe, helfen mir bei dem Prozess, mich selbst immer wieder neu inspirieren und definieren zu können. So verliere ich nie meinen anfänglichen Enthusiasmus. Ich bevorzuge knappe Informationen, die genug Raum für innovative und ausdrucksstarke Antworten lassen. Ich war stets darum bemüht, meine Arbeiten als Reproduktionen zu präsentieren und nicht so stark in den Galerien vertreten zu sein. Limitiertes Vorstellungsvermögen von dem, was Illustration ist, sollte man stets herausfordern.

NAME: Joel Lardner **LOCATION:** England **CONTACT:** info@heartagency.com **TOOLS:** Black Ink. **AGENT:** Heart <www.heartagency.com> **CLIENTS:** MIT/Technology Review, The Observer, The New York Times, BBC Radio One, Erotic Review, Res Magazine, Wrigley's Gum, Harvard Business Review.

Simone Legno

The best designers live looking at reality in a different perspective than most people. The designer looks, searches, stylizes, studies, filters and transforms continuously in his mind the elements around his daily life. Design is away to express myself, it's the way I am and communicate with people my inner self and my dreams. I see my art, childish and mature, traditional and alternative, as a balance between pure and provocative.

Les meilleurs illustrateurs voient la réalité sous un autre angle que la plupart des gens. L'illustrateurs observe, cherche, stylise, étudie, filtre et transforme en permanence dans sa tête les éléments qui font partie de sa vie quotidienne. L'illustration est un moyen de m'exprimer, c'est ce que je suis et la manière dont je communique aux gens mon moi intérieur et mes rêves. Pour moi, mon art est enfantin et mature, traditionnel et alternatif, c'est un équilibre entre la pureté et la provocation.

Gute Designer haben eine andere Perspektive bezüglich der Realität als die meisten Menschen. Der Designer schaut, forscht, stilisiert, filtert und transformiert in seinem Geist ständig die Elemente, die ihn in seinem täglichen Leben umgeben. Design gibt mir die Möglichkeit, mich selber auszudrücken, es ist die Essenz, von dem, was ich bin und wie ich mein Inneres und meine Träume den Mitmenschen mitteile. Ich betrachte meine Kunst sowohl als naiv und ausgereift, traditionell und alternativ, als auch als eine Balance zwischen Reinheit und Provokation.

www.tokidoki.it
www.designergokko.it
www.vianet.it

NAME: Simone Legno **LOCATION:** Los Angeles, CA, USA and Rome, Italy **CONTACT:** simone@tokidoki.it, info@vianet.it **TOOLS:** Adobe Illustrator, acrilic paintings.
AWARDS: Flash Film Festival. **CLIENTS:** Toyota, MTV, Daihatsu, Renault, Telecom, BenQ, John Galliano, Computer Arts.

Lillycat

The purpose isn't only to create a "nice" picture, but to use a given technique to express myself, and my own way of giving voice to my feelings is drawing.

L'objectif n'est pas seulement de créer une « belle » image mais d'utiliser une technique donnée pour m'exprimer. Et ma façon de donner voix à mes sentiments est le dessin.

Das Ziel ist es, nicht nur ein "schönes" Bild zu kreieren, sondern eine bestimmte Technik anzuwenden, die es mir erlaubt, mich selber auszudrücken. Ich zeichne, um meinen Gefühlen Ausdruck zu verleihen.

www.lillycat.net

NAME: Lillycat (Rachelle Bartel) **LOCATION:** Paris, France **CONTACT:** lillycat@lillycat.net **TOOLS:** Adobe Photoshop. **AGENT:** Lezilus <www.illustrissimo.com>
CLIENTS: Éditions les Humanoides Associés, Marithé + François Girbaud, Disney, Éditions Lito, Milan Presse, Éditions Magnard.

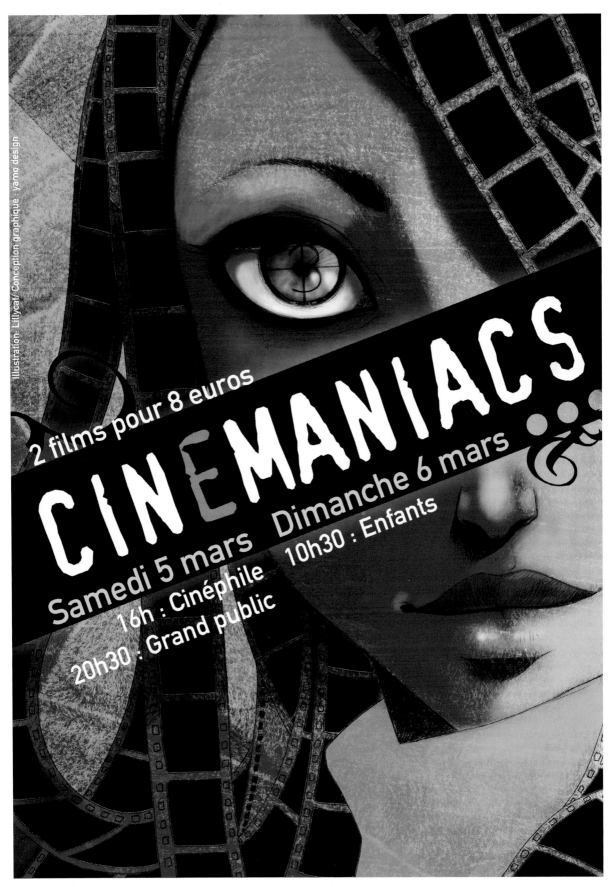

Illustration: Lillycat/Conception graphique: yamo design

2 films pour 8 euros

CINEMANIACS

Samedi 5 mars
16h : Cinéphile
20h30 : Grand public

Dimanche 6 mars
10h30 : Enfants

Daniel Lim

It's all about being creative. Don't show art directors what you don't want to paint.

Tout est une question de créativité. Ne montrez pas aux directeurs artistiques ce que vous ne voulez pas peindre.

Es dreht sich alles nur um Kreativität. Zeige niemals einem Art Director das, was du nicht malen möchtest.

www.daniel-lim.com

NAME: Daniel Hyun Lim **LOCATION:** New York, USA **CONTACT:** me@daniel-lim.com **TOOLS:** Adobe PhotoShop, color pencil, Adobe Illustrator, photography. **AWARDS:** American Illustration, Society of Illustrators Student Competition (Gold), Society of Illustrators NY Starr Foundation Scholarship, etc. **CLIENTS:** Laweekly, G4tv.com, Canadian Business, Television Weekly.

Richard Link

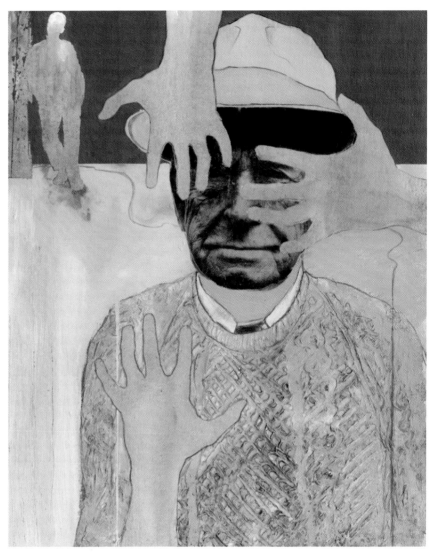

My work is about distilling the emotional essence of what makes the text interesting and then present-ing the response to the viewer, not in a tortuous linear fashion, but by capturing the emotional energy generated from a particular idea or moment in time. Sometimes conflictive, sometimes contemplative, my work attempts to reflect the interactions of people: illustrating what makes us violent or passive, still or in motion, beautiful or ugly.

Mon travail consiste à distiller l'essence émotionnelle de ce qui fait l'intérêt du texte, puis de présenter la réponse à l'observateur, non pas d'une façon linéaire sinueuse mais en capturant l'énergie émotion-nelle générée par une idée particulière ou un moment. Parfois conflictuel, parfois contemplatif, mon travail tente de refléter les relations entre les gens, il illustre ce qui nous rend violent ou passif, apaisé ou en mouvement, beau ou laid.

Bei meiner Arbeit findet ein Destillierungsprozess statt, bei dem ich versuche, die emotionale Essenz und das, was den Text interessant macht, herauszuheben und anschliessend das Ergebnis dem Kunden zu präsentieren, jedoch keinesfalls auf eine irritierend moderne Linienhaftigkeit, sondern vielmehr durch die aufgestaute emotionale Energie, resultierend aus einer ganz bestimmten Idee oder eines Zeitpunktes. Manchmal konfliktiv, manchmal nachdenklich, versuche ich, zwischenmenschliche Beziehungen zu reflek-tieren: zu illustrieren, was uns gewalttätig oder passiv macht, ruhig oder bewegt, schön oder hässlich.

www.richardlink.co.uk

NAME: Richard Link **LOCATION:** Maidstone, Kent, UK **CONTACT:** link_richard@hotmail.com **TOOLS:** Acrylic Paint. **AWARDS:** The John Hackett Book Award. **AGENT:** Between Beautiful <www.betweenbeautiful.com> **CLIENTS:** Maidstone Green Collective, David Hicken Associates, Not a Million Miles Away Productions.

MALMAS III
DARK SKIES

1. BRING IT ON
2. SAVIOUR
3. CAGE
4. SPIT
5. DREAMLAND
6. TIME TO KILL
    RISE
    CHANGELING
    NEW WORLD

7. REALMS OF TIME
    AWAKENING
    FIGHT BACK
    SWITCH/COMA

HORIZON

DREAMLANDS

Liz Lomax

Illustration is a wonderfully fascinating career that I am so fortunate to have. I enjoy the challenge of short deadlines, which allow me to completely immerse myself in a subject for a short enough time to hold my attention without losing interest in the project. The Rolling Stones was a commission that had to be sculpted in just four days, so I surrounded myself with tons of photos of the band members. I became an obsessed fan and listened to nothing but the Rolling Stones day and night in an attempt to absorb their character before I began sculpting so I could achieve not just their likeness, but their soul too.

Mon métier d'illustratrice est fascinant et me comble. J'aime le défi des délais brefs qui me permettent de m'immerger entièrement dans un thème pendant un temps suffisamment court pour retenir mon attention sans me faire perdre mon intérêt pour le projet. Les Rolling Stones étaient une commande qui devait être sculptée en quatre jours seulement. Je me suis alors entourée de tonnes de photos des membres du groupe. Je suis devenue une fan complètement obsédée et n'écoutais plus que les Rolling Stones, nuit et jour, pour m'imprégner de leur caractère avant de commencer à sculpter. Je voulais les reproduire fidèlement extérieurement et intérieurement.

Illustration ist eine wundervolle und faszinierende Karriere, und ich schätze mich glücklich, einen solchen Beruf ausüben zu können. Ich geniesse die Herausforderung einer Deadline, die es mir ermöglicht, mich voll und ganz auf mein Projekt einzulassen und meine gesamte Konzentration zu investieren, ohne dabei das Interesse an der Arbeit zu verlieren. In nur vier Tagen sollte ich eine Skulptur der Rolling Stones erschaffen. Also habe ich mich mit unzähligen Fotos der Bandmitglieder umgeben. Ich wurde zu einem besessenen Fan. Bevor ich mit der Skulptur begann, hörte ich Tag und Nacht nur Rolling Stones, um ihre Persönlichkeiten so ganz in mich aufnehmen zu können und nicht nur ihr Äusseres sondern auch ihre Seele widerzuspiegeln.

www.lizlomax.com

NAME: Liz Lomax **LOCATION:** New York, USA **CONTACT:** liz@lizlomax.com **TOOLS:** Super Sculpey (polymer clay), oil paint, wire, clay shapers, aluminum foil, digital camera and Adobe Photoshop. **AWARDS:** Society of Illustrators, American Illustration, Communication Arts, Dimensional Salon, SI-LA, RSVP, Dimensional Illustrators. **AGENT:** Levy Creative <www.levycreative.com> **CLIENTS:** Rolling Stone, TIME, Der Spiegel, MAD Magazine, VH1, Miramax, MTV, The Wall Street Journal, etc.

LizLomax

Mike LOOS

The subject of the illustration is the hero. Understanding the clients needs leads to the suitable formal concept.

Le sujet de l'illustration est le héros. Comprendre les besoins du client conduit au concept formel approprié.

Das Thema einer Illustration ist tonangebend. Den Kunden zu verstehen, bedeutet, ein passendes Konzept zu finden.

www.mike-loos.de

NAME: Mike Loos **LOCATION:** Augsburg, Germany **CONTACT:** mike.loos@t-online.de **TOOLS:** Ink, Adobe Photoshop, Scraperboard. **AWARDS:** ADC (Bronze); Illustrations for awarded Graphic Design works for different Agencies (ADC Awards) **AGENT:** Jutta Kleinert <www.kleinert.de> **CLIENTS:** Focus, Playboy, Spiegel, Stern, Rowohlt Verlag, Heye & Partner, Springer & Jacoby, RG Wiesmeier, and others.

Brigitta Garcia López

My three-dimensional works are modelled from diverse materials and then arranged and photographed in the photo studio. Most of my works get photographed by Felix Streuli.

Mes travaux en 3D sont modelés à partir de matériaux divers puis retravaillés en studio avant d'être photographiés. La plupart d'entre eux sont photographiés par Felix Streuli.

Meine 3D Arbeiten werden aus diversen Materialien Modelliert und danach im Fotostudio arangiert und Fotografiert. Die Meisten meiner Arbeiten werden von Felix Streuli Fotografiert.

www.brigitta-garcia-lopez.com

NAME: Brigitta Garcia López **LOCATION:** Zürich, Switzerland **CONTACT:** bgl@hispeed.ch **TOOLS:** Marzipan, Plastilin, Adobe Photoshop, Adobe Illustrator. **AWARDS:** Plakatwettbewerb Frankfurter Buchmesse, Die Besten 7 Bücher für junge Leser, Biennale der Illustration BIB, Werkbeitrag der STEO Stiftung. **CLIENTS:** Verlag Die Provinz in Zürich, atlantis Verlag Zürich, Bilderbuch Flieg,s Flengel flieg!, Erschienen im atlantis Verlag Zürich.

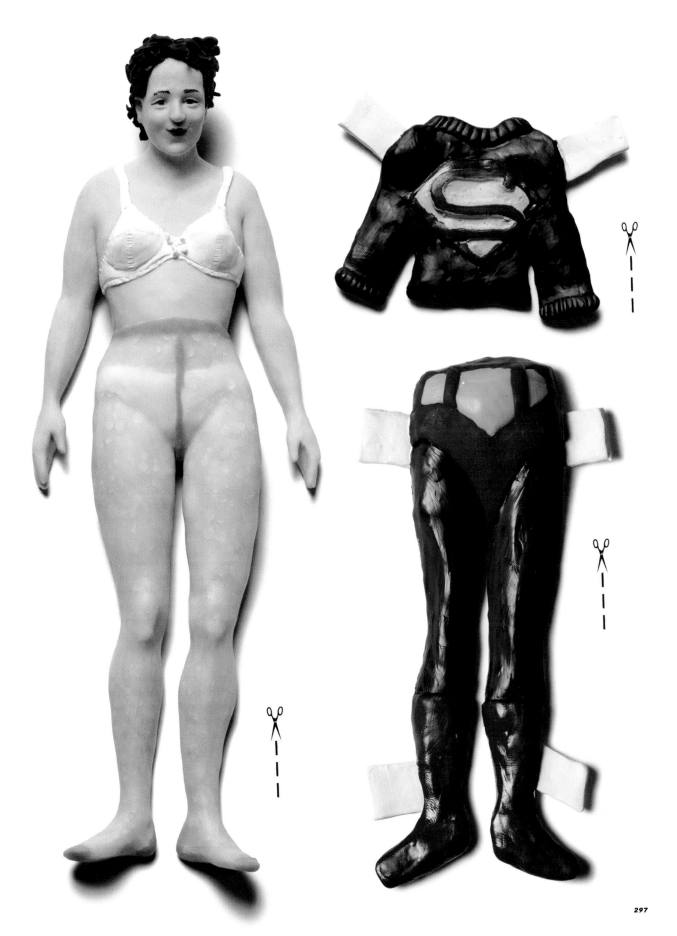

Iris Luckhaus

I work as a freelance illustrator, stylist and designer: different fields that all include visual storytelling. My inspiration is real life and real people, their stories and their attitude as well as versatile characters in books and movies. In illustration I appreciate the challenge of drawing in different styles related to projects, to keep learning and to stay curious. I have a passion for details that tell whole stories beyond what you see at first sight and add layers and life to a picture.

Je travaille comme illustratrice, styliste et designer freelance, des domaines divers qui ont pour point commun le fait de raconter une histoire visuelle. Je puise mon inspiration de la vraie vie et des vraies gens, de leurs histoires et de leurs attitudes. Je m'inspire également de personnages polyvalents trouvés dans des livres ou des films. Dans l'illustration, j'aime le défi de dessiner selon des styles différents liés à divers projets. Cela permet de continuer à apprendre et de rester curieux. J'ai une passion pour les détails qui racontent des histoires à eux seuls, au-delà de ce que l'on voit à première vue, et qui ajoutent de la profondeur et de la vie à une image.

Ich arbeite als freie Illustratorin, Stylistin und Designerin: unterschiedliche Gebiete, die alle die visuelle Erzählung von Geschichten beinhalten. Meine Inspiration sind das richtige Leben und echte Menschen, ihre Geschichten und ihr Ausdruck, ebenso wie vielschichtige Charaktere in Büchern und Filmen. Beim Illustrieren schätze ich die Herausforderung, projektbezogen stilistisch unterschiedlich zu zeichnen, ständig dazuzulernen und neugierig zu bleiben. Ich habe eine Leidenschaft für Details, die Geschichten erzählen und Bilder über den ersten Blick hinaus vielschichtig und lebendig erscheinen lassen.

www.irisluckhaus.com

NAME: Iris Luckhaus **LOCATION:** Wuppertal and Berlin, Germany; Paris, France **CONTACT:** irisluckhaus@web.de **TOOLS:** Ink, Fineliner, Pens & Pencils, Marker, Watercolours, Apple Computer. **CLIENTS:** Penthouse, Chiucchiu, Die Kolonie, Plan_B Media, Mogup, Karma, Ligaturdesign, Zeal, Formfaktion, Intergreeting Schott, Kawaii.

Bo Lundberg

So far I have found that it's not so much about being better, it's about being different. I also believe that for an image to have an impact it has to reflect something to which the viewer is able to relate. Strangely enough, the accustomed can become something very modern if it's done in the right way. And the same for movies, fashion and music. The result often turns out good if you flirt with themes that everybody recognises.

Ma vision des choses aujourd'hui est qu'il ne s'agit pas tant d'être meilleur que les autres que d'être différent. Je crois également que pour qu'une image ait un impact, elle doit refléter une chose avec laquelle l'observateur peut établir une relation. Étrangement, l'habituel peut devenir très moderne lorsqu'on s'y prend correctement. Et cela vaut aussi pour le cinéma, la mode et la musique. Le résultat est souvent bon lorsque l'on flirte avec des thèmes que tout un chacun reconnaît.

Bisher habe ich die Erkenntnis gemacht, dass es nicht darauf ankommt, besser zu sein, sondern vielmehr, anders zu sein. Ausserdem glaube ich, dass ein Bild nur dann eine Wirkung auf den Betrachter haben kann, wenn dieser sich damit identifizieren kann. Interessanterweise kann sich Altbekanntes in etwas sehr Modernes verwandeln, man muss es nur richtig angehen. Das gleiche gilt für Film, Mode und Musik. Das Ergebnis ist oft sehr zufriedenstellend, vorausgesetzt, du flirtest mit bekannten Themenbereichen, die jedermann wiedererkennt.

NAME: Bo Lundberg **LOCATION:** London, UK **CONTACT:** all@folioart.co.uk **TOOLS:** Adobe Illustrator, sometimes ink and paper. **AWARDS:** D&AD, Print Regional European Design, Swedish Golden Egg, Design Week Awards, etc. **AGENT:** Folio <www.folioart.co.uk>, Art Department (NY), Woo Agentur (Stockholm), Agent 002 (Paris) <www.agent002.com>, Agent Double (Tokyo) **CLIENTS:** Elle, Vogue, Wallpaper, Coca-Cola, Disney, H&M, Scandinavian Airlines, etc.

Margot Macé

Using aquarelle and ink pen my drawings associate precision and abstraction in a poetic sense.

Mêlant la technique de l'aquarelle et du stylo à plume, mes dessins associent précision et abstraction avec un sens poétique.

Durch die Anwendung von Aquarell und Tuschfeder verkörpern meine Zeichnungen sowohl Präzision als auch Abstraktion im poetischen Sinne.

NAME: Margot Macé **LOCATION:** Barbizon, France **CONTACT:** margot.jerome@wanadoo.fr **TOOLS:** watercolour, ink pen. **AGENT:** Illustrissimo <www.illustrissimo.com>
CLIENTS: Lancome, L'Oreal, Biotherm, Clarins, Guerlain, Do! Family (Japan), Vogue.

Berto Martínez

My vision of illustration is that of an art form of an ephemeral character that should describe something that happens at a given time and place. My intention is to provide the mediums of communication with a graphic alternative to the photograph. I try to create a multi-faceted closeness to a theme, a vision from different angles by means of the juxtaposition of elements searching for the cohesion of the text and image. I also get pleasure from the application of illustration to different mediums ranging from textile prints to interior decoration.

Ma vision de l'illustration est celle d'une forme d'art éphémère qui doit décrire un événement survenant à un endroit et à un moment donné. Mon intention est de fournir aux médias une alternative graphique à la photographie. J'essaie de créer une proximité à multiples facettes avec un thème, une vue sous plusieurs angles au moyen de la juxtaposition d'éléments, le but étant de trouver une cohésion entre le texte et l'image. J'aime aussi appliquer l'illustration à des supports aussi divers que les imprimés textiles ou la décoration intérieure.

Meine Vision von Illustration ist die einer kurzlebigen Kunstform, die eine Situation zu einer bestimmten Zeit an einem bestimmten Ort wiederzugeben vermag. Meine Absicht ist es, ein Medium der Kommunikation als grafische Alternative zur Fotografie zu schaffen. Ich versuche, eine vielschichtige Nähe zu einem bestimmten Thema zu schaffen sowie durch Gegenüberstellung und Suche von Zusammenhängen zwischen Bild und Text eine Vision aus unterschiedlichen Gesichtspunkten zu kreieren. Ausserdem macht es mir Spass, Illustration bei unterschiedlichen Medien anzuwenden, angefangen von Stoffdrucken bis hin zur Innendekoration.

www.bertomartinez.com

NAME: Berto Martínez **LOCATION:** Barcelona, Spain **CONTACT:** berto@bertomartinez.com **TOOLS:** Pencil, ink, watercolours. **AWARDS:** Best of Newspaper Design.
AGENT: Agent002 <www.agent002.com> **CLIENTS:** Custo Barcelona, Olympus, Pinaud, BNP, El País, Marie Claire, Woman, GQ, IO Donna, Frau Magazine, Casa Brutus, Fashionize, Man, Composite Magazine, Elle, Cosmogirl, The Creator Magazine, Fashionize.

coeur des muscles

Mateo

When it comes to illustration, I am always seeking to first understand what message the client wishes to express, followed by a rigorous refinement in which I attempt to get that message across with the most elegant and simple image I can develop. This doesn't mean that the image can't be detailed and nuanced. It simply means that every element within the illustration should help tell a very specific story.

En matière d'illustration, j'essaie toujours de comprendre d'abord le message que souhaite exprimer le client avant de passer à une phase d'approfondissement rigoureux dans laquelle j'essaie de transmettre ce message avec l'image la plus élégante et la plus simple dont je suis capable. Cela ne veut pas dire que l'image ne peut pas être détaillée ou nuancée. Cela signifie simplement que chaque élément de l'illustration doit contribuer à raconter une histoire très particulière.

Wenn es um Illustration geht, ist es zuerst immer meine Absicht, meinen Kunden und die Nachricht, die er vermitteln möchte, zu verstehen. Darauf folgt dann eine rigorose Auswahl meinerseits, um diese Nachricht in einem möglichst eleganten und klaren Design wiederzugeben. Das bedeutet nicht, dass dieses Bild weder Details noch Nuancen aufweisen könnte. Es bedeutet einfach nur, dass jedes Element der Illustration dazu beitragen sollte, eine ganz besondere Geschichte zu erzählen.

www.portfolios.com/mateo

NAME: Mateo (Matt Dineen) **LOCATION:** Berlin, Germany **CONTACT:** inkslingerx@yahoo.com **TOOLS:** pen, pencil, acrylic paint, Corel Painter, Adobe Photoshop.
AGENT: Manuela Hirsch <www.hirschpool.de> **CLIENTS:** Anhauser Busch, Central American Beans, The City of Fremont, Flying Lizard Motor Sports, Goodplanet Productions (Australia), Mattel, Oracle, Precision Chimney Care (Oregon), QBox, Tevnan Technologies, Williams-Sonoma, The Canvas Cafe (San Francisco).

Mateo

Mateo-Miguel Berthelot

Work based on the fascination of elegance, fashion, expressionism, extravagant creatures, theatre and dramatic attitudes. Something in between the art of pop and the interest for Japanese-line drawing.

Mon travail est basé sur ma fascination pour l'élégance, la mode, l'expressionnisme, les créatures extravagantes, le théâtre et les attitudes dramatiques. Quelque chose entre l'art populaire et un intérêt pour les dessins japonais.

Meine Arbeit basiert auf der Faszination von Eleganz, Mode, Expressionismus, extravaganten Kreaturen, Theater und dramatischen Charakterzügen. Etwas zwischen Popkunst und dem Interesse an japanischer Linienzeichnung.

NAME: Mateo-Miguel Berthelot **LOCATION:** Paris, France **CONTACT:** m.mateo@noos.fr **TOOLS:** pencil, Adobe Photoshop. **AGENT:** Agent 002 <agent002.com>
CLIENTS: Glamour (Germany), Io Donna (Italy); Senso, K-agency, BETC, Oui, Kouro Sivo, Diamant vert, Preview (France); Scene, Don't tell it (England), Euro RSCG (Belgium), Galeries Lafayettes, Ken Club, Select, Femina hebdo.

scenes
d'interieur
l'esprit créateurs.

JOANNA MOORE

LE PETIT CHAPERON ROUGE

dirigé par
EDOUARD DIMITRI

C'est un film pour adultes !

Satoshi Matsuzawa

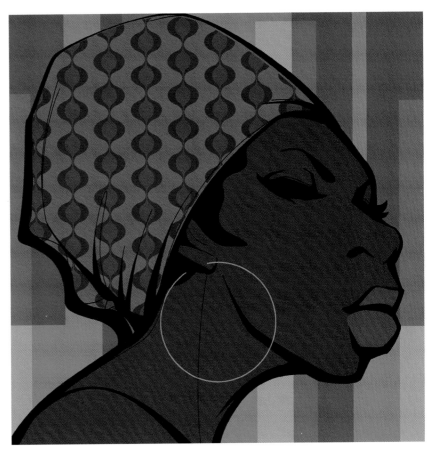

I'm inspired by 60's and 70's music, especially soul, jazz and funk music. I keep drawing music.

Je m'inspire de la musique des années 60 et 70 et particulièrement de la soul, du jazz et du funk. J'illustre en permanence de la musique.

Mich inspiriert Musik der 60er und 70er, vor allem Soul, Jazz und Funkmusik. Ich zeichne ständig Musik.

www.salboma.com

NAME: Satoshi Matsuzawa **LOCATION:** Shibuya, Tokyo, Japan **CONTACT:** mail@salboma.com **TOOLS:** pencil, Adobe Illustrator, Adobe PhotoShop. **CLIENTS:** Union Square Music, Avex, Toshiba EMI, Universal Music, BMG, EDWIN, Asics, K-SWISS, Shibuya 109, CYBIRD, J-WAVE, TBS, MTV.

Tara McPherson

Creating art about people and their odd ways, my characters seem to exude an idealized innocence with a glimpse of hard earned wisdom in their eyes. Recalling many issues from childhood and good old life experience, I create images that are thought provoking and seducing. People and their relationships are a central theme throughout my work.

Mes personnages semblent dégager une innocence idéalisée mêlée de sagesse durement gagnée que leurs yeux trahissent par instant. A partir de nombreux souvenirs d'enfance et d'événements du bon vieux temps, je crée des images que je veux à la fois provocantes et séduisantes. Les gens et les relations qui existent entre eux sont au centre de mon travail.

Bei der Kreation von Kunstwerken über Menschen und deren seltsamen Gewohnheiten, unterscheiden sich meine Charaktere durch eine idealisierte Unschuldigkeit, stets mit einem Funken hart erarbeiter Weisheit, die sich in ihren Augen reflektiert. Unter Einbeziehung einiger Kindheitserlebnisse und allgemeiner Lebenserfahrung, kreiere ich Bilder, die provozieren und gleichzeitig verführen sollen. Menschen und Beziehungen sind ein zentrales Thema, das sich durch alle meine Arbeiten hindurchzieht.

www.taramcpherson.com

NAME: Tara McPherson **LOCATION:** New York, USA **CONTACT:** tara@taramcpherson.com **TOOLS:** Acrylic, Oil, Pencil, Ink, Adobe Photoshop, Adobe Illustrator. **CLIENTS:** DC/Vertigo Comics, Fanta, Goldenvoice, McCann Erickson Dublin, Knitting Factory, House of Blues, Atomica Magazine, Art Rocker UK, Skratch Magazine, Alchera Essentials, Complete Control NYC Booking, Wyden and Kennedy, New York Is Book Country, Nike, etc.

Rafael Mendoza

You have to catch the eye! If you want to transmit an idea, first of all you have to catch the eye. We live in an age of images; everything is visual and competition is brutal, therefore, if you want to be seen you have to stand out. A good illustration must capture the viewer's attention instantly; it's hard to communicate a concept when nobody is watching you.

Il faut attraper l'œil ! Si vous voulez transmettre une idée, il faut d'abord que vous attrapiez l'œil ! Notre ère est celle de l'image, tout est visuel et la compétition est brutale. Si vous voulez être vu, vous devez donc vous démarquer. Une bonne illustration doit capturer l'attention de l'observateur instantanément, il est difficile de communiquer un concept quand personne ne vous regarde.

Du musst Aufmerksamkeit erregen. Um eine Idee weitergeben zu können, musst du zuerst Aufmerksamkeit erregen. Wir leben in einem Zeitalter, das durch Bilder geprägt wird; alles ist visuell und die Konkurrenz ist brutal, daher musst du hervorstechen, wenn du nicht übersehen werden willst. Eine gute Illustration muss sofort die Aufmerksamkeit des Beobachters auf sich ziehen; es ist schwer, ein Konzept verständlich zu machen, wenn dir keiner Aufmerksamkeit schenkt.

www.rafamendoza.com

NAME: Rafael Mendoza **LOCATION:** Mexico **CONTACT:** luzazul1@prodigy.net.mx **TOOLS:** Pencil, Macromedia Freehand, Extreme, Adobe Photoshop. **AGENT:** Agent002 <www.agent002.com> **CLIENTS:** Televisa, Editorial Expansion, FCB, Netmedia.

PRICE $3.95   THE   NOV. 22, 2004

NEW YORKER

My work is based on a lot of influences beginning in my childhood. Cartoons, TV serials, advertisements, music, design, art and photography from the 60's to now. From Bewitched to Warhol, from Gerald Mc Boing Boing to Tibor Kalman, from David Stone Martin to Le Corbusier, from Miroslav Sasek to Paul Rand.

Mon travail est le produit de nombreuses influences dont certaines remontent à mon enfance : dessins animés, séries télévisées, publicité, musique, design, art et photographie des années 60 à aujourd'hui. De Ma Sorcière Bien-Aimée à Warhol, de Gerald Mc Boing Boing à Tibor Kalman, de David Stone Martin à Le Corbusier, de Miroslav Sasek à Paul Rand.

Meine Arbeit ist durch viele Einflüsse geprägt, angefangen bei meiner Kindheit. Zeichentrick, Fernsehserien, Werbung, Musik, Design, Kunst und Fotografie der 60er Jahre bis heute. Von Bewitched bis Warhol, von Gerald Mc Boing Boing bis Tibor Kalman, von David Stone Martin bis Le Corbusier, von Miroslav Sasek bis Paul Rand.

NAME: José Luis Merino **LOCATION:** Barcelona, Spain **CONTACT:** kate@larkworthy.com **TOOLS:** Brush, watercolour, ink, digital mixed media. **AWARDS:** American Illustration, Communication Arts, D&AD, Premis Junceda, Premis Laus, The AOI, Print and SND. **AGENT:** Kate Larkworthy <www.larkworthy.com> **CLIENTS:** Elle, Forbes, Freixenet, Gourmet, GQ, LA Times Magazine, Playboy, The New York Times, The New Yorker, The Wall Street Journal.

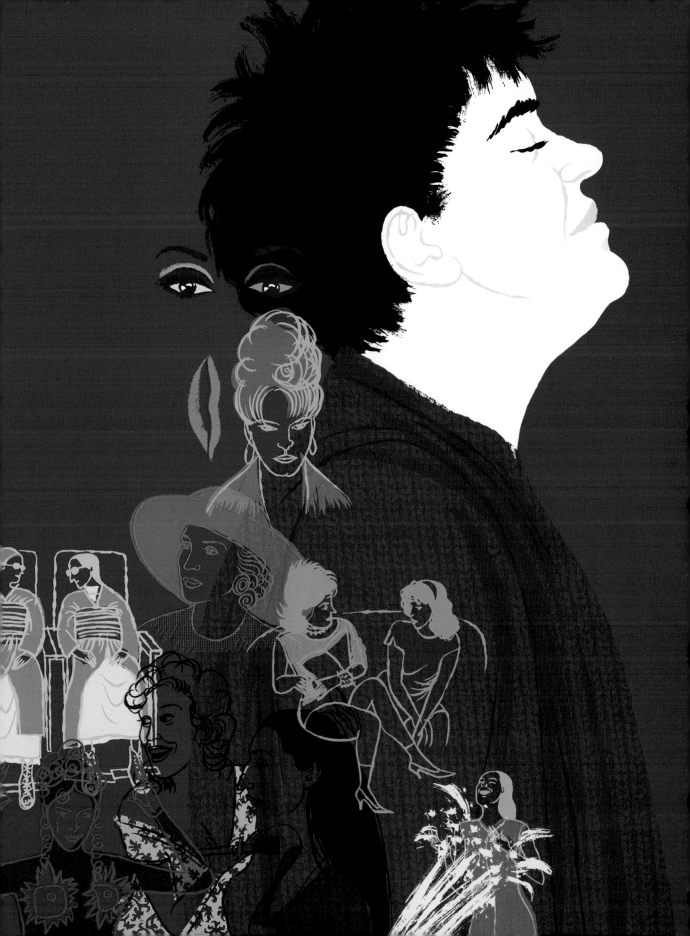

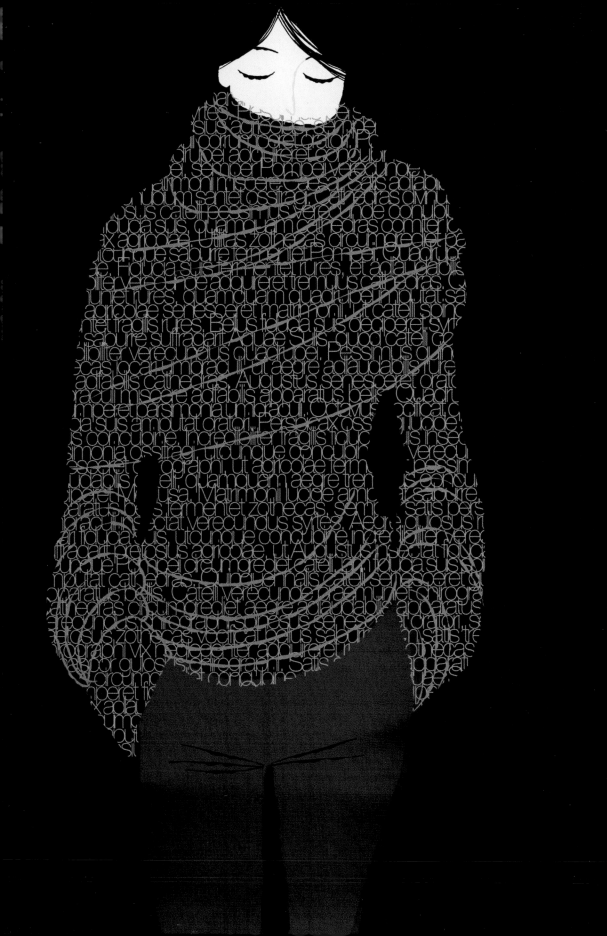

Mia

Although we are conscious of now, I want to draw illustrations from the heart which remain in people's minds forever.

Bien que je sois conscient du moment présent, j'aspire à concevoir des illustrations avec ma chair et à ce qu'elles restent dans l'esprit des gens pour toujours.

Auch wenn wir im vollen Bewusstsein der Gegenwart leben, bemühe ich mich darum, Illustrationen von Herzen zu zeichnen und sie für immer im Gedächtnis der Menschen zu verankern.

NAME: Mia **LOCATION:** Hyogo, Japan **CONTACT:** starfactory@dream-more.com; info@dutchuncle.co.uk **TOOLS:** Color ink, Pastel, Adobe Photoshop. **AWARDS:** Saga Art College, EST-1 graphic-arts, 5th fan picture competition. **AGENT:** Dream & More Co. (Japan) <www.starfactory.info>; Dutch Uncle (UK) <www.dutchuncle.co.uk> **CLIENTS:** Citty Hill, Tokyu Department Store, World, Point, Tokuma Shoten Publishing, Rainbow Entertainment, etc.

Micca

My drawing is about colour. But my colour doesn't dominate everything. There is enough room for the audience to get into it. I intend always to draw work, which has a sensitivity and softness to the design and text.

La couleur est ce qui définit le mieux mes dessins mais elle ne domine pas tout. Il y a assez de place pour le public. Mon intention est toujours de réaliser des travaux ayant une sensibilité et une douceur vis-à-vis du design et du texte.

Bei meinen Zeichnungen geht es um Farbe. Dennoch dominieren meine Farben nicht. Ich lasse genügend Raum für die Teilnahme der Betrachter. Ich versuche stets, Arbeiten zu zeichnen, die eine gewisse Sensibilität und Weichheit bezüglich des Designs und des Textes aufweisen.

NAME: Micca **LOCATION:** Tokyo, Japan **CONTACT:** starfactory@dream-more.com; info@dutchuncle.co.uk **TOOLS:** Pencil. **AGENT:** Dream & More Co. (Japan) <www.starfactory.info>; Dutch Uncle (UK) <www.dutchuncle.co.uk> **CLIENTS:** Stussy Australia, Kodansha, Genko-Sha, Sony magazine, Sony Music, Shueisha, EV by etvous, Magazine House.

Mari Mitsumi

I always try to make coincidence with humour, irony, hope and a little melancholy in my work. And try to find the elements of universality that exists in individual to free of possessiveness.

J'essaie toujours de faire coïncider mon travail avec de l'humour, de l'ironie, de l'espoir et un peu de mélancolie. Et j'essaie aussi de trouver les éléments universels qui existent dans chaque individu pour libérer de l'instinct de possession.

Ich bin stets darauf bedacht, Humor, Ironie, Hoffnung und ein wenig Melancholie in meine Arbeiten einfliessen zu lassen. Ausserdem versuche ich, Elemente von Allgemeingültigkeit, die in jedem Individuum existieren, zu finden, um es von Besitzgier zu befreien.

http://home.att.ne.jp/green/mari-m

NAME: Mari Mitsumi **LOCATION:** Tokyo, Japan **CONTACT:** mari-m@tkc.att.ne.jp **TOOLS:** Adobe Photoshop, acrylic color, gouache, canvas. **CLIENTS:** Magazine House, The Yomiuri Shimbun, Nihon Keizai Shimbun, Recruit, Columbia Music Entertainment, Shueisha, Bungei Shunju, The Asahi Shimbun, etc.

Patrick Morgan

Afternoon Tea

Work Hard Play Hard. Illustration is all about meeting people, working hard and producing the most boundary pushing material in the industry. Illustrators stand on the shoulders of giants pushing fashion, photography design. I work using all this knowledge and then applying it to my book of wonders (my sketch pad). Once collecting the images needed either from found material of location drawing I am ready for my Mac. I scan my drawings in maybe bitmapping for a raw edge of just playing with the levels to get real hard black.

« Work hard play hard ». Illustrer c'est rencontrer des gens, travailler dur et produire la matière repoussant le plus les limites dans ce secteur. Les illustrateurs se tiennent sur les épaules de géants faiseurs de mode, de photographie ou de design. Je travaille en me servant de toutes ces connaissances et les applique dans mon livre des merveilles (mon carnet d'esquisses). Après avoir recueilli les images à partir soit de documents que j'ai trouvés, soit de dessins d'ensemble, je me mets devant mon Mac.

Arbeite hart und dann geh aufs Ganze. Illustration definiert sich durch das Kennenlernen von Menschen, Vollgas im Job und die Kreation der besten Produkte eines Bereiches — keine Scheu vor Limits. Illustratoren sind diejenigen, die Mode und Fotodesign vorantreiben. Wenn ich arbeite, nutze ich all dieses Wissen und übertrage dies in mein „Buch der Wunder" (mein Sketchblock). Nachdem ich alle Bilder, Materialien und Zeichnungen, zusammengetragen habe (viele stammen von Mode- und Filmshootings), bin ich bereit für meinen Mac. Ich scanne meine Zeichnungen höchstwahrscheinlich im bitmap-Format, um mit dem Rohmaterial spielen sowie die verschiedenen Levels testen zu können, mit dem Ergebnis, ein reines Schwarz zu erhalten.

www.patrickmorgan.co.uk

NAME: Patrick Morgan **LOCATION:** London, UK **CONTACT:** patrick@patrickmorgan.co.uk **TOOLS:** Pencil, screen print, litho print, etching, woodcut, Adobe Photoshop, Adobe Illustrator, Sketch book, putty rubber, colouring pencils. **AGENT:** debut Art <www.debutart.com> **CLIENTS:** Virgin Airways, Thomson, BBC, Channel4, Timeout, BMG, Penguin, Guiness, Gordon's Gin, The Body Shop, Selfridges, Nokia, Siemens, HMV, Abbey National, Rank, Sainsbury's, Waitrose, Hewlett Packard, Levis, NARS, L&M.

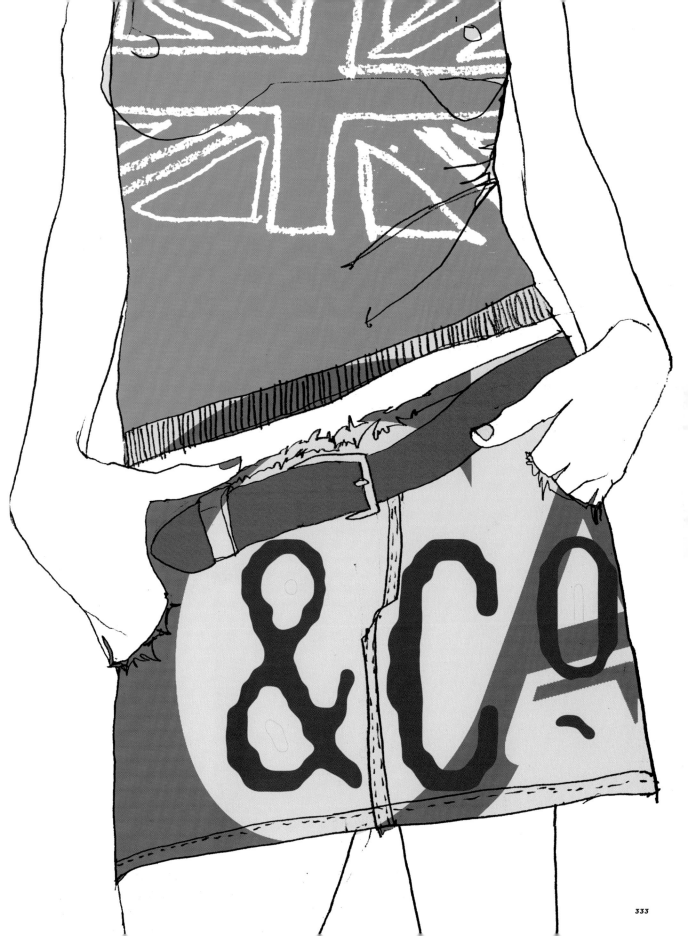

337

Joe Morse

My work flows from drawing and the expressive collision of pigment and solvent. In a gas mask and chemical gloves I work with materials that form images and informs my ideas. An illustration should be a powerful picture that is both immediate and haunting. I create art that defines the shape around popular culture, rather than adding more noise to blur it.

Mon travail découle du dessin et de la collision expressive des pigments et des solvants. Équipé d'un masque à gaz et de gants chimiques, je travaille avec des matériaux qui forment des images et guident mes idées. Une illustration se doit d'être une image efficace à la fois immédiate et obsédante. Je crée des œuvres d'art qui définissent une forme autour de la culture populaire plutôt que d'ajouter davantage de bruit et de la brouiller.

Meine Arbeit fliesst sowohl durch meine Zeichnungen als auch durch das ausdrucksstarke Aufeinanderprallen von Pigmenten und Lösungsmitteln. Mit Schutzmaske und Schutzhandschuhen arbeite ich mit Materialien, die meine Bilder formen und meine Ideen inspirieren. Eine Illustration sollte ein ausdrucksstarkes Bild sein, das sowohl direkt ist als auch den Betrachter gefangennimmt: ein Bild, das verfolgt. Ich kreiere Kunst, die populärer Kultur Form gibt, anstatt diese durch viel Lärm verschwimmen zu lassen.

www.joemorse.com

NAME: Joe Morse **LOCATION:** Toronto, Canada **CONTACT:** joe@joemorse.com **TOOLS:** Oil paint and dangerous chemicals combined on paper, acrylic, scanner, Adobe Photoshop. **AWARDS:** Awarded over 60 international awards: American Illustration, Communication Arts, Society of Illustrators, etc. **AGENT:** Heflinreps <www.heflinreps.com> **CLIENTS:** Universal Films, Nike, Coca Cola, LandRover, RollingStone, ESPN Magazine, Vibe, The New Yorker, Esquire, Los Angeles Times, etc.

Redefinition

Time to look once more at what "blackness" is all about.
BY SACHA JENKINS

Debra J. Dickerson, author of *The End of Blackness*, is rattlin' cages round this zoolike nation with her colorful words. Announces the tome's introduction: "The concept of 'blackness,' as it has come to be understood, (CONTINUED ON PAGE 42)

Illustration by **JOE MORSE**

341

Bee

Belinda Murphy

As an illustrator I am part of popular culture embedded in the Flotsom and Jetsom of daily life. I love that. In my work I am the architect of a world with in a frame, I love the making of the work creating the details, trying to make it right. My inspiration comes from the world around me, from people, travel, Nature and cocktail parties.

En tant qu'illustratrice, je fais partie intégrante de la culture populaire ancrée dans le bric-à-brac de la vie quotidienne. Dans mon travail, j'aime être l'architecte d'un monde encadré, j'aime créer des détails, et m'efforcer de faire mon travail correctement. Je puise mon inspiration dans le monde qui m'entoure, des gens, de voyages, de la nature et des cocktails.

Als Illustratorin sehe ich mich als Teil einer modernen Kultur, manifestiert im Treiben des täglichen Lebens. Ich liebe es. Bei meiner Arbeit agiere ich als Architektin und stelle sozusagen eingerahmte Welten her. Dabei gefällt mir besonders die Detailarbeit, der Versuch, alles perfekt zu gestalten. Meine Inspirationen erhalte ich aus meiner Umgebung, von Menschen, Reisen, in der Natur und auch von Cocktailparties.

www.supabee.com

NAME: Belinda Murphy "Bee" **LOCATION:** Los Angeles, USA **CONTACT:** bee@supabee.com **TOOLS:** Mechanical pencil, Adobe Illustrator, watercolours, Adobe Photoshop. **AGENT:** Kate Larkworthy <www.larkworthy.com> **CLIENTS:** Vogue, Flaunt Magazine, Herman Miller, Marcel Schurman, American Express, Grey Goose Vodka, Marie Claire, Lancome, Random House, Penguin Books, The Wall Street Journal, United Airlines, Elle, INStyle, Takashimaya, World (Japan).

Flaunt can fulfill at least one of Iggy Pop's must haves. We may not be able to provide "a dirty beach" or the "old car," but we can at least grant him Number 4. Iggy's new CD, Skull Ring, is out now.

1. A dirty beach
2. An old car
3. My hot girlfriend
4. A copy of some stupid magazine with my name in it
5. My corporate pimp
6. The money
7. John Coltrane
8. Mississippi Fred McDowell
9. Junior Kimbrough
10. My bad attitude

MUST-HAVES

by **Jean-Paul Gaultier** *Illustration by* **Bee**
Today's imperatives for the senses come wrapped in play. Below, the designer divulges a few things he can't do without.

1. A fiance
2. Minimum of 10 boxes of condoms
3. Television meal and a TV
4. A prayer chair
5. Justin Timberlake CD
6. A picture of Pete Burns (singer of Dead or Alive)
7. A holographic image of Marilyn Manson
8. Madonna's beret
9. A romper suit
10. A makeup kit

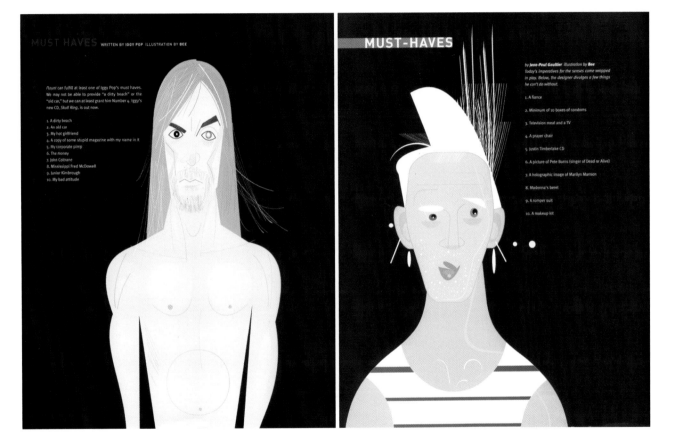

345

Gaku Nakagawa

The means for conveying quickly the contents and impression of a product to a target audience through vision.

Le moyen de véhiculer rapidement le contenu et l'impression d'un produit vers un public cible via la vue.

Schnell Inhalt und Eindruck eines Produktes einem ausgewählten Publikum visuell vermitteln.

NAME: Gaku Nakagawa **LOCATION:** Kyoto, Japan **CONTACT:** Japan: starfactory@dream-more.com; UK: info@DutchUncle.co.uk **TOOLS:** Adobe Illustrator. **AWARDS:** Amuse Artjam. **AGENT:** Dream and More Co. (Japan) <www.starfactory.info>; Dutch Uncle (UK) <www.dutchuncle.co.uk> **CLIENTS:** Hankyu, Seizan Fukakusa of Jodo-sect Motoyama vow temple, Gifu City, Kyoto Shinkyogoku shopping center, Higashi Honganji.

Miya Nakajima

I always want to represent the sense of fragility and mystery.

Je souhaite toujours représenter le sens de la fragilité et du mystère.

Ich bin stets darauf bedacht, ein Gefühl von Zerbrechlichkeit und Rätselhaftigkeit weiterzugeben.

www.nuances.cc

NAME: Miya Nakajima **LOCATION:** Tokyo, Japan **CONTACT:** miya@nuances.cc **TOOLS:** Acrylic, Oil. **AWARDS:** The Choice, Japan Art & Culture Association, Nippon Graphic Exhibition, Tokyo Illustrators Society. **CLIENTS:** AERA, Esquire Japan, Nikkei Business Publications, Sweden House, Tohokushinsha Film Corporation, GunHo Online Entertainment, Bungeishunju, Koudansha, Shougakkan, etc.

Nico

My theme is a girl! In her essence she is a retrospective girl, a modern girl, and a cute, happy one. My lifework is to express original "POP" = " NICOPOP".

Mon thème est une fille ! Par essence c'est une fille rétrospective, une fille moderne, jolie, heureuse. Le travail de ma vie consiste à exprimer un original "POP" = " NICOPOP".

Mein Thema ist ein Mädchen! In ihrem Ursprung ist sie ein modernes Mädchen, mit der Fähigkeit, auf Vergangenes zurückzublicken, ein süsses, glückliches Mädchen. Mein Lebenswerk besteht darin, echtes "POP" ="NICOPOP" auszudrücken.

NAME: Nico **LOCATION:** Osaka, Japan **CONTACT:** starfactory@dream-more.com; info@dutchuncle.co.uk **TOOLS:** Adobe Illustrator, Adobe Photoshop. **AWARDS:** T-shirt Exhibition; Small, Small Large Exhibition. **AGENT:** Dream & More Co. (Japan) <www.starfactory.info>; Dutch Uncle (UK) <www.dutchuncle.co.uk> **CLIENTS:** Toshiba, EMI, MS Record, Gunze, Takarajimasha, Shufu-to-seikatsusha, Forsouth, Tescom, Dhc, Pola, Nissen, For-side.com, Walkerplus, Starlab, etc.

Christoph Niemann

Probably because of my education as a graphic designer, my approach to illustration focuses more on problem solving than on artistic expression per se. I try to base my illustrations on the idea, and then find an appropriate style to best support the concept. Hence I try to use a wide variety of styles, from crude handmade drawings and slick illustrator renderings to simplistic pixel-icons.

Probablement du fait de ma formation de graphiste, mon approche de l'illustration se concentre plus sur la résolution de problèmes que sur une expression artistique en soi. J'essaie de baser mes illustrations sur l'idée puis de trouver un style approprié pour soutenir au mieux le concept. J'essaie en effet d'utiliser une grande variété de styles, du dessin brut fait à la main et de l'interprétation habile d'illustrateur aux images simplistes à base de pixels.

Wahrscheinlich liegt es an meiner Ausbildung zum Grafikdesigner, dass ich beim Medium Illustration eher Problemlösungen suche, als den künstlerischen Aspekt. Bei meinen Illustrationen ist die Idee die Basis und anschliessend suche ich den passenden Stil, der das Konzept zu tragen vermag. Folglich versuche ich, eine grosse Auswahl an Techniken anzuwenden, angefangen bei rohen, handgefertigten Zeichnungen, aalglatten Interpretationen bis hin zu stark vereinfachten Pixel-Ikonen.

www.christophniemann.com

NAME: Christoph Niemann **LOCATION:** New York, USA **CONTACT:** mail@christophniemann.com **TOOLS:** brush, ink, Adobe Illustrator, Adobe Photoshop. **AWARDS:** ADC of Germany - Talent of the Year, ID Forty under Thirty, Society of Publication Designer, AIGA, Art Directors Club NY, American Illustration, Member of Alliance Graphique Internationale, Design Triennial (Cooper Hewitt Design Museum New York). **CLIENTS:** New York Times, New Yorker, Nike, Google.

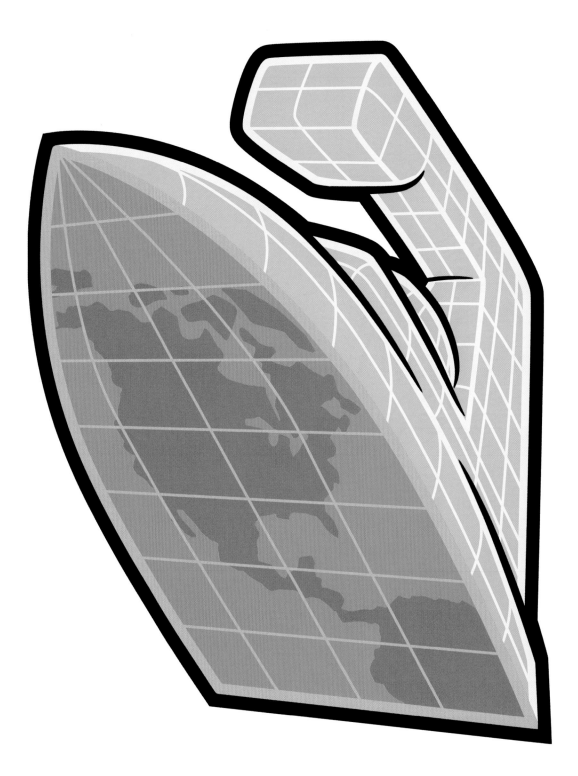

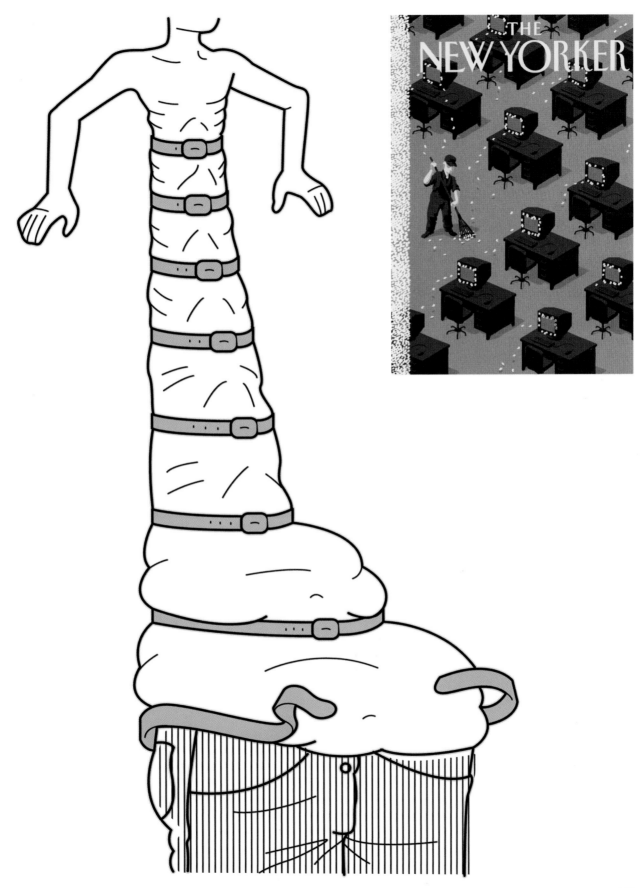

Anja Nolte

A good illustration is seductive. Sexy. Captures views, wakes up interest, makes appetite for more. The spectator gets the feeling. Illustration is a process of common transfer of written, thought and spoken words in a visual counterpart. A counterpart, which on the one hand substitutes and complements the contents, on the other hand enriches them and offers to the spectator additional, direct access to the subject. Illustration is to create expectations and to fulfill them simultaneously.

Une bonne illustration est séduisante. Sexy. Elle attire les regards, éveille l'intérêt, fait qu'on en redemande. C'est elle qui donne une sensation à l'observateur. L'illustration est un processus de transfert commun de mots écrits, pensés et parlés dans un équivalent visuel. Un équivalent qui sert de substitut et de complément au contenu, et enrichit ce dernier tout en offrant à l'observateur un accès supplémentaire et direct au sujet. Illustrer c'est créer des attentes tout en y répondant.

Eine gute Illustration ist verführerisch. Sexy. Zieht Blicke auf sich, weckt Interesse, macht Appetit auf mehr. Sie gibt dem Betrachter das bestimmte Gefühl. Illustration ist der Prozess der gemeinsamen Umsetzung von geschriebenem, gedachtem und gesprochenem Wort in ein bildhaftes Gegenüber. Ein Gegenüber, das den Inhalt zum Einen ergänzt und unterstützt, zum anderen bereichert und dem Betrachter einen zusätzlichen, sehr direkten und ganz eigenen Zugang zum Thema gibt. Illustration ist die Erweckung einer Erwartung und gleichzeitige Erfüllung derselbigen.

www.anjanolte.de

NAME: Anja Nolte **LOCATION:** Berlin, Germany **CONTACT:** mail@anjanolte.de **TOOLS:** Adobe Photoshop, Macromedia Flash, pencil. **AWARDS:** Label Netdays. **AGENT:** Margarethe Hubauer <www.margarethe-hubauer.de> **CLIENTS:** Barclays Bank PLC, BMW, BP, DM-Euro Magazin, La Roche, Max, Euro am Sonntag, Springer& Jacoby, National Museums Berlin (SMB), Die ZEIT, a.s.o. 2002- 04 Main Illustrator, Director & Art Director of the webbased Culture portal Kizzart / Pizzart S.A./ CH.

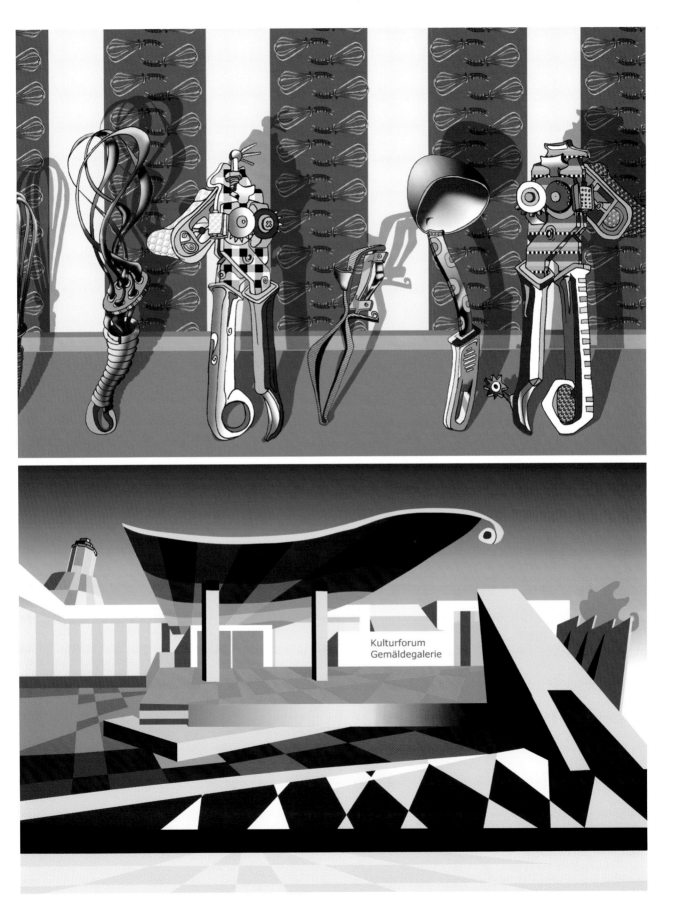

Kulturforum
Gemäldegalerie

Seiko Ohmori

尊き情熱、
歌うことは日々への祈り。
その瞳も唇も、歌うために開かれた。

うまち
上原知子

"Illustration" is a work for the ephemera (advertising, magazines, etc.) and it is in this transitory aspect that I have a great interest. Flash meeting for anyone who sees it – just for the reason that Illustration can deeply touch their subconscious. In a spirit of modernity, I hope to express the everlasting beauty. I also desire to incarnate women's strength, heartiness and flexibility in each piece of my work.

L' « illustration » est un travail qui a à avoir avec l'éphémère (publicité, magazines, etc.). C'est cet aspect transitoire qui m'intéresse tout particulièrement. La rencontre entre l'illustration et la personne qui la voit est une rencontre éclair mais qui peut toucher profondément le subconscient. Dans un esprit de modernité, j'espère exprimer une beauté intemporelle. J'aspire également à incarner la force, la vigueur et la flexibilité des femmes dans chacun de mes travaux.

"Illustration" ist eine Arbeit der Ephemera (Werbung, Zeitschriften, etc.) und ist sehr kurzlebig. Genau an diesem Durchlaufprozess habe ich grosses Interesse. Ein Flash für jeden, der offen dafür ist, allein schon wegen der Möglichkeit, Illustration könnte das Unterbewusstsein erreichen. Im Sinne der Modernität versuche ich, ewige Schönheit zum Ausdruck zu bringen. Mein Wunsch ist es auch, in meinen Arbeiten die Stärke der Frauen, Herzlichkeit sowie Flexibilität zu verkörpern.

www.se.batic2.com

NAME: Seiko Ohmori **LOCATION:** Tokyo, Japan **CONTACT:** seiko_426@ybb.ne.jp **TOOLS:** Cly, Gouache, Adobe Photoshop. **AWARDS:** Japan Art & Culture Association (Special Award), 3Dimentional and Digital Illustration Award Show USA (Bronze). **CLIENTS:** NHK, KIRIN, Shueisha, Magazine House, Kodansha, KAO, TENMAYA, Sony, etc.

Karen Oxman

I enjoy the playfulness and irony of juxtaposing reality, fantasy and abstraction. In treatment of the subjects I often attempt to create the poetical, lyrical world within a contemporary condition. My work often employs the hybridization of concepts and media and the integration of different sources. The images evoke the anonymity, aloofness and distance of classical century portrait paintings, through the ironic glare of a modern eye. However, beyond the lyrical qualities of the work, I am still looking for a way to be critical without caricature. I want to maintain a certain commitment to the beauty of my subjects. This duality and complexity is perhaps less traditional in illustration than it is in painting, or conceptual art.

J'aime ce qu'il y a de ludique et d'ironique à juxtaposer la réalité, la fantaisie et l'abstraction. Dans le traitement de mes sujets, j'essaie souvent de créer un univers poétique et lyrique dans un environnement contemporain. Mon travail repose souvent sur le métissage de concepts et de médias, et l'intégration de différentes sources. Mes images évoquent l'anonymat, la réserve et la distance des portraits du siècle classique à travers le regard ironique d'un œil moderne. Mais, au-delà des qualités lyriques de mon travail, je cherche toujours à être critique sans verser dans la caricature. Je tiens à maintenir un certain attachement à la beauté de mes sujets. Cette dualité et cette complexité sont peut-être moins traditionnelles en illustration qu'elles ne le sont en peinture ou en art conceptuel.

Ich geniesse das Spielerische und die Ironie bei der Gegenüberstellung von Realität, Fantasie und Abstraktion. Bei der Bearbeitung eines Projektes versuche ich oftmals, eine poetische, lyrische Welt unter zeitgenössischen Bedingungen zu kreieren. Bei meiner Arbeit verwende ich oft eine Mischung von Konzepten und Media und beziehe unterschiedliche Quellen mit ein. Die Bilder drücken eine gewisse Anonymität, Zurückhaltung und Distanzierung aus, vergleichbar mit einem klassischen Porträtgemälde des vergangenen Jahrhunderts, und all dies aus einem ironischen Blickwinkel der Moderne betrachtet. Trotz der lyrischen Qualitäten meiner Arbeiten versuche ich nicht nur durch Karikatur zu kritisieren. Ich möchte ein gewisse Verpflichtung bezüglich der Ästhetik meiner Werke aufrechterhalten. Wahrscheinlich ist diese Dualität und Komplexität in der Illustration weniger geläufig als bei Gemälden oder in der Conceptual art.

www.karenoxman.com

NAME: Karen Oxman **LOCATION:** London, England **CONTACT:** k@karenoxman.com **TOOLS:** Pencil, Adobe Photoshop, Adobe Illustrator. **AWARDS:** The Clore Scholarship Award; Society of Illustrators; WPP Atticus Magazine Award. **CLIENTS:** I.D Magazine, Flaunt Magazine, WYWS Magazine, Empty Magazine, Chrysalis Books Group, etc.

Dan **Page**

I love everything about illustration; always dealing with different subject matter on a daily basis, thinking of the ideas, bringing them to life in full colour, fuelled by the adrenalin rush of a deadline. At the core of what I do is the "idea" behind each image, communication with pictures or creating a thought provoking image is what makes me move forward. In the final, the application of colour becomes part of the overall concept.

J'aime tout dans l'illustration : aborder des thèmes différents chaque jour, chercher des idées, leur donner vie et couleurs, poussé par l'adrénaline d'un délai à respecter. Dans ce que je fais, l' « idée » est derrière chaque image. Communiquer avec des images ou créer une image évocatrice est ce qui me fait avancer. Au final, l'application de couleurs devient partie intégrante du concept dans son entier.

Ich liebe alles, was mit Illustration zu tun hat; das tägliche Behandeln unterschiedlicher Themenbereiche, auf Ideen kommen, diese in Farbe umsetzen, und das Ganze angespornt durch den Adrenalinstoss einer Deadline. Das Wichtigste ist mir die Idee, die hinter jedem Bild steckt, die Kommunikation der Bilder oder auch die Provokation eines Gedanken innerhalb eines Bildes. All dies treibt mich voran bei meiner Arbeit. Schliesslich trägt die Farbauswahl zum generellen Konzept bei.

www.danpage.net

NAME: Dan Page **LOCATION:** Canada **CONTACT:** danpage@rogers.com **TOOLS:** acrylic paint, Adobe Photoshop. **AWARDS:** American Illustration. **AGENT:** Gerald & Cullen Rapp <www.rappart.com> **CLIENTS:** Time, Business Week, Forbes, Popular Science, The New York Times, New Scientist, Fast Company, Wall Street Journal, Canadian Business, CFO, American Way, Newsweek, Shape, Random House, American Express, Booz Allen Hamilton.

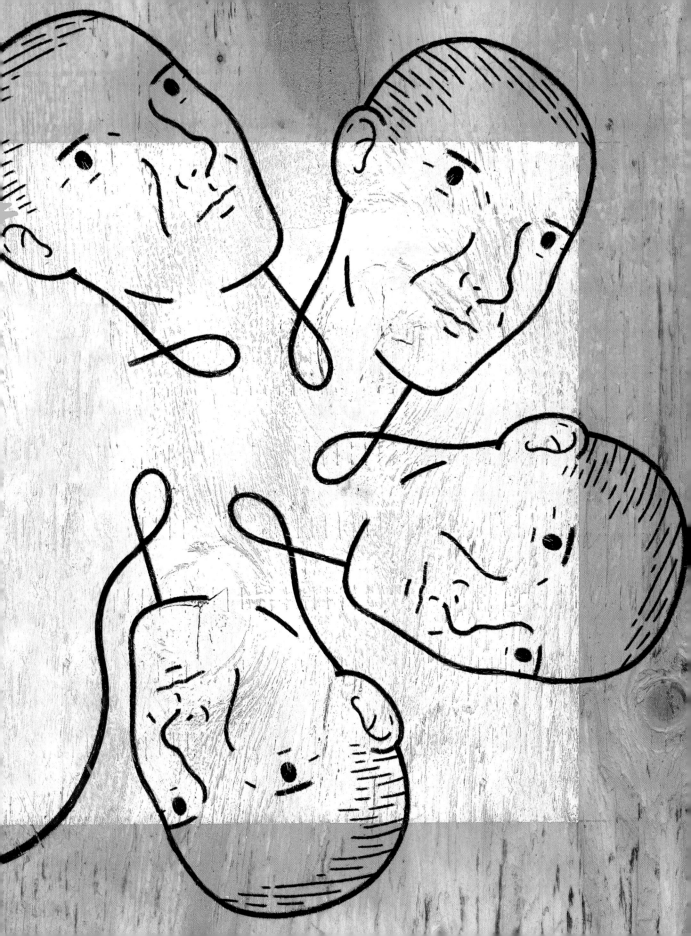

CANADIAN EDITION / DECEMBER 6, 2004

TIME

WHY BUSH'S TRIP TO CANADA MATTERS

ARE THE GREAT LAKES FOR SALE?

An inside look at the controversial proposal to export water from our precious resource

LAKE SUPERIOR

LAKE MICHIGAN

LAKE HURON

LAKE ONTARIO

LAKE ERIE

$4.95 CANADA

49>

0 72440 10091 6

www.timecanada.com AOL Keyword: TIMECANADA

Carlos **Pardo**

Creation is a lifelong hobby, that's why I'm always experimenting new media, changing my way of drawing and digging other themes. People and music are the very first sources of my daily inspiration for an ever-growing, dynamic and resourceful digital art, a wide and interesting new way of expressing feelings, showing and displaying things that sometimes words cannot say and our mere imagination cannot see.

Créer est pour moi un passe-temps de toujours. C'est pourquoi j'expérimente toujours de nouveaux supports en changeant ma façon de dessiner et creusant de nouveaux sujets. Les gens et la musique sont les sources essentielles de mon inspiration quotidienne, qui alimente un art numérique en constante croissance, dynamique et plein de ressources, un moyen vaste et intéressant d'exprimer des sentiments, de présenter des choses que les mots ne peuvent parfois pas décrire et que notre simple imagination ne peut voir.

Kreation ist ein lebenslanges Hobby, von daher experimentiere ich ständig mit neuen Medien, ändere meinen Zeichenstil und schaue mir andere Themenbereiche an. Menschen und Musik sind die erste Quelle meiner täglichen Inspiration, die mir zu Wachstum und Dynamik in der digitalen Kunst verhilft und einen breiten und interessanten Weg zum Ausdruck meiner Gefühle eröffnet. Dabei kommen Dinge zum Vorschein, die weder durch Worte ausgedrückt werden können, noch von unserem Vorstellungsvermögen erfasst werden.

www.m4de.com

NAME: Carlos Pardo (Made) **LOCATION:** Paris, France **CONTACT:** carlos@m4de.com **TOOLS:** Adobe Photoshop, pencil. **CLIENTS:** Orange, Nokia, EuroRSCG, SNCF, Artsonik, Ginger studios, Nina Ricci, Elektro Games; Docomo NTT, AU, Famitsu magazine (Japan); Mattel (USA); Conforama, Canal+, CarpeDiem, SFR, Vodaphone, France Telecom, Newt games; Telefónica, General Solutions (Spain); Mediamobsters (Denmark); Cakewalk, Manyc (Germany), etc.

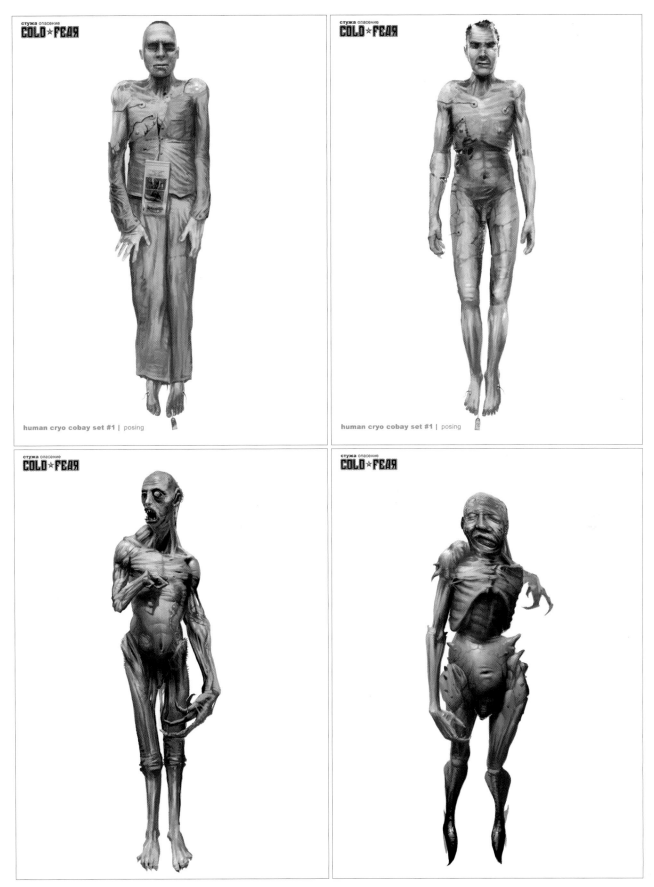

human cryo cobay set #1 | posing

human cryo cobay set #1 | posing

Susanne Paschke

A good illustration is always preceded by the exact observation of your environment. Only by the graphic studying of light and shadow can you also create this realistic effect with the help of vectors. Here it is important for me that the illustrations do not appear too perfect and soft because the human face is also not always free from edges and it is exactly these edges that form the character of every human. With this method I try to breathe some emotion and life into my illustrations.

Un illustrateur ne peut obtenir un bon résultat que s'il observe de façon précise son environnement. Ce n'est qu'avec l'étude graphique de la lumière et des ombres qu'il est possible de créer un effet réaliste à l'aide de vecteurs. Pour moi, il est important que les illustrations ne soient ni trop parfaites ni trop lisses car les visages humains ne sont pas non plus toujours exempts d'imperfections. Et ce sont justement ces imperfections qui font le caractère de chaque être humain. Avec cette méthode j'essaie d'insuffler un peu d'émotion et de vie à mes illustrations.

Einer guten Illustration geht stets eine genaue Beobachtung der Umgebung voraus. Nur durch grafische Analysierung von Licht und Schatten und mit Hilfe von Vektoren lässt sich dieser realistische Effekt erzielen. Hierbei ist es mir besonders wichtig, dass die Illustrationen nicht zu perfekt und weich erscheinen, denn vergleicht man sie mit dem menschlichen Gesicht, so stellt man fest, dass dieses selten ohne Ecken und Kanten ist, und genau dieses Fehlen an Perfektion charakterisiert den Menschen. Mit dieser Methode versuche ich, meinen Illustrationen Gefühl und Leben zu geben.

www.susannepaschke.de

NAME: Susanne Paschke **LOCATION:** Berlin, Germay **CONTACT:** SP@susannepaschke.de **TOOLS:** Macromedia Freehand. **CLIENTS:** Aperto AG, Meta Design (Sportscheck), Praxis Designagentur (Berlin Cosemtics), Iconmobile, Universal Strategic Marketing.

Frédéric Péault

I like to say many things with nothing, I love the old Japanese illustration, I love when an illustration is empty.

J'aime dire beaucoup de choses avec pas grand-chose, j'aime les illustrations japonaises anciennes, j'aime lorsqu'une illustration est vide.

Ich liebe es, Viel mit Nichts auszudrücken, ich liebe die alte japanische Illustration und mir gefallen leere Illustrationen.

www.fred-peault.com

NAME: Frédéric Péault **LOCATION:** Paris, France **CONTACT:** info@fred-peault.com **TOOLS:** Adobe Illustrator, Strata 3D. **AGENT:** Agency Virginie <www.virginie.fr>
CLIENTS: Total, Havas, Cégétel, Champion, Elle, Fur Die Frau, IBM, Lyonnaise des Eaux, Renault.

Stina Persson

Apart from making pretty things prettier, and ugly things at least more acceptable, it's all about problem solving, really. To follow directions but still manage to keep the work fresh, unique and personal. It is also important to be able to stay true to your style, while at the same time constantly challenging yourself and never get fat and lazy and afraid of trying new things.

A part rendre les belles choses plus belles encore et les choses laides au moins plus acceptables, illustrer, c'est véritablement résoudre des problèmes. Il s'agit en effet de suivre les instructions données tout en gardant une fraîcheur, une individualité et une personnalité. Il est également important de rester fidèle à son style mais en se lançant en permanence de nouveaux défis, en n'ayant pas peur d'expérimenter.

Abgesehen davon, dass man versucht, hübsche Dinge noch hübscher erscheinen zu lassen und hässliche Dinge zumindest akzeptabel, geht es hauptsächlich um Problemlösungen. Gewissen Normen folgend und die Arbeit dennoch natürlich, besonders und persönlich wirken zu lassen. Ausserdem ist es von grosser Wichtigkeit, seinem Stil treu zu bleiben und sich gleichzeitig ständig selbst herauszufordern. Und dabei nie müde zu werden, neue Dinge auszuprobieren.

www.stinapersson.com

NAME: Stina Persson **LOCATION:** Stockholm, Sweden **CONTACT:** stina@stinapersson.com **TOOLS:** Pen & Ink, Watercolor, Acrylic, Adobe Photoshop. **AWARDS:** Society of Illustrator. **AGENT:** CWC-I <agent@cwc-i.com>, CWC (Japan) <agents@cwctokyo.com> **CLIENTS:** Macy's, Bloomingdales, Nylon, Elle, Marie Claire, Björn Borg Collection, 2K Tshirts, Volvo Japan, Swedish Broadcasting, Goldwell, Amica.

LEO
(23 JULY – 23 AUG)

LOVE Let's be honest, you need to be loved and adored the way other people need oxygen. And, lucky you, you do seem to get more than the lion's share of affection. But the best way to receive all that loving attention right now is to spread it around. Until 28 August this won't be an issue but, after that, when the love spring dries up and has you almost panic-stricken, practise what comes naturally to Leos: making others feel special. The vibe will come back in spades.
SEX It is hot, it is heavy, and it is changing every time you turn around. There are possibilities literally everywhere you turn, which tells you two important things: one, don't plan on shacking up with anyone just yet. Two, you need to work out a little harder than usual since you will be spending so much of the summer and autumn in various states of undress...
MONEY Spending money has never been a problem for you, and from July till the end of August you may actually set a personal record. But sometime between 23 and 28 August, a light goes on in your head, making it very clear to you that if you have some big plans for the coming year, and if those plans involve shifting major amounts of capital, you'd better start saving now.

LEO will stay in tbut with Christian Louboutin's printed calfskin creation, and a hot Moschino frock (left)

VIRGO
(24 AUG – 23 SEPT)

LOVE In July you're spending so much time hanging out with your mates that you develop a crush on one of them. In August you'll be on to someone new – but don't get carried away. By 23 August you'll know if it's for real. September is your best love month, and after 26 October things really get cooking!
SEX Casual sex isn't your cup of tea, but with all the changes going on in the rest of your life it's hard to take commitment seriously. You start to get serious about someone in September, but he sends you mixed messages. Let him know he's not the only one with a libido.
MONEY There's no need for you to always get the first round, or dole out cab fare to cash-poor friends every time you're out. It's hard for you to say no, but you must if you're going to afford that new autumn wardrobe. After 16 September, you'll get a raise or new source of income, and around 9 October it gets even better!

VIRGO will be sitting pretty with a chic printed calfskin bag by Salvatore Ferragamo, and in neat, neat, neat Hermès (right)

LIBRA
(24 SEPT – 23 OCT)

LOVE They say guys think about sex every five minutes, but Libra girls think of romance at least that often. These days, however, it's probably down to twice an hour, thanks to your current workload. Naturally, you have your eye on the hottest guy in the office – but watch your step in September. There'll be a big change in your love life around 9 October, coming completely out of the blue.
SEX If you're not having the multiple orgasms you're accustomed to, don't blame him. Maybe you don't have the energy you need for such Olympic-level activity. Try leaving the office at a reasonable hour on 1 October and you'll realise he isn't. Plan a very special night in on 9 November. He'll never stray again.
MONEY You hate to think about it in the summer, but by the end of August reality catches up with you in the form of credit-card statements, and it's obvious you need to make sweeping economic reforms. Look out for ways to out right back in September, and by late October you'll be back in the black – black Prada, that is.

LIBRA will feel just swell-egant with Celine's printed calfskin boogie bag, and flirty Ungaro (left)

SCORPIO
(24 OCT – 22 NOV)

LOVE You've made a summer resolution to spice up your love life – but you're more interested in a buffet than a meal on a plate. The good news is there are plenty of luscious delicacies to choose from (the difficulty will be getting their names straight). On 10 October you're such a man magnet that friends are hanging around just to pick at your leftovers.
SEX There's 'wild and exciting' to the general populace, and there's 'wild and exciting' to a Scorpio on the prowl. You may find yourself exploring things that even you haven't got into before. You won't be able to control all the variables and that may freak you out from 29 July to 27 September. On a serious note, do make sure you have reliable protection. 9 November is a big day.
MONEY You're shrewd about finances, but you like to keep your money situation private. A chance to earn some cash with a partner after 28 August may force you to open up a little. This is worth taking a chance on, but don't expect instant results. However, a big eclipse in your money house on 23 November will bring six months of exciting opportunities. ▶

SCORPIO will be sex bomb-central with Jil Sander's leather shoulder bag, and in a come-hither number by Tom Ford for YSL Rive Gauche (right)

David Pfendler

I like to think of my work as urban lifestyle imagery with a bit of a fashion bent. The urban influence along with the "musicality" of style has changed the way we relate to our environment and how we present ourselves to the world. I try to capture emotional gestures informed by daily life. How all of this is represented continues to evolve along with changing tastes and influences.

Des images de mode de vie urbain teinté de mode, c'est ainsi que j'aime définir mon travail. L'influence urbaine et la « musicalité » stylistique ont changé notre relation à notre environnement et la façon dont nous nous présentons au monde. J'essaie de capturer des gestes émotionnels guidés par la vie quotidienne. La manière dont tout cela est représenté continue d'évoluer selon les goûts et les influences.

Ich betrachte meine Arbeit gerne als ein Bilderwerk urbanen Lebenstils mit modernem Touch. Die urbane Beeinflussung in Kombination mit einer gewissen "Musikalität" des Lebensstils hat unser Selbstverständnis und die Art und Weise, mit der wir unserer Umwelt begegnen, wesentlich verändert. Ich versuche, Gefühle und Verhaltensweisen im täglichen Leben einzufangen. Die Repräsentation all dessen ist ein konstanter Entwicklungsprozess mit ständig wechselnden Geschmäckern und Einflüssen.

www.davidpfendler.com

NAME: David Pfendler **LOCATION:** New York, USA **CONTACT:** dpfendler@nyc.rr.com **TOOLS:** Adobe Photoshop. **AGENT:** Carla Grande <cgrande@nyc.rr.com>
CLIENTS: Levi's, Calvin Klein, Flaunt magazine, YM magazine, Teen People, BET books.

It is my intent to capture on a piece of paper the things I love in the world around me. This is the way I make the world mine and then reintroduce to people the fashionable things around us with my own point of view. I simply paint things I like. I paint what I know, what I love. I am creating continuously. Non-stop... it's a constant focus. My obsession. And I think about creating that next illustration with no end, day and night, twenty-four seven.

Ce que je cherche, c'est capturer sur un bout de papier les choses que j'aime dans le monde qui m'entoure. C'est de cette manière que je m'approprie le monde et que je présente aux gens des objets en vogue tels que je les vois. Je peins simplement les choses que j'aime. Je peins ce que je connais, ce que j'aime. Je crée en permanence. Non-stop. . . C'est une activité de chaque instant. Une obsession. Et je pense constamment à ma prochaine illustration, je ne vois jamais de fin, je m'y consacre corps et âme, jour et nuit, 24h/24.

Die Dinge, die ich auf dieser Welt liebe, auf einem Stück Papier einzufangen – das ist meine Absicht. Auf diese Art und Weise mache ich mir die Dinge zueigen und gebe dann alles, was „hip, cool und in" in unserer Umgebung ist, -so wie ich es empfinde -, an mein Publikum weiter. Ich male nur die Dinge, die mir gefallen. Ich male das, was ich kenne, was ich liebe. Ich kreiere pausenlos. Nonstop....ständige Konzentration. Meine Besessenheit. Dauernd denke ich an meine nächste Illustration, vierundzwanzig Stunden, sieben Tage die Woche lang.

www.bellapilar.com

NAME: Bella Pilar **LOCATION:** Los Angeles, CA, USA **CONTACT:** bella@bellapilar.com **TOOLS:** gouache. **AGENT:** Magnet Reps <www.magnetreps.com>
CLIENTS: CosmoGirl, YM, Brides, Macy's New York, Hewlett Packard, Full Picture PR, Brand Building PR, Asha Fashion PR, MS Management Beauty Agency.

WhAt'S YoUr SiGn?

Your horoscopes for June and July! By Susan Miller

JUNE

GEMINI (MAY 21–JUNE 20)
In the days following the new moon on June 17, a family relationship becomes unexpectedly demanding and distracting. Travel to distant points will help you relax—so if friends want to organize a trip, find a way to join them.
LOVE FLASH: You can't shake an old flame. Try to be brave—moving on will bring good things.
BEST DATE NIGHTS: June 11 and 25

CANCER (JUNE 21–JULY 22)
Extra responsibilities have been challenging lately, but the bonus is that they've increased your poise, and now you know that you can handle whatever life throws your way. That new attitude is helping you to evolve into a shining star.
LOVE FLASH: You're tempted to date a friend's crush—but don't! (It's a no-win situation.)
BEST DATE NIGHTS: June 12 and 22

LEO (JULY 23–AUGUST 22)
After hibernating in early June, you'll be cheered on by four planets in your friends-and-fun sector, and you won't be alone after June 23. Pals will flock to you with amazing plans they want to include you in. You'll be ready for all the attention!
LOVE FLASH: Resist a big spender—there's a low-key guy friends will soon introduce you to.
BEST DATE NIGHTS: June 5 and 26

VIRGO (AUGUST 23–SEPTEMBER 22)
By the new moon on June 17, a super summer job op shows up. But don't assume it's yours after the interview—you'll have to fight for this plum spot. A well-written thank-you note and a solid reference letter will push you ahead of the rest.
LOVE FLASH: A moody crush is bringing you down. Move on—a fun new prospect awaits.
BEST DATE NIGHTS: June 12 and 25

LIBRA (SEPTEMBER 23–OCTOBER 22)
The huge workload at the end of the school year has drained you, but a treat is near—a friend or relative may invite you to visit. Don't think twice about accepting the generous offer—you deserve it, and the change of scene will do you good.
LOVE FLASH: After June 29, you and a special someone finally get much-needed time alone.
BEST DATE NIGHTS: June 12 and 30

SCORPIO (OCTOBER 23–NOVEMBER 22)
You may have to deal with some difficult times this month, but remember, you have true-blue friends who will support you through it. Your fierce determination will help you overcome these hurdles, and when you do, you'll be much stronger.
LOVE FLASH: Watch for the shy cutie who can't make the first move—do it for him instead!
BEST DATE NIGHTS: June 11 and 17

SAGITTARIUS (NOV. 23–DEC. 21)
A relationship matter that's been brewing will come to the surface, and June 3 is the perfect day to clear the air. But don't worry—Venus is protecting you, and your talk will be so successful you'll wonder why you didn't bring it up sooner.
LOVE FLASH: Try a new hairstyle after June 29, and you will intrigue two hotties!
BEST DATE NIGHTS: June 29 and 30

CAPRICORN (DECEMBER 22–JANUARY 19)
Restore your energy with lots of naps once school lets out. That way, you'll be raring to go the week after June 17—the perfect time to look for an interesting summer job (where you'll be likely to meet yummy romantic prospects as you work).
LOVE FLASH: Break away from the guy at school you just hang with—a more committed guy awaits.
BEST DATE NIGHTS: June 12 and 22

AQUARIUS (JANUARY 20–FEBRUARY 18)
On the full moon, June 3, a friend comes on strong with advice. Let her say what she wants, but don't let her opinions get you down or dissuade you from those last-minute interviews for summer internships—try to stay on track.
LOVE FLASH: Expect a surprising new love encounter at a rock concert or sporting event.
BEST DATE NIGHTS: June 22 and 27

PISCES (FEBRUARY 19–MARCH 20)
The start of June may bring news of a special award at school. Friends and family are sure to be impressed, so let them fuss over you. All the excitement will fill you with nervous energy, so pick your favorite way to unwind and set it free.
LOVE FLASH: Strike up a conversation with a cutie any time this month and be rewarded.
BEST DATE NIGHTS: June 5 and 12

ARIES (MARCH 21–APRIL 19)
Teachers will be harsh right now, so don't even think about asking for an extension on a final paper or to redo an exam. Take their attitude in stride and know that relief is in sight by month's end, when school stress will finally be behind you.
LOVE FLASH: An old friend you once had a crush on may reenter your life around June 10.
BEST DATE NIGHTS: June 5 and 26

TAURUS (APRIL 20–MAY 20)
Thank goodness you'll be out of the house a lot this month, working hard to earn extra money—because a cranky family member needs space now. Blame Saturn orbiting close to Mars and bite your tongue until his or her mood passes.
LOVE FLASH: You're running hot and cold now with your crush. June 29 brings a final verdict!
BEST DATE NIGHTS: June 25 and 29

WhAt'S YoUr SiGn?

Check out your horoscope for the coming month! By Susan Miller

PISCES (FEBRUARY 19–MARCH 20)
Though you're known as the most creative zodiac sign, rarely have you come up with artistic ideas *this* original. So pick up a camera, a paintbrush, or a needle and thread and get to work. A pursuit that's dear to your heart will finally come to fruition this month.
LOVE FLASH: In this perfect month, your love life should be dazzling. With Venus and Mars sweetly positioned, you'll find the words to spark your crush's interest.
BEST DAYS FOR LOVE: March 6 and 19

ARIES (MARCH 21–APRIL 19)
A girlfriend turns out to be a lifesaver when it comes to homework during the first 10 days of March—together you both ace your exams. Celebrate with a trip to the mall, but plan how much you want to spend, or you (and your mom) will be horrified at the totals.
LOVE FLASH: You're bored with the guys your crowd has been hanging out with and are eager to meet new people. A first date early in the month will work out well.
BEST DAYS FOR LOVE: March 6 and 20

TAURUS (APRIL 20–MAY 20)
You are positively *dripping* with charisma this month! Suddenly everyone wants to be near you, hoping your sparkle will rub off on them. This is the moment for fun, so gather your girlfriends and throw the party of the season during the full moon on March 6.
LOVE FLASH: With love planet Venus in your sign, make sure to take extra care with your looks. You never know who you'll bump into at the movies!
BEST DAYS FOR LOVE: March 11 and 16

GEMINI (MAY 21–JUNE 20)
Scan the school bulletin board for things to try out for (like a spring play). Go for the gold—in this made-for-Gemini month, *nothing* is impossible. By March 21, energy planet Mars surges even more power to you. If others underestimate you, they'd better watch out.
LOVE FLASH: With all your energy in other areas, love is on the back burner until March 21. That's the day you'll feel ready to strike up conversations with cuties.
BEST DAYS FOR LOVE: March 3 and 23

CANCER (JUNE 21–JULY 22)
During March's third week, your spirits will get a boost from the raves you receive on a paper. After that, you feel justified in hanging loose; schoolwork's been demanding, so get away—even a short hop over spring break would do you a world of good.
LOVE FLASH: You won't have to try very hard this month to meet a sweet, hip guy, but a cool new haircut might make him notice you sooner.
BEST DAYS FOR LOVE: March 1 and 18

LEO (JULY 23–AUGUST 22)
Odd jobs are hard to come by, but this month you have a knack for finding them. One boss is particularly generous on March 6, thanks to a link between the full moon and Jupiter. And the independence you feel from not having to ask your parents for cash? Priceless!
LOVE FLASH: A person you just met is more interested in flirting than in a relationship. Throw this fish back in the sea and wait for someone better next month.
BEST DAYS FOR LOVE: March 5 and 20

Arthur de Pins

I started to make illustrations because French animation studios always ask illustrators to make their character design. When I was working for TV series, I felt very frustrated to draw other people's characters and I decided to make my own ones... That's how it began. Since then , Illustration is my #1 job.

J'ai commencé à faire des illustrations parce que les studios français d'animation demandent toujours aux illustrateurs de créer leur propre design de personnages. Lorsque je travaillais pour des séries TV, j'étais très frustré de devoir dessiner les personnages créés par d'autres et c'est ainsi que j'ai décidé de créer les miens. C'est comme ça que tout a commencé. Depuis, l'illustration est ce que je préfère.

Französische Animationsstudios setzen die Kreation von Charakteren bei einem Illustrator voraus und so begann ich mit meinen ersten Illustrationen. Als ich für Fernsehserien arbeitete, frustierte es mich, für andere die Charaktere zeichnen zu müssen und so entschloss ich, meine eigenen zu kreieren... So fing alles an. Seit diesem Zeitpunkt ist Illustration mein Job Nummer Eins.

www.arthurdepins.com

NAME: Arthur de Pins **LOCATION:** Paris, France **CONTACT:** mail@arthurdepins.com **TOOLS:** Adobe Illustrator, Macromedia Flash, Adobe Photoshop. **AWARDS:** Mostly in animation (Annecy, Ottawa, Roma, etc). **AGENT:** Lezilus <www.lezilus.com> **CLIENTS:** Acme Filmworks, Spirou, Max-Magazine, Carrefour, Wombat, ADAε, Wagram Music, etc...

Hanoch Piven

Illustration to me is first of all about capturing an audience. You need to create an image that has enough appeal to initially attract a viewer. Then it is about communication. I like my images to communicate just enough that the viewer would be invited to continue my thought process himself. Therefore I like my caricatures not to be recognized immediately. I like to think of them as puzzles that need to be solved within certain amount of time.

Pour moi, une bonne illustration doit capter l'attention. Il faut créer une image qui a suffisamment d'attraits pour attirer le regard. Ensuite, tout est une question de communication. J'aime que mes images communiquent juste ce qu'il faut pour que l'observateur soit invité à prolonger lui-même mon processus de pensée. C'est pour cette raison que je préfère que mes caricatures ne soient pas instantanément reconnaissables. J'aime l'idée qu'elles soient comme des puzzles qu'il faut un peu de temps pour reconstituer.

Das Wichtigste bei der Illustration ist für mich, ein Publikum zu haben. Man muss ein Bild schaffen können, das genügend Ausdruck hat, um den Betrachter anzuziehen. In zweiter Linie geht es um die Kommunikation. Meine Bilder sollen genau so viel aussagen, dass der Betrachter von selbst meinen Gedankengang zu Ende führen kann. Von daher möchte ich auch nicht, dass meine Karikaturen sofort erkannt werden können. Ich stelle sie mir gerne als Puzzle vor, dessen Teile unter einem bestimmten Zeitaufwand zusammengeführt werden müssen.

www.pivenworld.com

NAME: Hanoch Piven **LOCATION:** Barcelona, Spain **CONTACT:** hanoch@pivenworld.com **TOOLS:** glue gun. **AWARDS:** Society of Illustrators NY (Gold), Society of Publication Designers (Silver), Biennial Dimensional Salon - Society of Illustrators NY (Silver), 3D Art Directors & Illustrators Show, Art Directors Club NY (Bronze). **AGENT:** Heflinreps <www.heflinreps.com> **CLIENTS:** Rolling Stone, Time, Newsweek, The New Yorker, The New York Times, Premiere, BMG/Arista, etc.

piven

piven

Yvonne Poepperl

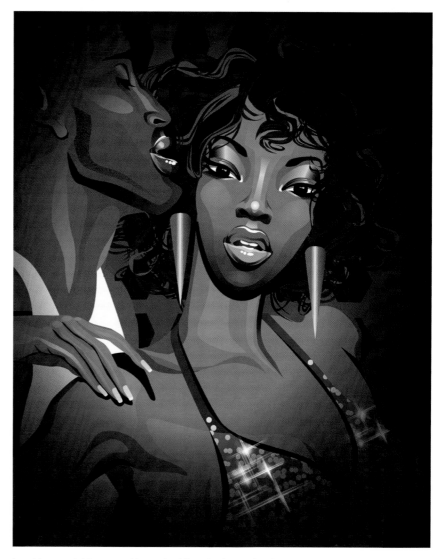

I would say my job has something to do with aspiration, and with passion.

Je dirais que mon travail a à voir avec l'aspiration et avec la passion.

Ich würde sagen, mein Job hat mit Sehnsucht zu tun. Und mit Leidenschaft.

www.illyp.de

NAME: Yvonne Poepperl **LOCATION:** Hamburg, Germany **CONTACT:** yvonnepoepperl@web.de **TOOLS:** Macromedia Freehand, Adobe Photoshop, Mixed media, Collage, Acrylic. **AGENT:** Hirschpool Berlin <www.hirschpool.de>; Eye Candy <www.eyecandy.co.uk> **CLIENTS:** Allegra, Blond, Cosmopolitan, Eurocentres, Goldmann TB, Hinnerk, Knaur, Max, Rowohlt/Wunderlich, Sat 1, Sony Music Germany, Springer & Jacoby, TBWA, Universal Music, Wellfit.

Emiliano Ponzi

It's a challenge between my hand and my mind to capture an abstract idea and make it visible and tangible through the marks of my optic pen. The more the brushstrokes are fluid and fast, and the more the illustration is faithful to the concept – the more weightless I become. Sometimes I think I have chosen this career just for pure hedonism.

Entre ma main et mon esprit, il y a le défi de capturer une idée abstraite et de la rendre visible et tangible par l'empreinte de mon crayon optique. Plus les coups de crayons sont fluides et rapides, plus l'illustration est fidèle au concept et plus je me sens en apesanteur. Parfois je pense que j'ai choisi cette carrière par pur hédonisme.

Die Erfassung einer abstrakten Idee ist eine Herausforderung für meine Hände sowie meinen Geist, und noch mehr, diese durch die Striche meines optischen Stiftes sichtbar und fühlbar zu machen. Je flüssiger und schneller meine Pinselstriche, und je mehr die Illustration ihrem Konzept gleicht, desto schwereloser fühle ich mich. Manchmal habe ich den Eindruck, meinen Beruf aus reinem Hedonismus heraus gewählt zu haben.

www.emilianoponzi.com

NAME: Emiliano Ponzi **LOCATION:** Milano, Italy **CONTACT:** e.ponzi@fastwebnet.it **TOOLS:** Pencil and Corel Painter **AWARDS:** Communication Arts, Torino Città di Cultura, Acqua S.Bernardo, etc. **AGENT:** Magnet Reps <www.magnetreps.com> **CLIENTS:** L.A. Times, HR Magazine, Princeton Alumni Weekly, Nuvo Magazine, Swatch Group, Elle, Smart Money Custom Solution, Delta Airlines, Artes de Mexico, Centurion Publishing Group (UK), Corriere della Sera (Italy), and more.

Voice SIMON SEBAG MONTEFIORE

DRUNK WITH POWER

Stalin's feasts were endurance tests for the members of his Politburo – all of
them desperate to keep the dictator happy. Illustration by Emiliano Ponzi

"THOSE SLEEPING AT STALIN'S TABLE came to a bad end," said Khrushchev, who ultimately succeeded him as Soviet leader. Stalin's all-male dinners were not merely feats of eating and drinking that lasted all night: men's lives were decided. Indeed, the whole Soviet Empire was ruled from these terrifying banquets, especially during the dictator's last years.

No one would dare refuse an invitation. But the boozing, vomiting, dancing, and practical jokes more resembled a rowdy stag night than a meeting of the rulers of the world's biggest empire.

Dinner *chez* Stalin always began after midnight, when the guests would arrive at his Kuntsevo mansion on the outskirts of Moscow. They entered a huge dining room with high windows covered by long drapes. The centrepiece was a long table with 14 chairs along each side.

Stalin always sat to the left of the head of the table with Lavrenti Beria, his terrifying chief of secret police, at its head, and the guest of honour on Stalin's left. Both Stalin and Beria came from the Georgian Caucasus region by the Black Sea, where traditions were very different to that of Russia. And so their meals were exotic, spicy Georgian feasts, during which Beria would act as *tamada* or toastmaster.

As soon as they sat down, the drinking started. At first it was civilised, with a few bottles of wine and Crimean champagne, which Stalin greatly enjoyed. The guests used to bring wine but Stalin was so suspicious that he always asked them to try it first, in case it was poisoned.

As the evening wore on, the toasts of vodka, pepper vodka and brandy became more insistent until even these iron-bellied drinkers, all members of the ruling Politburo, would be under the influence. "Let's get you drunk and see what kind of person you really are," Stalin would tell his guests.

"He forced us to drink to untie our tongues," wrote one of them, Mikoyan. The leader liked the drinking game of guessing the temperature: everyone had to make a guess and drink a bumper of vodka for every degree they were out.

Once, three of the guests were able to suborn a waitress into serving them brown-coloured water instead of brandy, but the ploy floundered when one of the trio betrayed his allies. Stalin was furious. "Want to be smarter than the rest?" he fumed. "See you don't regret it later!" Stalin sometimes got drunk himself but, more often, he would drink a weak mix of wine and water out of his own carafe.

During summer, the guests would stagger outside on to the verandahs. The standard of drunken horseplay was not much better than an American frathouse. So regularly were diners pushed into the pond that Stalin's guards, fearful that sooner or later a guest would end up drowned, discreetly drained the water.

Meanwhile, in the dining room, the maids would emerge with an array of Georgian dishes that they laid on the sideboard or on the other end of the long table, before disappearing. Among these Georgian favourites were usually *satsivi*, a spicy chicken dish, *khachapuri*, a pastry covered with melted cheese rather like a pizza, and *lobio*, hot red-and-green beans in a piquant sauce. Other Georgian delicacies were made of vegetables with herbs and crushed walnuts, while the main course was either fish or lamb kebabs. The guests served themselves, then joined Stalin at the other end of the table.

As he grew older, Stalin began to take a keen interest in food. The weary dictator fuelled his failing energy with, "quantities of food enormous for a much larger man… He ate at least twice as much as I did," wrote Mikoyan. "He took a deep plate, mixed two soups in it, then in a country custom that I knew from my own village, crumbled bread into the hot soup. Then there would be entrées, the main course and lots of meat."

He enjoyed ordering fish, particularly herring, but "he also liked game – guinea-fowl, ducks, chickens," and quails. Stalin also proudly invented a new dish that he called *aragvi*. This was made of aubergines, tomatoes, potatoes, black pepper and mutton, all in a spicy sauce. He would order *aragvi* frequently.

At about 4am, there would be a short rest for the guests to wash their hands, then it was back to the dinner, which now sank to even lower levels. Sometimes Stalin himself "got so drunk he took such liberties," said Khrushchev. "He would throw a tomato at you." Encouraged by Stalin, Beria would often slip old tomatoes into Mikoyan's suits and then press him against the wall so they burst. Mikoyan's response was to bring spare pairs of trousers to dinner.

As the night wore on, Stalin would stagger over to the gramophone and play his favourite records. He would then, an observer once noted, "shuffle around with his arms spread out" in true Georgian style, although he did have, apparently, "a sense of rhythm". But Stalin's greatest amusement was to make the men slow dance together while he watched, beaming roguishly.

STALIN'S GREATEST AMUSEMENT WAS TO MAKE THE MEN SLOW DANCE TOGETHER WHILE HE WATCHED, BEAMING ROGUISHLY

At about 5am, Stalin would finally dismiss his exhausted and inebriated comrades. Cars were summoned and chauffeurs dragged away their charges. The guests were relieved to be alive. "One never knows," whispered a survivor, "if one's going home or to prison." It was dawn. Dinner was over.

'Stalin: The Court of the Red Tsar' is published by Phoenix, priced £9.99. For details of how to order a copy at a specially discounted price, turn to page 102.

Andy Potts

My illustration style is an energetic fusion of traditional and new techniques, creating exciting and colourful visuals from a blend of hand crafted elements, digital collage, 3d and photography. I infuse the work with spontaneity, as though it were made without computer. Greeting happy accidents with open arms, I favour genuine textures over filters and like to roughen the edges a little. Controlled chaos if you like.

Mon style d'illustration est une fusion énergique de techniques traditionnelles et modernes, et consiste à créer des visuels attrayants et colorés à partir d'un mélange d'éléments faits à la main, de collages numériques, d'images en 3D et de photos. J'aime instiller une dose de spontanéité dans mon travail, comme si je ne me servais pas d'un ordinateur. Accueillant les accidents heureux à bras ouverts, je privilégie les textures authentiques par rapport aux filtres et aime donner un léger aspect rugueux aux contours. Un chaos contrôlé en un sens.

Meinen Illustrationsstil könnte man als eine energetische Fusion aus traditionellen sowie neuen Techniken beschreiben, eine Kreation von aufregenden und farbenfrohen Dingen, die eine Mischung aus selbstgemachten Elementen, digitalen Kollagen sowie 3D und Fotografie sind. Ich gebe meinen Arbeiten gerne den Anschein von Spontanität, gerade so, als seien sie ohne Computerbearbeitung erstellt. Kleine Unfälle sind mir immer willkommen, ich ziehe die natürliche Begebenheit einer Filtrierung vor und rauhe Kanten gefallen mir. Man könnte das Ganze auch ein kontrolliertes Chaos nennen.

www.andy-potts.com

NAME: Andy Potts **LOCATION:** London, UK **CONTACT:** info@andy-potts.com **TOOLS:** Pencil, Paintbrush, Biro, Scanner, Adobe Photoshop, Adobe Illustrator, Adobe AfterEffects. **AWARDS:** AOI Images (Gold). **AGENT:** Thorogood (UK) <draw@thorogood.net>; Anna Goodson Management (USA) <www.agoodson.com> **CLIENTS:** Random, TBWA/GGT, HSBC, BBC, Design Week, Time Out, The Guardian, The Independent, Dazed & Confused, Fast Company, Men's Health, Computer Arts.

Shonagh **Rae**

Ideas come first, but they are shaped by the way I produce the image, I use technology to combine the more traditional illustration media of drawing and photography. I find the possibilities of putting images through a process exciting, but ultimately my favourite gadget is still the pencil.

Les idées viennent en premier mais sont façonnées par la manière dont je produis l'image. J'utilise la technologie pour combiner le dessin, moyen d'illustration le plus traditionnel, avec la photographie. Je trouve que les possibilités d'insérer des images via un processus sont fascinantes mais en définitive, mon gadget préféré est le crayon.

Zuerst zählt die Idee, doch sie wird durch die Art und Weise geformt, wie ich ein Bild kreiere. Ich wende Techniken an, um das eher traditionelle Medium der Illustration mit Fotografie zu verbinden. Die Möglichkeit, Bilder durch einen Prozess laufen zu lassen, finde ich aufregend. Trotz allem ist mein Lieblingsspielzeug immer noch der Bleistift.

www.shonaghrae.com

NAME: Shonagh Rae **LOCATION:** London, UK **CONTACT:** shonagh@shonaghrae.com **TOOLS:** Pen, brush, print, collage, Adobe Photoshop. **AGENT:** Heart <www.heartagency.com>, Illustrissimo (Paris) <www.illustrissimo.com> **CLIENTS:** Levis, The Guardian, The Independent, Penguin Books, Simon and Schuster, Hodder and Stoughton, etc.

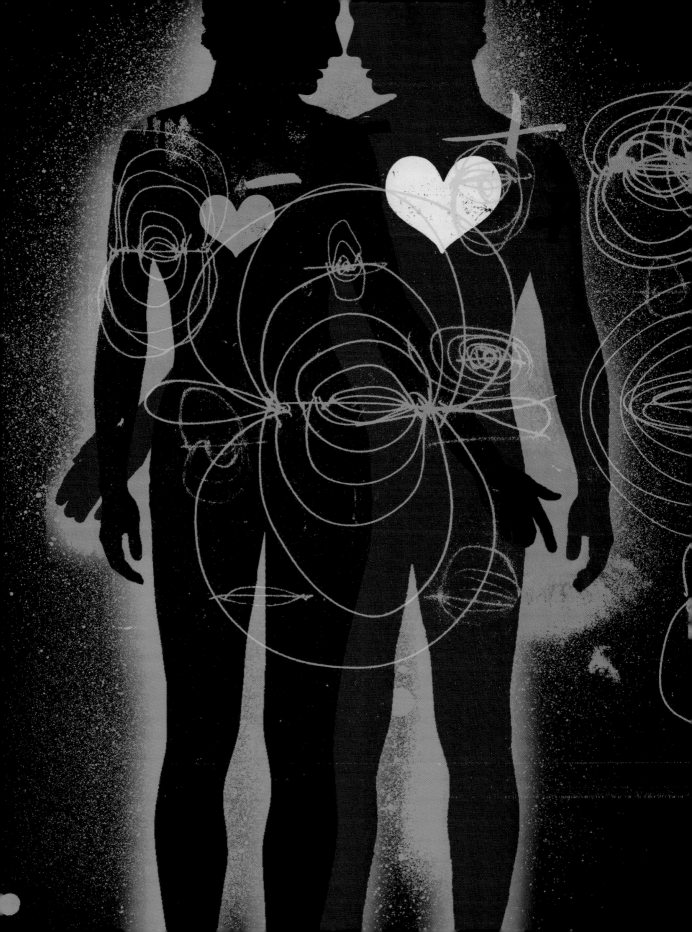

Calvin Rambler

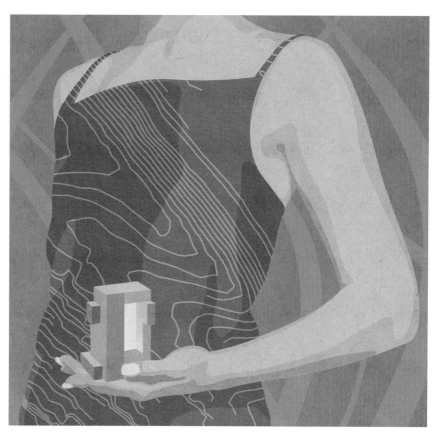

Illustration offers the reader a chance to make connections between what he/she is seeing and what they are reading -- the audience bridges the gap between the image shown and the body copy that accompanies it. I try not to illustrate what the title suggests in a literal way -- instead, the fun comes from offering visual clues as to the content of the piece without giving away the entire thought or idea contained in the text.

L'illustration donne au lecteur la possibilité de faire la relation entre ce qu'il voit et ce qu'il lit. Le public fait le lien entre l'image et le texte imprimé qui l'accompagne. J'essaie de ne pas illustrer de façon littérale ce que le titre suggère. En effet, ce qui est amusant, c'est de proposer des indices visuels quant au contenu sans révéler la pensée ou l'idée du texte dans son intégralité.

Das Medium der Illustration gibt dem Betrachter die Möglichkeit, Verbindungen zwischen dem, was er sieht, und dem, was er liest, herzustellen — so wird die Kluft zwischen dem gezeigten Image und der dazugehörigen Kopie ohne Schwierigkeiten überbrückt. Ich beabsichtige nicht, durch meine Illustration den Titel im Wortsinn wiederzugeben, sondern vielmehr durch visuelle Anhaltspunkte auf den Inhalt eines Werkes aufmerksam machen, ohne dabei die gesamte Textidee preiszugeben.

NAME: Calvin Rambler **LOCATION:** Vancouver, British Columbia, Canada **CONTACT:** crambler@telus.net **TOOLS:** Adobe Photoshop, pencil, Adobe Illustrator. **AGENT:** Magnet Reps <www.magnetreps.com> **CLIENTS:** AOL Time Warner, EMI Records, Sierra, Dwell, Continental Airlines, Smart Money, Bloomberg Wealth Manager, MBA Jungle, Harvard Business Review, American Way, Cougar Paper Company, Organic Style, The Wall Street Journal, Seventeen, Out Magazine, among others.

trains, planes, & pains

**WHAT'S THE BEST WAY TO GET FROM POINT A TO POINT B?
AMTRAK'S HIGH-SPEED RAIL TAKES ON THE AIRLINES.**

CONTRAILS SLASH DAWN'S ROSY LIGHT high above Manhattan. Headlights stream down the West Side Highway, and the morning's first ferry churns across the Hudson. I'm up early, rushing to a lunch meeting 215 miles away in Boston. I'll catch Amtrak's new high-speed train to Massachusetts, then fly home on the Delta shuttle. My schizophrenic itinerary has a purpose: I want to compare the two modes of travel head-to-head, assessing comfort, practicality, and cost—both to my bank account and to society, in environmental impacts.

Not many travelers—especially those on business trips—consider environmental effects when crafting their itineraries. Yet the societal benefits gained by putting green issues on the short list with legroom, arrival time, and quality of onboard peanuts could add up quickly: The kind of short hop I'm taking makes up 20 percent of all miles traveled.

In the 1970s, diesel trains sputtered between New York City and my North Carolina hometown. Leaning perilously on decaying tracks, they crept south past cotton fields and tobacco barns. Once, the engine hit a cow and later caught fire, extending an 8-hour trip to a 14-hour overnight. A few years later, a grueling 5-hour ride to Boston was ruining a budding long-distance romance. I gave up and hailed cabs to LaGuardia instead.

But recently I shot 345 miles overland from Osaka to central Tokyo in just 2.5 hours. Now it's time to give Amtrak's latest, fastest train a fair test. At 8:30, I leave Times Square. I could take a taxi, or one of seven subway lines to centrally located Penn Station. Instead, I hoof the eight blocks past shuttered theaters, claiming my $119 Internet-booked ticket from Amtrak's machine ten minutes later. Waiting to board the 9:03, I settle into a sleek Acela Express lounge. For the first time ever in Penn Station, I relax my grip on my purse; only ticketed Acela passengers are admitted to its Plexiglas-enclosed waiting area.

The room is crowded, a reflection of the fact that Amtrak's share of the Boston–New York market has jumped from 17 to 33 percent since 1997. I eavesdrop. Some riders are spooked by post–September 11 air travel. One man waves a *Wall Street Journal* article about how layoffs of mechanics may threaten aircraft maintenance. (Autos aren't so safe either—highway deaths accounted for 94 percent of transportation fatalities in 2001, according to the National Transportation Safety Board.) And how 'bout the weather? When blizzards lashed the Northeast last winter, Amtrak was the only thing moving. Between New York and Boston, 90 percent of scheduled trains soldiered on, carrying stranded motorists and fliers.

Passenger rail once thrived in America. The introduction of steam locomotives in the early 1800s inspired long-distance travel and settlement of the

BY BLAIR TINDALL ILLUSTRATIONS BY CALVIN RAMBLER

Red Nose Studio

For me, the camera is my eye, the sculpture is not the finished piece, how the piece is lit and composed can make or break a 3-D illustration. A beautiful sculpture can look like crap with poor photography. But a slapdash sculpture can look great if it is shot like a painting. The concept is the heart and soul of an illustration, if you don't have that as a foundation, the illustration will not hold up, no matter how it looks.

Mon appareil photo est mon œil. La sculpture n'est pas le produit fini. La façon dont le sujet est éclairé et composé peut faire une illustration 3D ou la détruire. Une belle sculpture peut ne ressembler à rien si elle est mal photographiée. A l'inverse, une sculpture bâclée peut être grandiose si elle est photographiée comme une peinture. Le concept est le cœur et l'âme d'une illustration. Si votre illustration en est dépourvue, elle ne tiendra pas la route peu importe à quoi elle ressemble.

Die Kamera ist mein Auge. Eine Skulptur ist kein Endresultat, sondern so wie sie komponiert und beleuchtet ist, kann sie zu einer 3D-Illustration werden oder nicht. Eine wunderschöne Skulptur kann durch schlechte Fotografie hässlich erscheinen. Eine weniger überzeugende Skulptur hingegen - wird sie als Gemälde betrachtet und fotografiert -kann an Schönheit gewinnen. Das Geheimnis liegt beim Illustratoren, hat er dieses Konzept nicht als Basis, so kann keine Illustration überzeugen, ganz gleich, wie sie aussieht.

www.rednosestudio.com

NAME: Red Nose Studio (Chris Sickels) **LOCATION:** Indiana, USA **CONTACT:** chris@rednosestudio.com **TOOLS:** Clay, X-acto knife and other tools, paper, cardboard, china markers, acrylics, 4x5 camera, lights, needle and thread, wire, found objects, water, chocolate covered expresso beans and a hairdryer **AWARDS:** Society of Illustrators, Best of Show How Magazines, American Illustration, and more. **AGENT:** Magnet Reps <www.magnetreps.com> **CLIENTS:** The New York Times, MTV, etc.

red mose
studio

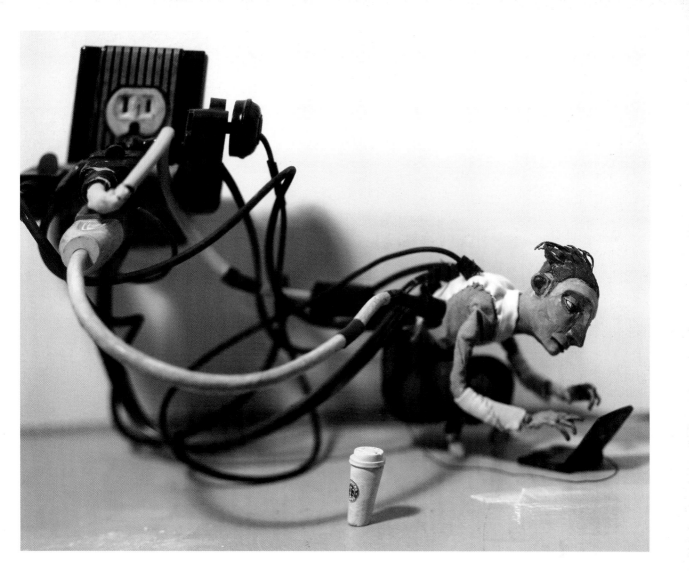

Maria Rendón

I see both illustration and personal work as an opportunity to explore new ways of communicating visually. I put together all kinds of materials (wood, metals, glass, paint, found objects, crafted objects) to convey the meaning in the work. In addition, I find myself using openings or 'windows' to contain, shelter and give importance to ideas. I steal from both personal work and illustration to feed the other.

Pour moi, les illustrations de commande et le travail personnel sont une opportunité d'explorer de nouveaux moyens de communiquer visuellement. Je rassemble des matériaux très variés (bois, métal, verre, peinture, objets trouvés, objets d'artisanat) pour véhiculer la signification dans mon travail. J'utilise de plus des ouvertures ou « fenêtres » pour contenir, abriter et donner de l'importance à des idées. Mon travail personnel et mon travail d'illustrateur s'alimentent l'un l'autre.

Ich betrachte sowohl Illustration als auch persönliche Arbeiten als Möglichkeit, neue Wege visueller Kommunikation ausfindig zu machen. Ich verwende ganz unterschiedliche Materialien (Holz, Metall, Glas, Farbe, gefundene Objekte, Kunstgegenstände), um die Bedeutung einer Arbeit vermitteln zu können. Darüber hinaus nutze ich Öffnungen oder 'Fenster', um Ideen ihre Wichtigkeit zukommen zu lassen und diese zu sammeln und zu schützen. Ich bediene mich sowohl persönlicher Arbeiten, um Illustration zu bereichern als auch umgekehrt.

www.mariarendon.com

NAME: Maria Rendón **LOCATION:** Santa Barbara, California, USA **CONTACT:** maria@mariarendon.com **TOOLS:** Power Tools (scroll saw, sander, drill press, table saw); Materials (wood, wire, foam, metals, glass, clay); Found Objects (old and new); Acrylic and Oil Paint. **AWARDS:** Communication Arts, 3Dimensional Illustration Awards Show, Society of Illustrators, American Illustration Website. **CLIENTS:** Bloomberg, Business Week, Computerworld, Discover Magazine, Harper's, etc.

Hands-on Approach

Mutual funds make investing so simple that one might get lulled into complacency. When is the last time you looked—really looked— at your portfolio? Sometimes a little reallocation can have a big payoff.

BY NILES HOWARD

FOR BLOOMBERG

One of the great appeals of mutual funds is that they're the closest thing you can get to one-stop investing. All you have to do is write a check. The fund manager takes care of the rest—research, diversification, trade execution, and recordkeeping. What's not to like? * Unfortunately, too many investors take this hands-off approach to the extreme. They settle on a handful of funds and rarely look back, other than to complain when a fund doesn't live up to expectations. By confusing buy-and-hold with

ILLUSTRATION BY MARIA RENDON

ILLUSTRATION BY MARIA RENDON

They rode **round and round** the Dynegy gas-swap fraud. They say they never saw **what was coming.** All the lawyers did was help make it possible. Does running structured **finance deals** mean never having to say **you're sorry?**

WEARING BLINDERS

IN MARCH, BEFORE HE SUFFERED THE criminal sentence that rocked corporate America, Jamie Olis made a last-ditch plea for leniency. The former midlevel tax planner at Houston's Dynegy Inc. had been convicted of conspiracy and fraud in late 2003 for helping disguise a $300 million loan to Dynegy as cash flow from a gas trade. The crime had allowed the company to puff up its balance sheet. But once it was discovered, Dynegy's stock price dropped, and investors lost millions.

Olis faced more than 24 years in prison. But in a motion filed with U.S. district court judge Sim Lake of Houston, Olis offered a just-following-orders defense. Olis claimed that Dynegy's bankers (Citigroup Inc. was the lead bank) and lawyers (Houston's Vinson & Elkins) had understood that the purported gas trade, called Project Alpha, was in substance a loan. Olis's crime included conspiring to hide information from Arthur Andersen LLP so that the now defunct accounting firm would not characterize the deal as debt. But Olis noted that he had never been accused of hiding information from Dynegy's bankers and lawyers.

"Some of the most brilliant lawyers in this coun-

try took part in the ultimate resolution of [Alpha]," said Olis's criminal lawyer, Terry Yates of Houston, during an April interview. "They approved of this transaction." Yates points the finger not only at V&E but also Bracewell & Patterson and Milbank, Tweed, Hadley & McCloy, both of which represented Citigroup. At least one other firm, Houston's Andrews Kurth, was heavily involved in Alpha, as counsel to other banks that helped finance the project. "[Olis] is just a lowly accountant," said Yates. "So, he is stuck holding the bucket?"

So far, yes. In March, Lake handed him the maximum sentence: 24 years, four months, with no chance of parole. Olis, 38, headed to federal prison in May, leaving behind his wife and infant daughter. But the question remains: What about the professionals who helped bring Alpha to life? The bankers have gotten their due, at least financially. In July 2003 the Securities and Exchange Commission fined Citigroup $18.75 million, twice its fee, for its role in Alpha. The SEC concluded that the bank knew that Alpha was essentially a loan and was further aware that Dynegy would use the deal to falsely pump up its financial statements. Citi-

By Nathan Koppel

Paul Rogers

Rather than rely on one style or technique in my work, I choose to draw from a variety of references and influences from throughout the 20th Century. Style becomes an important part of the communication.

Plutôt que d'être fidèle à un seul style ou à une seule technique, je préfère puiser dans toute une variété de références et d'influences de l'ensemble du 20e siècle. Le style devient une part importante de la communication.

Anstatt mich von einem Stil oder einer Technik abhängig zu machen, bediene ich mich viel eher unterschiedlicher Referenzen und Einflüsse aus dem gesamten 20. Jahrhundert. Stil ist ein wichtiger Teil der Kommunikation.

www.paulrogersstudio.com

NAME: Paul Rogers **LOCATION:** Pasadena, CA, USA **CONTACT:** paulrogers@attglobal.net **TOOLS:** Adobe Illustrator, airbrush, rapidograph. **AWARDS:** American Illustration, Association of Illustrators, Communication Arts, Graphis Poster, Print Magazine, Society of Illustrators NY. **AGENT:** Heflinreps <www.heflinreps.com>
CLIENTS: Amtrak, HBO, Arts & Sciences, Pixar Pictures, Playboy Jazz Festival, The Wall Street Journal, Warner Bros. Studio, and The Washington Post.

Kerry Roper

My work is an amalgamation of photography, typography and traditional illustration. Although it's all created on the computer I am a firm believer that it remains spontaneous and organic.

Mon travail est un amalgame de photographie, de typographie et d'illustration traditionnelle. Bien que je travaille uniquement sur ordinateur, je crois véritablement que le résultat reste spontané et authentique.

Meine Arbeit ist eine Mischung aus Fotografie, Typografie und traditioneller Illustration. Ausserdem kreiere ich alles am Computer und bin fest davon überzeugt, dass ich sowohl Spontanität als auch Organik herrüberbringe.

NAME: Kerry Roper **LOCATION:** London, UK **CONTACT:** all@folioart.co.uk **TOOLS:** Adobe Photoshop, Adobe Illustrator. **AGENT:** Folio <www.folioart.co.uk> **CLIENTS:** Adidas, Snickers, Future Publishing, Paragon Publishing, Dennis Publishing, Time Out, and The Big Issue.

Graham Roumieu

I'm not a particularly religious person but sometimes I wonder if what I am doing with every little absurd scenario I draw is really laying down the blue print for my afterlife. I also wonder if I should work in a better-ventilated space. Either way I am quite scared. I use that in my work too.

Je ne suis pas particulièrement croyant mais parfois je me demande si ce que je fais avec le moindre petit scénario absurde que j'illustre m'ouvrira véritablement les portes de l'au-delà. Je me demande également si je ne devrais pas travailler dans un espace mieux ventilé. Ces deux interrogations ne me rassurent pas. Je me sers de cela aussi dans mon travail.

Ich würde mich nicht unbedingt als religiös bezeichnen, aber manchmal frage ich mich, ob ich vielleicht mit jeder absurden Szene, die ich zeichne, einen Plan für mein Leben nach dem Tod entwerfe. Auch frage ich mich manchmal, ob ich vielleicht in einem besser durchlüfteten Raum arbeiten sollte. Wie dem auch sei, ich habe einfach Angst. Auch das verarbeite ich in meinen Arbeiten.

www.roumieu.com

NAME: Graham Roumieu **LOCATION:** Toronto, Ontario, Canada **CONTACT:** g@roumieu.com **TOOLS:** Watercolor, ink, some mixed media and digital. **AWARDS:** American Illustration, Applied Arts Magazine, Canadian National Magazine Awards, Coupe Magazine, Advertising, Design Club of Canada. **AGENT:** Magnet Reps <www.magnetreps.com> **CLIENTS:** New York Times, Wall Street Journal, Harper's, Penguin USA, The Walrus Magazine, The Washington Post, The Globe and Mail.

SUPER FUN ROCKET

Jim Salvati

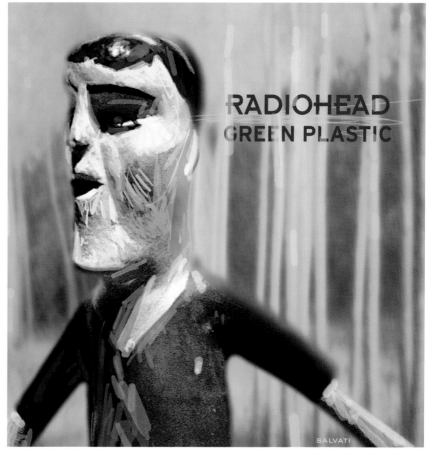

RADIOHEAD
GREEN PLASTIC

25 years as an artist I have lived by the simple work ethic of "work hard and play hard". Growing up a surfer has influenced every aspect of my life as an artist, working hard to travel and surf with my family. Art now influences me in every aspect of my life. As an artist and art collector I have been fortunate enough to collect and to continue my life as a surfer and artist.

Depuis 25 ans que je suis artiste, je suis fidèle à cette simple éthique de travail : « work hard and play hard ». J'ai grandi avec le surf et il influence entièrement ma vie d'artiste puisque je dois travailler dur pour pouvoir voyager et surfer avec ma famille. Aujourd'hui, l'art influence également ma vie dans ses moindres détails. Étant aussi collectionneur d'art, j'ai eu beaucoup de chance de pouvoir me consacrer à cette passion tout en poursuivant mes activités de surfeur et d'artiste.

25 Jahre lang habe ich als Künstler nach dem Motto "hart arbeiten und aufs Ganze gehen" gelebt. Die Tatsache, dass ich als Surfer aufgewachsen bin, und hart arbeiten musste, um mit meiner Familie gemeinsam reisen und surfen zu können, hat mein Leben als Künstler in jeder Hinsicht stark beeinflusst. Heute dreht sich bei mir alles um Kunst und ich kann mich glücklich schätzen, stets die Möglichkeit zu haben, als Kunstsammler, Surfer und Künstler tätig zu sein.

www.salvatidesign.com

NAME: Jim Salvati **LOCATION:** West Hills, California, USA **CONTACT:** salvatidesign@earthlink.net **TOOLS:** Oil, Goauche, Adobe Photoshop, Painter. **AWARDS:** selected published 200 Best Illustrators Worldwide, Commuication Arts, American Illustration, 50 Top Illustrators working Today Book. **AGENT:** Hedge Graphics and Motion Artists **CLIENTS:** Warner Bros. Pictures , Disney Fine Arts , Collectors Editions, Sony Pictures, Dalmatian Press, Bostonia.

Allan **Sanders**

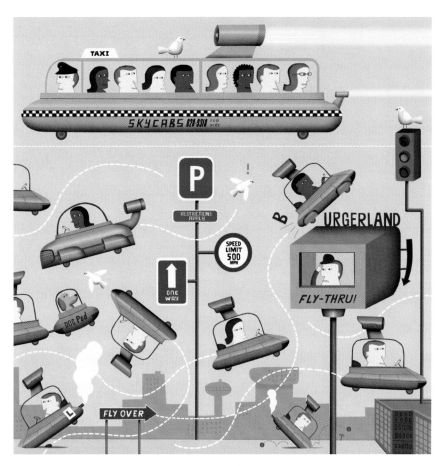

I like to communicate through ideas that avoid cliché but have a sense of individuality. Characters are central to my work. Their relationship with technology, their environment and other characters are often situations that I find I can exploit to produce humour and a sense of quirkiness. Visually I employ a graphic approach, which is simple but very precise; simplicity with sophistication is something I strive toward.

J'aime communiquer avec des idées qui évitent le cliché mais ont un côté individuel. Les personnages sont au centre de mon travail. Leur relation avec la technologie, avec leur environnement et avec les autres personnages créent souvent des situations que je pense pouvoir exploiter pour susciter un effet comique et un côté excentrique. Visuellement, j'emploie une approche graphique simple mais très précise. Mêler simplicité et sophistication est l'un des buts que je recherche.

Ich kommuniziere gerne mittels Ideen, die Klischees vermeiden und einen Sinn für Individualität haben. Charaktere bilden den Schwerpunkt meiner Arbeiten. Ihre Beziehung zu Technologie, zu ihrer Umgebung und zu anderen Charakteren führen oft zu Situationen, die mir die Möglichkeit geben, daraus etwas Humorvolles, aber auch Verschrobenes zu produzieren. Meine Grafik ist einfach, doch sehr genau. Ein klares Design, intelligent angewandt, das ist das, was mich vorantreibt.

NAME: Allan Sanders **LOCATION:** England **CONTACT:** info@heartagency.com **TOOLS:** Adobe Photoshop, Pilot supergrip 0.5mm Pencil, Canon Scanner. **AGENT:** Heart <www.heartagency.com> **CLIENTS:** New Scientist, The Guardian, New York Times, The Independent, The Science Museum, The Economist, Time Out, Smart Money, FIFA, The Sunday Times, The Builder Group, Spiral Productions, Studio AKA.

Béatrice Sautereau

To me illustration confers a tone and an atmosphere to a picture. Each artist develops his/her personality in a drawing. Mine is to mix humour and fashion, smart and genuine characters. My characters are often inspired by people seen in the streets or in magazines. And so when I draw a character, an object or a place I try to find out the most distinctive features. My objective is to be simple with a few sticking details.

Pour moi l'illustration confère un ton et une atmosphère à une image. Chaque artiste développe sa personnalité dans ses dessins. La mienne est de mêler l'humour, la mode et des personnages élégants et authentiques. Mes personnages sont souvent inspirés de gens rencontrés dans la rue ou vus dans des magazines. Lorsque je dessine un personnage, un objet ou un endroit, j'essaie d'en refléter les traits les plus distinctifs. Mon objectif est de faire simple tout en apportant quelques détails marquants.

Meiner Meinung nach gibt die Illustration dem Bild einen bestimmten Ton und eine Atmosphäre. Jeder Künstler entwickelt seine/ihre Persönlichkeit beim Zeichnen. Ich vermische Humor und Mode, intelligente und reelle Charaktere. Ich hole mir die Inspiration für meine Charaktere oft bei Leuten, die ich auf der Strasse oder in Zeitschriften sehe. Wenn ich dann eine Figur, ein Objekt oder einen Ort zeichne, versuche ich, die ganz besonderen Eigenheiten widerzuspiegeln. Unkompliziert und doch einen bleibenden Eindruck hinterlasssend, das ist mein Ziel.

NAME: Béatrice Sautereau **LOCATION:** Paris, France **CONTACT:** bsautereau@ free.fr **TOOLS:** Adobe Photoshop. **AGENT:** Agent 002 <agent002.com>
CLIENTS: CosmoGirl NY, Marie Claire, Heart Magazine, TGV Magazine, Challenge.

TRIBU(t) savignac

Marguerite Sauvage

I just love image. That is stronger than everything. Child I did comics all nights long and published in fanzines. I didn't study art, but when I finished my University diploma, it was necessary for me to become an illustrator. Inspiration is everywhere. I just want people to be happy to see my illustrations, to create joyful and light images pleasant to be seen, to bring a little of freshness.

J'aime tout simplement les images. C'est plus fort que tout. Petite, je passais des nuits à dessiner des BD que je publiais dans des fanzines. Je n'ai pas étudié l'art mais après avoir obtenu mon diplôme universitaire, il était nécessaire pour moi que je devienne illustratrice. Je puise mon inspiration partout. Je veux juste que mes illustrations rendent les gens heureux, je veux créer des images légères et joyeuses plaisantes à regarder, pour apporter un peu de fraîcheur.

Ich liebe Bilder über alles. Visuelle Kunst steht für mich über allem. Als Kind habe ich nächtelang Comics gezeichnet und sie dann veröffentlicht. Ich habe nie Kunst studiert, aber als ich die Universität abgeschlossen hatte, wollte ich Illustratorin werden. Inspiration gibt es überall. Ich möchte Menschen durch meine Illustrationen glücklich machen, fröhliche Bilder entwerfen, schön anzusehen und mit einem Hauch von Leichtigkeit und Frische.

www.margueritesauvage.com

NAME: Marguerite Sauvage **LOCATION:** Paris, France **CONTACT:** contact@margueritesauvage.com **TOOLS:** pencil, Adobe Photoshop. **AGENT:** Magnet Reps (USA) <www.magnetreps.com>; Virgine (France) <www.virginie.fr>; Taiko & Associates (Japan) <www.ua-net.com> **CLIENTS:** Paul and Joe, Galeries Lafayette, Apple, Citröen, St Dupont, Flaunt, Elle, Cosmopolitan, CosmoGirl, Non No, Continental Airlines.

marguerite sauvage

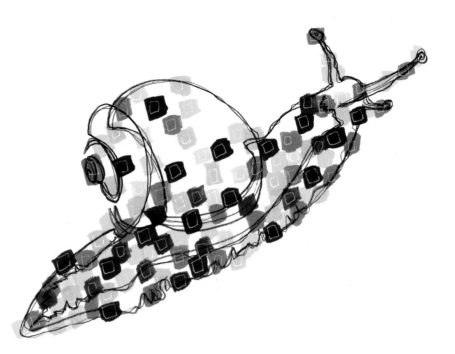

Illustration (lat. illustrare) means to 'enlighten' and to 'focus light' on something, literally as well in the figurative sense. It brings up things, which were not noticed yet; it discovers and makes recognition stronger. My wish is to find a clear, expressive and powerful solution with simple tools and techniques.

Illustrer (illustrare en latin) signifie « mettre en lumière » quelque chose, aussi bien au sens littéral qu'au sens figuré. C'est mettre au jour l'invisible, c'est découvrir et rendre l'identification plus forte. Mon souhait est de trouver une solution claire, expressive et efficace à l'aide d'outils et de techniques simples.

Illustrieren (lat. Illustrare) bedeutet so viel wie 'beleuchten' und 'erhellen'; im wörtlichen, wie im übertragenen Sinne. Es bringt nicht Gesehenes zum Vorschein, macht schon Erkanntes noch deutlicher. Mein Anliegen ist es, mit möglichst einfachen Mitteln ein klares Ergebnis mit viel Ausdruck aufs Papier zu bringen.

www.helenschiffer.de

NAME: Helen Schiffer **LOCATION:** Frankfurt, Germany **CONTACT:** info@helenschiffer.de **TOOLS:** Ink, Felt pen on paper, Acrylic, Adobe Photoshop, QuarkXpress, Macromedia Freehand. **CLIENTS:** F.A.Z., Süddeutsche Zeitung, Für Sie, Hörzu, Journal Frankfurt, Deutscher Taschenbuchverlag, Langenscheidt-Longmann, Jill Sander, Lufthansa, DaimlerChrysler, Walt Disney, Ogilvy & Mather, Scholz & Friends, JW Thompson.

441

Dan Seagrave

One way I develop ideas for commissioned works is to approach a subject from a slightly theatrical viewpoint, and to visualise the art as a potentially 3D production. With a commission there is the opportunity to explore an idea that you might otherwise not in a personal painting, or a subject that provokes a different way of thinking or rendering. I believe that as an artist naturally evolves, so too must the illustration.

J'ai une manière de développer des idées pour des travaux de commande qui consiste à approcher un sujet d'un point de vue légèrement théâtral et à visualiser l'art en tant que production potentiellement en 3D. Une commande est une opportunité d'explorer une idée que l'on ne creuserait pas dans une peinture personnelle, ou d'explorer un sujet qui provoque une manière différente de penser ou d'interpréter. Je crois qu'un artiste évolue de façon naturelle, comme ce doit être le cas de l'illustration.

Eine mögliche Form von Ideenfindung bei einer in Auftrag gegebenen Illustration ist ein eher theatralischer Gesichtspunkt, das heisst, sich die Kunst als eine potentielle 3D-Produktion vorzustellen. Durch einen Auftrag hat man die Möglichkeit, neue Ideen auszuprobieren, auf die man bei einer persönlichen Arbeit gar nicht käme, Themen, die zu neuen Denkanstössen und Anwendungsmöglichkeiten verleiten. Genauso wie ein Künstler sich ständig weiterentwickelt, muss dies auch bei einer Illustration der Fall sein.

www.danseagrave.com

NAME: Dan Seagrave **LOCATION:** UK and Toronto, Canada **CONTACT:** dan@danseagrave.com **TOOLS:** Acrylic, Adobe Photoshop, pencil. **CLIENTS:** Wizards of the Coast, Hasbro, Scandecor Marketing, Wizard & Genius, Unique Leader Records, Karmageddon Media, Relapse Records, RoadRunner Records, Solid State Records, Earache Records, Buck Productions, Fuse Gallery. Ferral House Books, Titan Books, Nuclear Blast Records.

Shibuya

Tadaomi

Hand painted illustration is for me softer and warmer than computer created graphics, I believe this way helps create a warmer bond between the creator and the audience.

Les illustrations peintes à la main sont pour moi plus douces et plus chaleureuses que les graphismes créés par ordinateur. Je crois que cette technique contribue à créer un lien plus fort entre le créateur et le public.

Handgemalte Illustration ist für mich weicher und wärmer als per Computer erstellte Grafiken. Sie verhelfen dazu, eine wärmere Verbindung zwischen Künstler und Publikum herzustellen.

NAME: Tadaomi Shibuya **LOCATION:** Yokohama, Japan **CONTACT:** love-is-not-a-game@docomo.ne.jp **TOOLS:** Watercolour Paint. **AWARDS:** The Choice. **AGENT:** Dutch Uncle (UK) <www.dutchuncle.co.uk> **CLIENTS:** Mizuno, Is-ness, Bbs (Fashion), Music Conception.

Yuko **Shimizu**

Some people say, "Illustration is dead". Is that true? I believe it is illustrators' job now to show how exciting and powerful illustration can be, to show the possibilities outside of the regular boundaries of what people would think it can do.

Certains disent que l'illustration est morte. Est-ce vrai ? Je crois que c'est aux illustrateurs de montrer combien l'illustration peut être excitante et forte, de montrer ses possibilités en dehors des limites que les gens veulent lui prêter.

Manche sagen, "Die Illustration ist tot". Stimmt das? Ich denke, es ist heute die Aufgabe der Illustratoren, zu zeigen, wie aufregend und stark das Medium der Illustration sein kann, und die Möglichkeiten, die es gibt, sich über bereits geglaubte Grenzen hinwegzusetzen.

www.yukoart.com

NAME: Yuko Shimizu **LOCATION:** New York, USA **CONTACT:** yuko@yukoart.com **TOOLS:** Japanese calligraphy brushes to draw, Adobe Photoshop to color. **AWARDS:** American Illustration, Society of Illustrators, Society of Publication Designers SPOTS, SPD Awards, New American Paintings. **CLIENTS:** Rolling Stone, Interview, Entertainment Weekly, The New Yorker, The New York Times, M.A.C. Cosmetics, Esquire, Financial Times Magazine, etc.

Skwak

My illustrations are colourful, exaggerated and a bit crazy. They are composed of elements which have no connections and which bang together in the page. It's up to the spectator to build the story told by the illustration.

Mes illustrations sont colorées, exagérées et un peu folles. Elles sont composées d'éléments entre lesquels n'existe aucun lien et qui s'entrechoquent dans la page. C'est à l'observateur de construire l'histoire racontée par l'illustration.

Meine Illustrationen sind farbenfroh, übertrieben und ein bisschen verrückt. Sie sind aus Elementen zusammengestellt, die keinerlei Verbindung aufweisen und auf der Seite zusammenprallen. Es ist die Aufgabe des Zuschauers, eine Geschichte aus der Illustration zusammenzustellen.

www.skwak.com

NAME: SKWAK **LOCATION:** Lille, France **CONTACT:** contact@skwak.com **TOOLS:** macromedia flash, Adobe Illustrator, Adobe Photoshop, and a pen.
CLIENTS: BeautifulDecay magazine, papaetmaman.com, yakuta, wedodatdesign, uailab...

Laura **Smith**

My graphic approach to illustration has been inspired by some of the great poster artists of the first half of the 20th century. Those who have influenced my the most have done so because of their simplicity and directness in terms of graphic elements, and their ability to communicate an idea quickly and efficiently. Economy in imagery and design have always been the motivating forces behind my art.

Mon approche graphique de l'illustration est inspirée de certains des plus grands auteurs d'affiches de la première moitié du 20ème siècle. Certains m'ont influencée plus que d'autres du fait de leur simplicité et de leur authenticité en termes d'éléments graphiques, ainsi que de part leur aptitude à communiquer une idée rapidement et efficacement. En imagerie et en graphisme, l'économie a toujours été la force motrice de mon art.

Meine grafische Annäherung an Illustration wurde durch einige grossartige Posterkünstler aus der ersten Hälfte des 20. Jahrhunderts beeinflusst. Dabei hat mich besonders ihre Einfachheit und Direktheit bezüglich der grafischen Elemente, sowie ihre Fähigkeit, Ideen schnell und effizient zu kommunizieren, beeindruckt. Der Aspekt Wirtschaft war stets eine Motivationskraft bei meinen Bildern und Designarbeiten.

www.laurasmithart.com

NAME: Laura Smith **LOCATION:** Hollywood, CA, USA **CONTACT:** Laura@laurasmithart.com **TOOLS:** Acrylic Paint. **CLIENTS:** HBO, Microsoft, Capitol Records, Japan Airlines, Bols (Liqueur), Heineken, Time, Newsweek, Mercedes-Benz, Budweiser, Levi's, The Walt Disney Company, etc.

SEABISCUIT

the BEVERLY HILLS POLO LOUNGE

DEC. 15, 2003

LAURA SMITH

Owen Smith

My paintings reflect my interest in figure painting from 1900 to 1950. I tend to exaggerate proportions and emphasize volume and movement. The figures crowd the frame and overlap each other in angular or swirling compositions. I'm often called to depict scenes of sexual tension or implied violence. Whether the subject is serious or pure kitsch, my work is always about human interaction or isolation.

Mes peintures reflètent mon intérêt pour les peintures figuratives de la première moitié du 20ème siècle. J'ai tendance à exagérer les proportions et à accentuer les volumes et les mouvements. Le cadre est bourré de personnages qui se chevauchent en des compositions angulaires ou ondoyantes. On me demande souvent de représenter des scènes de tension sexuelle ou de violence implicite. Que le sujet soit sérieux ou relève du kitsch pur, mon travail reflète toujours les relations humaines ou l'isolement.

Meine Gemälde reflektieren mein Interesse an bildhafter Malerei von 1900 bis 1950. Ich tendiere dazu, Proportionen übertrieben darzustellen, sowie Grösse und Bewegung besonders hervorzuheben. Die Figuren füllen den Rahmen und überschneiden sich gegenseitig in angularen sowie verdrehten Kompositionen. Man sagt mir oft die bildliche Darstellung von sexueller Spannung oder angewandter Gewalt nach. Ob es sich nun um einen ernsten oder total kitschigen Inhalt handelt, befassen sich meine Arbeiten stets mit zwischenmenschlichen Beziehungen oder Isolation.

NAME: Owen Smith **LOCATION:** Alameda, California, USA **CONTACT:** owensmith@alamedanet.net **TOOLS:** Oil Paint, Charcoal. **AWARDS:** American Illustration, Society of Illustrators, CA, SPD Spots, SPD Annual, Print Magazine, Society of Illustrators NY. **CLIENTS:** The New Yorker, Rolling Stone, Sports Illustrated, GQ, Esquire, Time, Random House, Simon and Schuster, St. Martin's Press, Viking Penguin, Sony Music, San Francisco Opera, United Nations, etc.

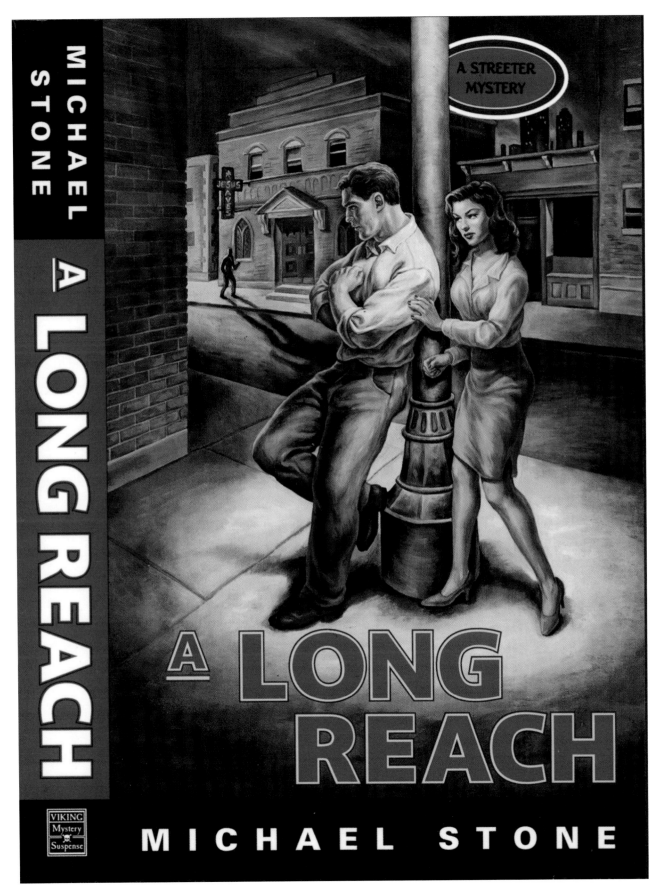

A STREETER MYSTERY

JESUS SAVES

A LONG REACH

A LONG REACH

MICHAEL STONE

MICHAEL STONE

VIKING
Mystery
Suspense

Michael **Sowa**

For commercial work the pattern is: A quick idea, a quick and usable realisation, good pay. Then there is more time for everything else: book illustrations, my own pictures, gardening, reading the newspapers and also playing with the kids or talking to the wife.

Pour les travaux commerciaux, ce qui compte c'est une idée rapide, une mise en pratique rapide et valable, et une bonne rémunération. Il reste: illustrer des livres, se consacrer à ses propres tableaux, s'occuper du jardin, lire le journal, jouer avec ses enfants ou parler avec sa femme.

Für kommerzielle Arbeiten gilt: Schnelle Idee, schnelle und brauchbare Umsetzung, gutes Honorar. Dann bleibt mehr Zeit für alles andere: Buchillustrationen, eigene Bilder, um den Garten kümmern, Zeitung lesen und auch mal mit den Kindern spielen oder mit meiner Frau sprechen.

NAME: Michael Sowa **LOCATION:** Berlin, Germany **CONTACT:** info@hubauer.com **TOOLS:** pencil and ink **AWARDS:** a lot of them **AGENT:** Margareth Hubauer <www.hubauer.com> **CLIENTS:** New Yorker, The New York Times, Der Spiegel, etc.

Deanna **Staffo**

Keep it simple and remember that each drawing will have my name on it.

Mon credo est de rester simple et de me rappeler que chacun de mes dessins sera signé de mon nom.

In der Einfachheit liegt das Geheimnis und vergiss nicht, dass alle Zeichnungen meinen Namen tragen.

www.deannastaffo.com

NAME: Deanna Staffo **LOCATION:** Philadelphia, Pennsylvania, USA **CONTACT:** d@deannastaffo.com **TOOLS:** charcoal pencils, watercolors, acrylic, gouache. **CLIENTS:** BlackBook Magazine, The Baltimore Citypaper, Bust, Centre Stage, MovieMaker, Orlando Weekly, Paper, The Progressive, UTNE, The Washington DC Citypaper.

François Supiot

I try to look at the text I am about to illustrate in my own way, in order to find personal things I see in it. The images point to the subject while expressing my own obsessions. I find myself working with a symbolic system that draws on recurring figures from my own universe: parts of the body, a mixture of human and mechanical forms, pipes, etc..."

J'essaie de considérer le texte que je vais illustrer à ma façon afin d'y trouver des choses personnelles. Les images renvoient au sujet tout en exprimant les obsessions qui sont les miennes. Je travaille avec un système symbolique qui puise dans les figures récurrentes de mon propre univers : parties du corps, un mélange de formes humaines et mécaniques, des tuyaux, etc.

Ich versuche stets den Text, den ich in eine Illustration verwandle, auf meine Art und Weise zu betrachten, um darin persönliche Dinge zu finden. Die Bilder weisen auf den Inhalt hin, während ich meine eigenen Verrücktheiten dabei ausdrücke. Ich arbeite nach einem symbolischen System, bei dem ich Figuren und Charaktere meines eigenen Universums wieder auftauchen lasse: Körperteile, eine Mischung aus menschlichen und mechanischen Formen, Rohre, etc....

www.supiot.com

NAME: François Supiot **LOCATION:** Paris, France **CONTACT:** supiot@wanadoo.fr **TOOLS:** Adobe Photoshop. **AGENT:** Illustrissimo <www.illustrissimo.com>
CLIENTS: Strategies, Le Monde, Libération, Le Monde Diplomatique, Psychologies Magazine, Le point, Éditions du Seuil, Le Nouvel Observateur, Autrement Éditions.

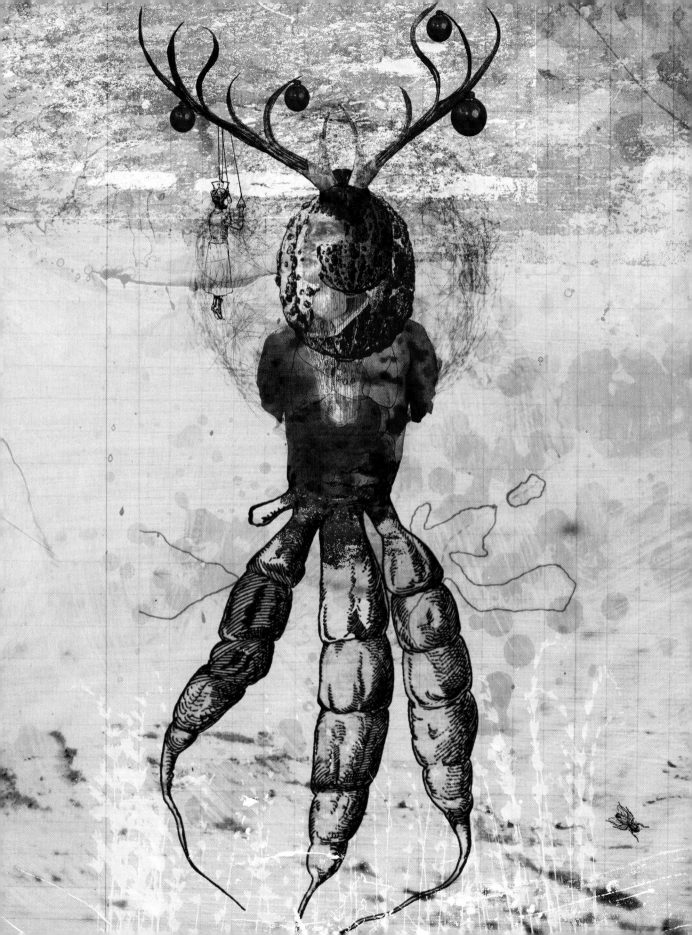

Tanja Székessy

DAS MAGAZIN

GEGRÜNDET 1924 IN BERLIN — JULI 2004 / EURO 2,50

DUSTIN HOFFMAN
EIN EWIGER CLOWN?
INTERVIEW

NACHTS
IN DEUTSCHEN
SCHLAFZIMMERN

MENSCHING
RETTET OMA

BUCHMESSE:
WAS WURDE
AUS DEN
FRÄULEIN-
WUNDERN?

Große
Liebe
ZUFALL ODER PLAN: REZEPTLISTE
VOM ZENTRALKOMITEE FÜR GEFÜHLE

Illustrators have: 1.the possibility of using ancient manual as well as brand new technical means and everything in between (which brings some variety into it), they are. 2. not restricted to a particular place and can. 3. diffuse in the public perception their way of looking at things, as regards figurativeness and content, more or less modestly.

Les illustrateurs ont: 1. la possibilité d'utiliser les moyens techniques manuels anciens aussi bien que les plus récents et les moins récents (pour garantir une certaine variété), ils ne sont pas. 2. limités à un lieu particulier et peuvent. 3. diffuser auprès du public leur manière de voir les choses, concernant la figuration et le contenu, de façon plus ou moins modeste.

Illustratoren haben: 1. Die möglichkeit, uralte manuelle, brandneue technische Mittel und alles, was dazwischen liegt, zum Einsatz zu bringen (was die Sache abwechslungsreich macht) sie sind. 2. An keinen bestimmten Ort gebunden und können. 3. In mehr oder weniger bescheidenem Umfang ihre bildliche und inhaltliche Sichtweise in die öffentliche wahrnehmung diffundieren lassen.

www.szekessy.net

NAME: Tanja Székessy **LOCATION:** Berlin, Germany **CONTACT:** tanja@szekessy.net **TOOLS:** pencil, gouache, Adobe Photoshop. **CLIENTS:** Bacardi Rigo, Benteli, Coca-Cola, Cornelsen, Granini Cuaro, Das Magazin, Die Zeit, Mare, NordSüd Verlag, Duden Paetec, Volk&Wissen, Ufa-Medien, etc.

Tatsuya Taniguchi

An illustration can enrich the heart anf life. That is the most important to me as an illustrator.

Une illustration peut enrichir le cœur et la vie. C'est ce qui est le plus important pour moi en tant qu'illustrateur.

Eine Illustration kann sowohl ein Herz, als auch ein ganzes Leben bereichern. Das ist für mich als Illustratorin das Wichtigste.

NAME: Tatsuya Taniguchi (Buggy) **LOCATION:** Osaka, Japan **CONTACT:** starfactory@dream-more.com; info@dutchuncle.co.uk **TOOLS:** Pencil and Acrylic. **AGENT:** Dream & More Co. (Japan) <www.starfactory.info>; Dutch Uncle (UK) <www.DutchUncle.co.uk> **CLIENTS:** Toshiba EMI, Kamueru, Gahodo, Vodafone, NTT, Master Piece.

LOUIS VUITTON

Tavish

Even though it is fictional, my art is focused around the people in my images. It's important to me that these characters capture the viewer's imagination. I focus largely on mood and personality, communicating it through body language and expression. Stylistically I've synthesized a wide range of influences from all over the world, an international outlook that owes largely to my cultural origins, as a Chinese / Scottish Canadian.

Même s'il est imaginaire, mon art se concentre sur les gens qui peuplent mes images. Il est important pour moi que ces personnages capturent l'imagination de l'observateur. Je m'attache particulièrement aux détails révélant une humeur ou une personnalité et les communique à travers le langage et l'expression du corps. D'un point de vue stylistique, j'ai synthétisé un large éventail d'influences du monde entier, une perspective internationale que je dois beaucoup à mes origines culturelles de Canadien écossais/chinois.

Auch wenn es nur Fiktion ist, konzentriere ich mich bei meinen Bildern auf die Menschen um mich herum. Mir liegt viel daran, durch meine Charaktere die Phantasie des Betrachters anzuregen. Ich konzentriere mich hauptsächlich auf Stimmung und Persönlichkeit und versuche diese Komponenten durch Körpersprache und Ausdruck zu vermitteln. Meinen Stil habe ich dank weltweiter Einflüsse ausgebaut, eine internationale Orientierung, die nicht zuletzt mit meiner Abstammung als chinesisch-schottischer Kanadier zu tun hat.

www.acidtwist.com

NAME: Tavish **LOCATION:** Montreal, Quebec, Canada **CONTACT:** tavish@acidtwist.com **TOOLS:** Graphite, Adobe Photoshop. **CLIENTS:** Private collectors, Freeset Interactive Entertainment, Epoxy Communications, Cloudraker Marketing, CCM Publishing, HorizonZero Magazine, Audiogram Records, Relentless SkateWorks, Android 8 Toys, Madame Italia, Android&Toys.

Gary Taxali

GOOD LOVER

I like to be selective about the kinds of jobs I take. It's important for me to find something in the project that I can attach on to and have the freedom from the client to explore visually. When that creative liberty is offered by the client, it often results in a picture we are both pleased with.

J'aime choisir avec discernement les travaux que l'on me propose. Pour moi, il est important que je puisse trouver quelque chose à quoi me rattacher dans le projet. Il est également essentiel que le client m'accorde la liberté d'effectuer une exploration visuelle. Lorsque cette liberté m'est donnée par le client, nous sommes souvent tous deux ravis du résultat.

Ich bin wählerisch mit den Arbeiten, die ich annehme. Es ist für mich ganz wichtig, einen Beziehungs-punkt zu einem Projekt zu finden und von dem Kunden die Freiheit zu bekommen, das Projekt visuell zu erforschen. Wird mir diese visuelle Freiheit von meinem Kunden gewährt, so ist das Ergebnis meist ein Bild, mit dem wir beide sehr zufrieden sind.

www.garytaxali.com
www.chumptoys.com

NAME: Gary Taxali **LOCATION:** Toronto, Ontario, Canada **CONTACT:** gary@garytaxali.com **TOOLS:** alkyd oils on masonite, screen printing, pen and ink, mixed media, collage, etc. **AWARDS:** American Illustration, Communication Arts, Society of Illustrators (Silver), Society of Publication Designers, National Magazine (Gold), Advertising & Design Club of Canada. **CLIENTS:** Time, Rolling Stone, Esquire, Newsweek, The New York Times, Fortune, Sony, Levi's, MTV, Coca-Cola, etc.

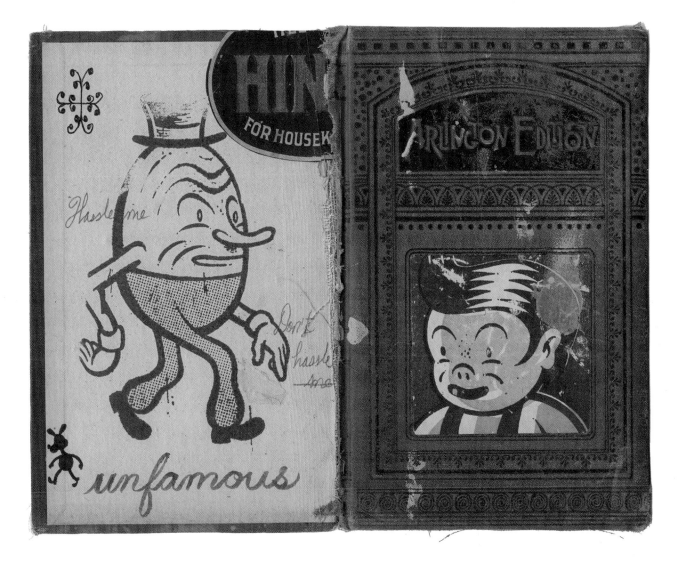

STEWART O'NAN

THE
NIGHT COUNTRY

Javali

Mike Thompson

I spend a lot of time crafting each painting. I won't step away from it till I feel it's right. You are only as good as your last piece, that's just real. The two worst things you can do in this profession are, "miss a deadline, and put out a bad piece." I also try to make each piece better than the last. People tend to get bored pretty quickly.

Je passe beaucoup de temps sur chacune de mes peintures. Je ne m'en détache pas tant que je n'ai obtenu le résultat souhaité. On est jugé à l'aune de ses derniers travaux. Dépasser un délai et livrer un mauvais travail sont les deux pires faux-pas dans cette profession. J'essaie toujours de faire en sorte que chaque travail soit meilleur que le précédent. Les gens ont tendance à s'ennuyer assez rapidement.

Ich verbringe viel Zeit damit, ein Gemälde künstlerisch zu perfektionieren. Ich höre nicht auf, bis ich das Gefühl habe, es fertiggestellt zu haben. Tatsache ist, dass du selbst nur soviel wert bist wie dein zuletzt hergestelltes Werk. Die zwei schlimmsten Fehler, die dir in diesem Beruf unterlaufen können, ist es, "eine Deadline zu verpassen oder eine schlechte Arbeit anzubieten." Ich versuche, jede meiner Arbeiten besser zu erledigen als die vorherige. Denn die Menschen sehen sich sonst schnell satt.

www.miketartworks.com

NAME: Mike Thompson (MikeT) **LOCATION:** Beltsville, MD, USA **CONTACT:** mike@miketartworks.com **TOOLS:** Adobe Photoshop, Corel Painter, Acrylics, Wacom Pad.
CLIENTS: Coca-Cola, Electronic Arts, Ecko, Reebok, the ROC, Atlantic Records, HBO, Brown & Williamson.

Ella Tjader

My passion lies in drawing beautiful, often sexy-ugly women as an abstract fashion statement. I am inspired my many things, but fashion, costume history, and nature have a major influence on my work.

Ma passion est de dessiner des femmes souvent moitié sexy moitié laides comme s'il s'agissait d'une déclaration de mode abstraite. Beaucoup de choses m'inspirent mais la mode, l'histoire des costumes et la nature ont une influence majeure sur mon travail.

Meine Passion liegt darin, schöne, sexy oder auch hässliche Frauen zu zeichnen, und das als abstraktes Fashion-Statement zu verstehen. Mich inspirieren viele Dinge, doch Mode, Geschichte der Kleidung und Natur haben einen besonderen Einfluss auf meine Arbeiten.

www.artlaundry.com

NAME: Ella Tjader **LOCATION:** United Kingdom **CONTACT:** contact@artlaundry.com **TOOLS:** Adobe Illustrator, black pen, Adobe Photoshop. **AGENT:** Illustration Agency <www.illustrationweb.com > **CLIENTS:** Reader's Digest, Here's Health, Scholastic, Deco Home (Germany), Candis, Spirit & Destiny, Hart McLeod, and Eve BBC.

Pedro Toledo

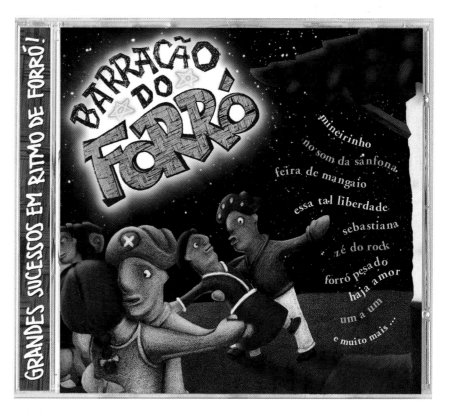

In the beginning of the 90's I started my degree in graphic design. During this time I had the chance to meet some really talented people, in special an illustration teacher called Amador Perez who had influenced my work and my resolution about living from my drawings.

J'ai commencé à étudier les arts graphiques dans les années 90. Pendant cette période j'ai eu la chance de rencontrer des gens vraiment très talentueux et particulièrement Amador Perez, un professeur d'illustration qui a influencé mon travail et ma décision de gagner ma vie avec mes dessins.

Anfang der 90er begann ich mein Studium des Grafikdesign. Während dieser Zeit hatte ich das Glück, viele talentierte Menschen kennenzulernen. Darunter einen gewissen Amador Perez, Professor in Illustrationsdesign, der grossen Einfluss auf meine Arbeiten als auch meine Entscheidung, von meinen Zeichnungen zu leben, hatte.

www.pedrotoledo.com.br

NAME: Pedro Toledo **LOCATION:** Rio de Janeiro, Brazil **CONTACT:** contato@pedrotoledo.com.br **TOOLS:** Pencil, Adobe Photoshop, Corel Painter, Discreet 3D Max Studio. **CLIENTS:** Universal Music, Sony Music, IBM, Coca-Cola, Telemar, O Globo, etc.

Eric Tranchefeux

Depending on the demands of his customers and the functional purpose of his illustrations, his work deals with very different subject areas. His personal work is mainly oil paintings covering subjects such as fantasy, dreams, visions and surrealism. This feeling of being close to the great masters of the past, the seeking of philosophical contents, the moments of reflection and the pleasure of suppressing the reality that surrounds us, all this influences the very true realisation of his work.

Ses illustrations ont des sujets très variées en fonctions des différentes demande de ses clients et de leurs utilisations. Ses création personnelle, pour la plupart des peintures à l'huile évoque des thèmes fantastiques, oniriques, visionnaires et surréalistes. Ce sentent proche des maîtres du passé, il recherche un contenue philosophiques un moment de réflexion et le plaisir de sublimer la réalité qui nous entour par le traité très réaliste de ses œuvres.

Seine Illustrationen behandeln sehr unterschiedliche Themenbereiche, abhängig von den Anforderungen seiner Kunden und ihrer Funktionalität. Seine persönlichen Arbeiten sind zum grössten Teil Ölgemälde, die Themen wie Phantasie, Traumvorstellungen, Visionen und Surrealismus behandeln. Dieses Gefühl, den grossen Meistern der Vergangenheit nahe zu sein, das Suchen von philosophischen Inhalten, Momente der Reflexion und der Genuss bei der Unterdrückung der Realität, die uns umgibt, all das fliesst in die sehr realistische Umsetzung seiner Werke mit ein.

www.tranchefeux.com

NAME: Eric Tranchefeux **LOCATION:** Paris, France **CONTACT:** studio@tranchefeux.com **TOOLS:** Adobe Photoshop, Corel Painter, Discreet 3D Studio Max, pencil, oil.
AWARDS: CG Talk, 3DVF. **CLIENTS:** Peugeot, Disney, TF1 Video, Kinder, Vitelle, Lu, Finger, Milka, Poster Movie Titus, Poster Escrime, jaquettes video: Bisounours, Gasper, Transformers, Marine National, Gaterpillard, Packaging big distributions, etc.

Gina Triplett

Illustration has served as a means for me to make art on a daily basis. The visual language I use in my personal work has evolved, and is evolving, in the jobs I do for others. In some jobs, I'm detached from the content, so it is in the building of the image that I stay engaged. Most often, and of course ideally, the assignment has an aspect that engages me on a conceptual level as well. It's at this point that the line between my personal art and commissioned work is most thin. I like these times best.

Le travail d'illustration est pour moi un moyen de faire de l'art de façon quotidienne. La langue visuelle que j'utilise dans mon travail personnel a évolué et évolue dans les travaux que j'effectue pour d'autres. Dans certaines illustrations, je me détache du contenu et c'est donc dans la construction de l'image que je reste engagée. Le plus souvent, et idéalement bien sûr, les travaux de commande comportent un aspect qui m'engage à un niveau conceptuel également.

Illustration gibt mir die Möglichkeit, Kunst auf einer täglichen Basis zu produzieren. Die visuelle Sprache, die ich bei meinen Arbeiten anwende, befindet sich in einem ständigen Entwicklungsprozess, sowohl auf persönlicher Ebene als auch bei den Arbeiten für meine Kunden. Bei einigen Arbeiten bin ich der inhaltlichen Aussage gegenüber eher distanziert eingestellt, doch während der Kreation des Bildes finde ich die Verbindung zum Projekt. Oftmals, und das ist natürlich der Idealfall, hat ein Auftrag einen konzeptionellen Aspekt, der mich gefangennimmt.

www.ginatriplett.com

NAME: Gina Triplett **LOCATION:** Philadelphia, PA, USA **CONTACT:** ginatriplett@comcast.net **TOOLS:** ink, acrylic. **AWARDS:** American Illustration, Communication Arts, Society of Illustrators, Print Magazine. **AGENT:** Frank Sturges <www.sturgesreps.com> **CLIENTS:** Rolling Stone, Converse Shoes, RCA Records, IBM, New York Times, Entertainment Weekly.

Mark Ulriksen

I aim to please myself. I am my own toughest critic. I figure that when I am satisfied my client will be as well. I compose my images in a drawn collage fashion, layering each element to create a composition I find successful. I take pains to make sure that each element (a face, body language, back ground etc) is well crafted, stylized and interesting.

J'aime me faire plaisir. Je suis mon plus farouche critique. Je me dis que lorsque je suis satisfait, mon client le sera également. Je compose mes images à partir de collages dessinés, en disposant chaque élément par couche afin de créer une composition réussie. J'investis beaucoup d'efforts pour que chaque élément (un visage, le langage du corps, le cadre, etc.) soit bien conçu, stylisé et intéressant.

Ich muss mich selbst zufriedenstellen. Ich bin mir selbst mein schärfster Kritiker. Wenn ich selbst mit mir zufrieden bin, dann ist es mein Kunde auch. Ich komponiere meine Bilder durch das Zeichnen moderner Kollagen, indem ich Element über Element anordne, um so eine erfolgsversprechende Komposition zu erreichen. Ich gehe bis an die Schmerzgrenze, um mich zu vergewissern, dass jedes Element (Gesicht, Körpersprache, Hintergrund etc.) das passende Aussehen, Stil sowie Ausdruck hat.

www.markulriksen.com

NAME: Mark Ulriksen **LOCATION:** San Francisco, California, USA **CONTACT:** ulriksen@prodigy.net **TOOLS:** HB pencil, kneeded eraser, acrylics. **AWARDS:** Society of Illustrators (Gold/Silver), American Illustration, Communication Arts Illustration. **AGENT:** Maslov/Weinberg <www.theispot.com> **CLIENTS:** The New Yorker, The New York Times, Time, Newsweek, The Wall Street Journal, Rolling Stone, Nike, EMI Capital, San Francisco Jazz Festival, Simon and Schuster, etc.

Price $3.00

Feb. 14, 2000

THE NEW YORKER

Like most people, I draw what entertains me. Dancing ladies, animals wearing outfits, abstract thought, celebrities, clowns... the variety keeps me enthusiastic about my work. I also try to use colours reminiscent of candy, or glowing disco floors, or fireworks. There's a compression of energy that takes place between a chaotic pencil sketch and a digital illustration. After I squeegee out the inessentials, I hope the finished product is not only visually exciting, but also delicious and fragrant.

Comme la plupart des gens, je dessine ce qui m'amuse. Danseuses, animaux habillés, pensées abstraites, célébrités, clowns, etc., la variété maintient mon enthousiasme pour mon travail. J'essaie toujours d'utiliser des couleurs rappelant les bonbons, les sols de discothèque flamboyants ou encore les feux d'artifices. Un concentré d'énergie prend place entre une esquisse chaotique au crayon et une l'illustration numérique. Après avoir éliminé tout ce qui est superflu, il ne me reste plus qu'à espérer que le produit fini soit non seulement captivant d'un point de vue visuel mais aussi délicieux et enchanteur.

Wie die meisten Menschen zeichne ich das, was mir Spass macht. Tanzende Damen, verkleidete Tiere, abstrakte Gedanken, Berühmtheiten, Clowns...die Vielfalt sichert meinen Enthusiasmus bei der Arbeit. Ich versuche, Farben zu benutzen, die an Bonbons, glänzende Diskoböden oder Feuerwerke erinnern. Es kommt zu einem Druckausgleich zwischen der freigesetzten Energie bei der Herstellung eines chaotischen Bleistiftsketches oder einer digitalen Illustration. Nachdem ich dann alle Unwichtigkeiten entfernt habe, hoffe ich, dass das Endprodukt nicht nur visuell ansprechend ist, sondern gleichzeitig köstlich und wohlriechend erscheint.

www.kirstenulve.com

NAME: Kirsten Ulve **LOCATION:** New York, USA **CONTACT:** kirsten@kirstenulve.com **TOOLS:** Adobe Illustrator. **AWARDS:** American Illustration, Art director's Club Distinctive Merit. **AGENT:** Holly Hahn (H2 + Co.) <www.hollyhahn.com>; CWC Toyko <www.cwctokyo.com> **CLIENTS:** Target, Hasbro, Mattel, The Chicago Tribune, The New York Times, Dariya Corporation (Japan), Entertainment Weekly.

Julie Verhoeven

Practice makes perfect and no pains, no gains.

La pratique mène à la perfection et sans effort, pas de résultat.

Durch Praxis zur Perfektion und ohne Schmerz kein Preis.

NAME: Julie Verhoeven **LOCATION:** London, UK **CONTACT:** julie.verhoeven@virgin.net **TOOLS:** Pilot hi-tecpoint pen, pencil, Tip-ex. **AGENT:** CLM <www.clmuk.com>
CLIENTS: Gibo, Dazed and Confused, www.showstudio.com, Louis Vuitton, Martine Sitbon, Central Saint Martins, Tache-Levy Gallery.

Annabelle Verhoye

Chine colle is a style that combines delicate layers of delightful patterns, precious webs of Chinese & Japanese rice papers that are amalgamated with a precise and sophisticated line drawing. Both Annabelle's commissioned illustrations and art work seeks to restore *beauty in itself*. She wants the viewer to pause and catch their breath in a moment of suspended delight. Her art lead us to seek out other beautiful things. In this way beauty replicates itself, without our help.

Le chine collé est une technique qui combine des couches de motifs ravissants et de précieuses toiles de feuilles de papier de riz chinois et japonais amalgamées avec un dessin à base de lignes sophistiquées et précises. Les illustrations de commande et les œuvres d'art d'Annabelle cherchent à restituer la *beauté elle-même*. L'artiste veut que l'observateur s'arrête et retienne sa respiration dans un moment de ravissement suspendu. Son art nous incite à la recherche d'autres belles choses. De cette façon la beauté se renouvelle, sans notre aide.

„Chine colle" ist eine Technik, die delikate Schichten aus chinesischem und japanischem Reispapier in wunderschönen Mustern und vielfältigen Verflechtungen miteinander kombiniert, welche dann zu präzisen und anspruchsvollen Linienzeichnungen verschmelzen. Annabelles Illustrationen und ihre Kunst möchten Schönheit als Ganzes neu definieren. Die Intention ist es, dem Betrachter zu einem Moment der Ruhe und unbestimmter Glückseligkeit verhelfen. Dank ihrer Kunst entdecken wir wiederum andere schöne Dinge. Auf diese Weise vervielfältigt sich Schönheit ganz von selbst, ohne jegliche Mithilfe.

www.annabelleverhoye.com

NAME: Annabelle Verhoye **LOCATION:** New York, USA **CONTACT:** anna@annabelleverhoye.com **TOOLS:** Chinese & Japanese rice papers, Acrylic Colors, Pen & Ink, Adobe Photoshop, Plexiglas. **AWARDS:** The Society of Illustrators, American Illustration. **CLIENTS:** The New Yorker, The New York Times Magazine, Tatler, Vogue, Elle, Gourmet, Nylon, Playboy, The Wall Street Journal, Disney, BMW, La Samaritaine, Atlantic Records, Bride, Gruner & Jahr, and more.

Je t'aime.
Happy Valentine's Day.

Miu Miu
On him: Canvas cape, button-down shirt, and canvas pants. On her: Wool-gauze collared dress.

Issey Miyake
Plant foam stole and paper tumbler foam dress.

Gordon Wiebe

I view illustration as an arena in which I may play, ponder, learn and ultimately grow. It is a place where things such as law, politics and religion are replaced by colour, shape, line, etc... It is a world brought to life by commission and nurtured by collaboration. It is in this reality I find, more often than not, that I am unhappy with the printing reproduction.

Je vois le domaine de l'illustration comme une arène dans laquelle je peux jouer, méditer, apprendre et grandir. C'est un domaine dans lequel des concepts tels que la justice, la politique et la religion sont remplacés par des couleurs, des formes, des lignes, etc. C'est un univers né de commandes et nourri par la collaboration. C'est dans cette réalité que je ressens la plupart du temps que je n'aime pas les reproductions imprimées.

Für mich ist Illustration vergleichbar mit einer Arena, in der ich spielen, nachdenken, lernen und letztlich auch wachsen kann. Illustration ermöglicht es, Gesetze, Politik und Religion durch Farben, Formen und Linien etc. zu ersetzen... Eine Welt, die durch Aufträge und Zusammenarbeit genährt wird. Allerdings stellen mich die Drucke der Reproduktionen nicht zufrieden.

www.gordonwiebe.com

NAME: Gordon Wiebe **LOCATION:** Toronto, Canada **CONTACT:** gord@gordonwiebe.com **TOOLS:** paper, glue. **AWARDS:** American Illustration, Applied Arts Illustration.
AGENT: Magnet Reps <www.magnetreps.com> **CLIENTS:** Bloomberg, HOW magazine, Mckinsey Quarterly, Murphy Design, Smart Money, The Hospital for Sick Children, THIS magazine, Bank of Montreal, The Globe and Mail, The National Post.

positively charged

By Henry Canaday
Illustrations by Gordon Wiebe

How to improve sales performance — from new-hires to experienced pros

HIRE SMART How do you pick successful salespeople? If you simply look for people who most resemble your current top producers you may not be looking in the right places, says Dave Barnett of Cedar Hill, Texas-based The Barnett Group.

"Veterans simply don't work like rookies," emphasizes Barnett, who tests sales recruits for major companies. Experienced reps have networks of prospects from which they can pick the best, and they do not always make many cold calls. A new-hire who worked that way would probably fail.

What about personality tests? Character counts, for both new and old reps, Barnett acknowledges. But testing for personality may not work very well. Pure personality doesn't count for much in business-to-business selling. And it is hard to know how a new rep will really behave a few months after the first job interview.

The bottom line, according to Barnett: "If you are using a test to hire new salespeople, make sure it is 'normed' to your good salespeople who have been on the job for a short time. Don't 'test the test' by giving it to veterans. Successful selling behaviors change over time."

Barnett studies his own tests regularly. He has to prove to his clients that they measure something real and useful in hiring. He calls this analysis his SalesMAP, which he gave to 200 veteran and rookie reps.

SalesMAP measured 21 behaviors associated with selling success, from such qualities as energy and decisiveness to skills including upselling and call frequency. Barnett discovered that veterans tended to outscore rookies consistently in some areas, while the best rookies beat the veterans regularly in other areas (see sidebar).

Consequently, try to hire people who "look like" your most successful rookies, Barnett advises. In other words, good new reps tend to be very consistent in how they answer prospects' questions, unlike veterans who may be confident enough to vary their response each time they encounter a different situation. Young salespeople tend to be more empathetic with prospects, perhaps because they themselves fear rejection. And rookies often find initial telephone contacts easier to handle. So look for consistent answers, empathy and comfort with cold calls in new hires.

Veterans, on the other hand, regularly outscore rookies in confidence, working hard toward definite goals and the ability to economize with time by eliminating distractions. Don't expect recruits to have all these qualities until they get a little experience. And look out for false confidence that will melt with a few rejections.

Lars Winsel

Deserve has got nothing to do with it.

Le mérite n'a rien à voir avec cela.

Verdienst spielt hier gar keine Rolle.

http://larswinsel.illustration.de

NAME: Lars Winsel **LOCATION:** Hannover, Germany **TOOLS:** Acryl, Gouache, Polychromos. **CLIENTS:** Focus, Playboy, Freundin, Quick, Wirtschaftswoche, Junge Karriere, Amica, Max, Cinema, Tomorrow, Das Magazin, Eulenspiegel, Red Herring, Du.

Yihsin **Wu**

As an uptight personality, through illustration bring me to a bizarre world. Under the drawings, I always image myself as every character I have created and secretly think of their life as my other life. Sometimes people say they are ugly but I would like to think they are unique and have a strong personality just like us.

Étant de nature réservée, l'illustration me mène dans un monde étrange. Derrière mes dessins, je m'imagine toujours dans la peau des personnages que je crée et vois secrètement leur vie comme étant ma propre vie. Certaines personnes disent d'elles-mêmes qu'elles sont laides mais j'aimerais croire qu'elles sont uniques et dotées d'une forte personnalité comme les autres.

Da ich eine eher angespannte Person bin, hilft mir die Illustration, mich in einer andersartigen Welt wiederzufinden. Beim Zeichnen schlüpfe ich in die Rolle der Charaktere, die ich kreiere und versetze mich heimlich in ihr Leben, so als wäre es mein eigenes. Manchmal sagen mir Leute, meine Charaktere seien hässlich, aber ich bevorzuge, sie einfach als „besonders" zu bezeichnen, mit einer starken Persönlichkeit, genauso, wie wir auch.

www.yihsin.net

NAME: Yihsin Wu **LOCATION:** New York, USA **CONTACT:** cocoyi@yahoo.com **TOOLS:** magazines, paper, pencil, acrylic. **AWARDS:** Society of Illustrators.
CLIENTS: Southern Poverty Law Center, Liberty Times of Taiwan.

Hiroshi **Yoshii**

I embody invisible ideas. I create a visual surprise with colour and form. Moreover, I like covering it with a humorous impression.

J'incarne des idées invisibles. Je crée des surprises visuelles avec de la couleur et des formes. Et j'aime couronner le tout d'une touche d'humour.

Ich verleihe unsichtbaren Ideen eine Gestalt. Ich kreiere eine visuelle Überraschung mit Farbe und Form. Ein humorvoller Ausdruck vervollständigt das Ganze.

www.yoshii.com

NAME: Hiroshi Yoshii **LOCATION:** Tokyo, Japan **CONTACT:** hiroshi@yoshii.com **TOOLS:** Corel Painter, Pixologic ZBrush. **AWARDS:** Meta Creations Beyond the Canvas Digital Art Competition. **AGENT:** Costume 3 Pieces <www.costume3pieces.com> **CLIENTS:** Le Point, L'équipe, SVM Mac, Total, Peugeot, ROCHE, Scholastic, Gloria Jean's Gourmet Coffees, Group Publishing, Matsushita Electric Works, Benesse, Takarajimasha, Gakken, Ascii, Alc Press.

Yukinori Tokoro

I always try to make my own worlds which nobody else can create.

J'essaie en permanence de concevoir des mondes que personne d'autre ne peut créer.

Ich versuche stets, mir meine eigenen Welten zu schaffen, die niemand sonst kreieren kann.

www.tokoroyukinori.com

NAME: Tokoro Yukinori **LOCATION:** Tokyo, Japan **CONTACT:** info@tokoroyukinori.com **TOOLS:** Adobe Photoshop, Hasselblad camera. **AWARDS:** Canon Prize in Graphic Show. **CLIENTS:** Coca Cola, Nike, West, Canon, Sony, Panasonic and various magazines.

ALDERETE, Jorge: p.20 - "Acapulco Tiki", personal work, Silkscreen, 2004. / p.21 - "Rapa Nui", cover illustration, Phophecy magazine, USA 2004. / p.22 - "Kassim Ouma", editorial illustration, Deep magazine, Mexico 2005. / p.23 - "Fobia al Picnic", Show poster, Mexico 2003. / p.23 - "Hog Wild", cover illustration, Students of the Unusual magazine, USA 2004.

AMANO, Miki: p.24 - Untitled, 2004, personal work. / p.25 - Untitled, 2004, personal work. / p.26 - Untitled, 2004, personal work. / p.27 - "The Power of Imagination", 2004, client: CosmoGirl!

ANGLES, Jean-Marie: p.28 - "Newspaper Stall", France Telecom/Phone card, photographer: Fabrice Besse. / p.29 - "Tiki Bar", personal work, photographer: Pascal Legrand.

ARÉVALO, Jorge: p.30 - "Eminem", published in a special supplement devoted to MTV of "EL Mundo" newspaper (Barcelona edition), 2003. / p.31 - "Monika Belluci", Personal work, 2004.

BAGAYAN, Ana: p.32 - "Portrait of Avril Lavigne", Rolling Stone Magazine, 2004. / p.33 - "Bad Seed", 2005, personal work.

BANYAI, Istvan: p.34 - "Parenting". / p.35 - "Sexual Etiquette". / p.36 - "Island Color", FINITO. / p.37 - Art Collector, FINITO, Ist-One. / p.38-39 - Covers for New Yorker Magazine.

BARBER, Shawn: p.40 - "Playful", Converse, 2005. / p.41 - "Rob Halford", Out Magazine, 2004. / p.42 - "Van Morrison", Rolling Stone Magazine, 2004. / p.43 - "Tupac Shakur", Rolling Stone Magazine, 2003. / p.44 - "Elvis Costello", Vancouver Magazine, 2003. / p.45 - Hoffman Bikes, Target at Woodward West, Stallion Springs, CA, 2004.

BARTHOLD, Christian: p.46 - "In the mood for love", 2005, Personal Work. / p.47 - "Rise", 2005, Personal Work. / p.48-49 - "Winter", 2005, Personal Work.

BASEMAN, Gary: p.50 - "Dumb Luck", book cover. / p.51 - Halloween cover of LA Times. / p.52-53 - Entertainer of the Year in EW. / p.54 left - New Yorker Cover. / p.54 right - Next!, Los Angeles Times Magazine. / p.55 - Teacher's Pet art.

BASSEWITZ, David von: p.56 - Materia prima, 2004, Publicis Erlangen. / p.57 top - no title, 2004, personal work. / p.57 middle - Harddisc-cat, 2002, Rotstift Verlag. / p.57 bottom - Netrunner, 2002, Rotstift Verlag.

BECK, Melinda: p.58-61 - Personal works.

BEETSON, Sarah: p.62 - "Miss Sherbet Dip", 2002, a personal work from a collection which was later featured in FAQ magazine (UK), for the theme 'Embark'. / p.63 - "The Rose of Kaluhua" (sailor boys), 2004, From the collection 'Mail Order Boys', created for 'ARTY' magazine.

BILDBAD: p.64 - Free work. / p.65 - "Schwester", book illustration. / p.66-67 - Free work, African football player.

BILLOUT, Guy: p.68 - Fortitude, The Atlantic Monthly. / p.69 - Civil Engeneering, The Atlantic Monthly. / p.70 - Leak, The Atlantic Monthly. / p.71 - Evening News, The Atlantic Monthly.

BONNKE, Jens: p.72 - Please do not feed!, Das Magazin, Berlin, 2004. / p.73 - Perpetual, 2004, UlfTone Records, rock group "Kingdom Come". / p.74 - Life Insurance, Berliner Zeitung, Berlin, 2004. / p.75 - New World Order, StadtRevue, Cologne, 2003.

BRAUN, Dieter: p.76 - Andy Warhol, Personal Work, 2004. / p.77 - San Juan, Cover for United Hemispheres Magazine, 2004. / p.78 - Homeexchange (Wohnungstausch), ADAC Reisemagazin-Traveller, 2005. / p.79 - Quentin Tarantino, Personal Work, 2004.

BROOKS, Jason: p.80 - Disco Heaven. / p.81 - Elle Breakfast for Elle Magazine. / p.82-83 - Warhol. / p.84 top - Speedboad. / p.85 bottom - Beach House. / p.85 top - Redken Packaging. / p.85 bottom - Safilo BB Catalogue.

BROWNFIELD, Mick: p.86 - For the G2 section of the Guardian newspaper in 1998. It was a feature about the dumbing down of television. / p.87 - A self promotion piece based on the Alfred E. Newman character in Mad magazine. It was used as a sticky label for packaging, 2002.

BURNS, Charles: p.88 - E.T. illustration. / p.89 - illustration for Esquire Magazine. / p.90 - Illustration on Drew Barrymore. / p.91 - Illustration for Black Hole Comic Book.

CABALLERO, Paula Sanz: p.92 - Illustration for El Mundo Magazine swiming suit special, 2004. / p.93 - R la B. Vison for "Roger la Borde" cards, 2002. / p.94 - Another chance encounter between Mr. X and Mrs.Y, Exhibited in "My name's Lolita art", solo exhibition, Madrid. / p.95 - Vanity, made for the exhibition "Small is beatifull", Central Flowers gallery, London 2004-5. / p.96 - made for "Roger la Borde", 2002. / p.97 top left - Outdoor for Telva. / p.97 top right - Illustration for bags, Coredo, Japan (blue) and Nice Day, Spain (Pink). / p.97 bottom left - Book cover. / p.97 bottom right - Outdoor for Telva.

CAMPBELL-NOTMAN, Finn: p.98 - Peckham. / p.99 - "Placa Reial" (Artbook).

CARDELLI, Maria: p.100 - Aquarius. / p.101 - Woman with accessories.

CASSON, Alison: p.102 - Bone Amie for Chantal Menard. / p.103 - "I Do", self promotion.

CHANG, Daniel: p.104 - "Elephant", 2004, Bloomberg Wealth Manager. / p.105 - "3-Headed Bird", 2005, Storage. / p.106 - "Winged Horse", 2005, Sturges Reps Calendar. / p.107 above - "Tatooed Arm", 2003, Storage. / p.107 below - "Boat", 2003, Pennsylvania Gazette.

CHIN, Marcos: p.108 - "Domestic Goddess", 2004, Time. / p.109 - "Charged", 2005, Sports Illustrated. / p.110 - "Moby", 2002, Rolling Stone. / p.111 - "It's Raining Men", 2003, Lavalife.

CIARDIELLO, Joe: p.112 - Frog, 2004, Dellas Graphics. / p.113 - Eric Clapton, 2003, Japanese Playboy Magazine.

Credits

CLARKE, Greg: p.114 - "Winter Page-Turners", 2004, The New Yorker/Condé Nast Publications, Art Director: Françoise Mouly. / p.115 - "Walking the Dot", 2004, picturemechanics.com, Art Director: Gary Taxali.

COBURN, Tavis: p.116 - Time Magazine, Cover: Understanding Anxiety, Art Director: Arthur Hochstein, 2002, Not Published. / p.117 - Inc. Magazine, Feature: The New Face of Confidence, Art Director: Linda Koury, 2003. / p.118 - Technology Review, Feature: Stopping Pain, Art Director: Linda Koury, 2003. / p.119 - CIO Magazine, Feature: A Land were Giants Rule, Art Director: George Lee, 2004. / p.120 - Vibe Magazine, Feature: Broken Hit Factory, Art Director: Florian Bachleda, 2004.

COHEN, Fernanda: p.122 - Coming Soon, 2004. / p.123 - Kid Shopping, 2003, Awards-Communication Arts Illustration Annual 45, 2004. / p.124 Title: Poop Weighs, 2004. / p.125 - The New York Times Sunday Magazine, COVER Article: His Calculations, Cover article on president George W. Bush and the issue on taxes and social security in the United States, Sunday January 16th, 2005.

CRONIN, Brian: p.126 - One in a series of six Book Jacket Illustrations by Graham Greene "End of The Affair", Designer Paul, Penguin USA, 2004. / p.127 - Full page Illustration for a short story in The New Yorker 2004. / p.128 - inside cover Illustration (part of a series of five drawings that appeared on the CD "Sweetheart", various artists, Hear Music USA, 2004. / p.129 - "Orange", limited edition print, 2004. All images Acrylic on watercolor paper. / p.130 - Cover Illustration for a large format catalogue for the Canadian Furniture furniture "BARONET", "2005 year of the monkey", Canada, 2004. / p.131 - One in a series of six Book Jacket Illustrations by Graham Greene "Travels with My Aunt", Penguin USA, 2004.

DANNENBERG, Thomas: p.132 - "The Three and Many Wishes of Jason Reid", book cover illustration, Annick Press, Art Director: Sheryl Shapiro, 2000. / p.133 - "Vegging out", Newspaper cover illustration, Globe and Mail newspaper, Art Director: David Woodside, 2003.

DELICATESSEN: p.134 - "Tango", YOU magazine, UK, 2004. / p.135 - "Cry Baby Cry", American Baby magazine, USA, 2004. / p.136 above left - Cancer. / p.136 above right: Leo. / p.136 below left - Taurus. / p.136 below right: Piscis. Four of a series of 12 horoscope signs, Cosmopolitan (D) 2005.

DELL, Vanessa: p.138 - Grooming Part One, personal work, 2003. / p.139 - Portrait of Dizzy, 2004, Private commission. / p.140 - Grooming Part Three, 2003, personal work. / p.141 upper image: Gallagher brothers, 1995, Time Out Magazine. / p.141 lower image: Kippers, 2004, Good Housekeeping Magazine.

eBOY: p.142 - Paul Smith. / p.143 top - Coca Cola, Mother, London, 2004. / p.143 bottom - New York Times Magazine, 2004. / p.144-145 - personal work (Poster A0), 2005. / p.146 - New York Times, 2005. / p.147 above left - New York Times Illustration, 2005. / p.147 above right - MacUser Cover Illustration, 2004. / p.147 below - Paul Smith bag, 2005.

FEINDT, Jan: p.148-149 - Personal work.

FIEDLER, Joseph Daniel: p.150 - "Heaven", 2002, Murphy Design Inc. / p.151 - "El Stigmatismo", 2001, Murphy Design Inc.

FIGOWY, Fernando: p.152 - "Abax", 2004, La Distillerie (France). / p.153 - "Mujer con perro", 2005, personal work. / p.154 - "Mujer sentada", 2005, personal work. / p.155 - "Telefono movil", 2005, CBM Media (Argentina).

FOREVER YOUNG: p.156 - Withe widow, 2005, personal work. / p.157 - Lust garden, 2005, personal work. Forever Young@Creative Syndicate.

FRASER, Douglas: p.158 - "A Pugilist's Alchemy" or "PULP", 2004, BLAB! #15 - Fantagraphics. / p.159 - "Unleash", 2004, Formica & Carmichael Lynch. / p.159-160 - "Dead Space", 2003, SciFi Western, Last Gasp Publishing.

FRAZIER, Craig: p.162 - "Wet Paint", 2004, Navigant Consulting Inc. / p.163 - "Santa Cruz Guitar Co.", 2003, Santa Cruz Guitar Co. / p.164 - "Underwater", 2004, Personal Work. / p.165 - "Potholes", 2002, Peninsula Community Foundation.

FU, Chu Keng: p.166 - "Kinman", 2004, Kinman in Kinmen. / p.167 above - "Peipei", 2004, for my sister's birthday. / p.167 below - "Bottle", 2003, Old Taiwan Series.

GARCÍA HUERTA, Carmen: p.168 - "October in New York", 2005, Custo Barcelona (Calendar 2005). / p.169 - "Elephant Girl", 2004, Custo Barcelona (Summer/Spring collection 2005). / p.170-171 - "Hypnosis session", 2005, Project for Hint Magazine, featuring Charles Anastase Summer/Spring collection 2005. / p.172 - "I love Rolls Royces", 2004, Custo Barcelona (Summer/Spring collection 2005). / p.173 above - "Taj Mahal", 2005, Carrera & Carrera jewelry featuring Anna Cortina stores. / p.173 below - Vogue Spain illustrations and Paperchic catalogue from the exhibition.

GEFE, Andreas: p.174 - Ile St., Vibrations magazin, 2004. / p.175 - "Aschenbrödel", personal work, 2003 / p.176 - "Bachata Fina", Strapazin, Comic-Magazin, 2004. / p.177 top - "Tillsammans", poster and flyer for an open air film release, 2004. / p.177 bottom - Cover for own comic book: "Mein Bruder Flo" released in Zurich, 2002.

GOMES, Marcio: p.178-179 - personal work.

GOSS, Ben: p.180 - Corker Food Illustraded, UK. / p.181 - Promotional Postcard for Larkworthy. / p.182-183 - Illustration on an article on financial climate in Asia, Asia Week Magazine. / p.184 - Illustration based on a Valentino Fabric Design, Loaded Magazine, UK. / p.185 left - Magazine Cover, The Australian. / p.185 right - Book Cover, Picador.

GRÖTZ, Ulli: p.186 - "Aquarius", 2003, young miss. / p.187 - "Draft", 2004, personal work.

HAAKE, Martin: p.188 - "Gaius Julius Gates", Playboy (D), Art Director: Achim Matschiner, 2004. / p.189 - "Las Vegas Hacker", Playboy (D), Art Director: Achim Matschiner, 2004. / p.190 - "Flexibility", Bloomberg Wealth Manager (USA), Art Director: Laura Zavetz, 2004. / p.191 left - "Love Man", Peix (D), Art Director: Karsten Szepka, 2004. / p.191 right - "Rocket", Peix (D), Art Director: Karsten Szepka 2004.

HAJEK, Olaf: p.192 - "Broken Chair", 2004, Bloomberg Wealth Manager. / p.193 - "Sly and the Family Stone", 2004, Rolling Stone. / p.194 - Michael Moore,2004, Playboy. / p.195 - "Shoes", 2004, Departmentstore Quartier 206, Berlin. / p.196 - "It's in your face" (Helmut Lang), 2004, Maxim Fashion. / p.197 - "It's in your face" (Yves Sain Laurent), 2004, Maxim Fashion.

HANUKA, Asaf: p.198 - LA Times. / p.199 - USN&WR. / p.200 - Bipolar Comics. / p.201 - The Source.

HANUKA, Tomer: p.202 - Side Magazine, for a story about a personal mission of a former CIA Agent in Irak. / p.203 - Out Side Magazine. / p.204 - Flaunt Magazine, for a stoty entitled Indignity. / p.205 - Album cover for Bazooka Thooth by Rap Artist Aesop Rock. / p.206-207 - Premiere Magazine, for the movie release Eternal Sunshine of the Spotless Mind.

HEISE, Warren: p.208 - editorial illustration, unpublished. / p.209 - editorial illustration published by SBS Digital Design Magazine.

HENDRIX, John: p.210 - "Bells & Whistles", 2005, Plan Sponsor Magazine. / p.211 - "Reckless", 2004, Knopf Delacorte Dell Publishing. / p.212 top - "I Will Raise a Storm", 2003, Personal work. / p.212 bottom - "Priests & Paramedics", 2004, Personal work. / p.213 - "To the 5 Boroughs", 2004, Rolling Stone.

HEWGILL, Jody: p.214 - "Seasons". / p.215 - "David Bowie". / p.216 - "Jerry Lee Lewis". / p.217 left - "M. Buterfly Flyer". / p.217 right - "Garden Party" wine bottle. / p.218 - Time Magazine cover, courtesy of Time Magazine. / p.219 - "Halle Berry".

HOLLAND, Brad: p.220-223 - Personal works.

HUNDLEY, Sterling: p.224 - "My Lady Richmond", VCU Adcenter, comissioned by Dinesh Kapoor at Arnika, 2003. / p.225 - "Stevie Wonder", comissioned by Kory Kennedy, Rolling Stone Magazine, created in 2004 for the "Immortals" issue.

HUNGRY DOG STUDIO: p.226 - "Amazing Baby", 2003, Murphy Design, Calendar piece with the theme of "Super Heros". / p.227 - "50 Cent", 2003, Rolling Stone Magazine, Lead artwork for the Record Review, Department of the magazine. / p.228 - "Carlos Santana", 2004, Commissioned for a private collection. / p.229 - "X Marks The Spot", 2004, Personal art.

ILIĆ, Mirko: p.230 - "Halt-Before I make you listen to Matchbox 20 again", 2005, Best Life magazine. / p.231 - "Love Hurts", 2005, VIBE magazine. / p.232 - "Uho, grlo, nož", 2002, AGM (book cover), Art Director: Kruno Lokotar. / p.233 - "I'd Leave My Country, But My Wife Won't Let Me", 2004, Village Voice newspaper. / p.234-235 - "Data Trail", 2003, National Geographic.

ISIP, Jordin: p.236 - "West Nile Virus", 2001, Playboy. / p.237 - "Benny's Heart", 2005, Priest Media, Reader's Digest.

JACEY: p.238 - Computer Arts Cover. / p.239-241 - Free work.

JASINSKI, Aaron: p.242 - "Swing States" for Student Ministry Publishing, 2005. / p.243 - "Micro Moog", personal piece, 2003. / p.244 - "Faded Rockstars", personal piece, 2004. / p.245 - "Priests of Preoccupation" for Dezart Gallery (Palm Springs CA), exhibition, 2004.

JEAN, James: p.246 - "Green Arrow 49", 2004, DC Comics. / p.247 - "Recess Wave", 2004, Personal Work.

KIRCHNER, Ben: p.248 - "Edinburgh Festivals", 2004, The Guardian. / p.249 - "The Beach Boys", 2005, personal work.

KITAOKA, Kumiko: p.250 - Poster, personal work. / p.251 - Mandolin. / p.252-253 - Astrology.

KNAPPE, Joachim: p.254 - Book cover "Die Medlevinger", Verlag Friedrich Oetinger, 2004. / p.255 top - Book cover for "Quin", Arena Verlag, 2005. / p.255 bottom - "Patient zwischen Psychoanalyse und Verhaltenstherapie", Stern Magazine.

KUGLER, Olivier: p.256 - "Portrait of Maurice Biriotti", 2004, SHM Ltd. / p.257 - "Double Portrait", 2004, Private commission.

KUHLENBECK, Thomas: all images have the same client: Playboy; Art Director: Achim Matschiner. / p.258 - "Roter Stern über Baden Baden", 2004. / p.259 top - "Schleuser", 2004. / p.259 bottom - "Radiation Rangers", 2003. / p.260-261 - "Roter Stern über Baden Baden", 2004.

KUNZ, Anita: p.262 - "U2", 2004, Rolling Stone Magazine, Art Director: Devin Pedzwater. / p.263 - "Carlos Santana", 2002, Rolling Stone Magazine, Art Director: Andy Cowles. / p.264 - "F is for fish", 2003, Part of An Anthropomorphic Alphabet, personal work. / p.265 - "Juggler", 2004, Poster illustration for The Illustration Academy, Art Director: John English. / p.266 - "In Pursuit of Doped Excellence", 2004, The New York Times Magazine, Art director: Nancy Harris. / p.267 left - "That Vision Thing", 2003, The New Yorker Magazine, Art Editor: Francoise Mouly. / p.267 right - "Puppetmaster", 2001, The New Yorker Magazine, Art Editor: Francoise Mouly.

KYONG, Yunmee: p.268 - "She cried for 21 days.", part of the Sofa book, 2001, Personal work. / p.269 Top - "After Life", 2002, Personal work. / p.269 bottom - "Gods' Bath", 2002, Personal work.

LARDNER, Joel: p.270 - "Word of Mouth", Art Direction: Malonedesign.co.uk, The Blueskins (Domino Records), 2004. / p.271 - "Spanish Girl", The Erotic Review UK, 2004.

LEGNO, Simone: p.272 - "Buon appetito!", 2004, work for Tokidoki brand promotion (trade show wallpaper, promo "uchiwa" plastic fans). / p.273 - "Primavera meets little Cloudia", 2004, personal work, printed on Tokidoki skateboards and promo posters. / p.274 - "Tokidoki Koen", 2003, personal work, compilation of Tokidoki licensed characters. / p.275 - "Clio Banzai", 2002, Renault, Agency: Saatchi&Saatchi Milano.

LILLYCAT: p.276 - "Under Control", 2004, personal work. / p.277 - "Geisha", 2004, Pop Up magazine. / p.278 - "Les Masques", 2004, personnal work. / p.279 - "Cinemaniaque", 2005, Cinema Festival.

LIM, Daniel: p.280 - "Dream Girls", 2004-2005, personal work. / p.281 top - "Ramification", 2003-2004, personal work, credits: Aaron Smith, Mark Murphy. / p.281 bottom - "So much of Nobody", 2002-2003, personal work, Credits: Alex Gross, Rob Clayton, David Morcarski, Richard Keyes.

LINK, Richard: p.282 - "A Small Family Business", 2002, Personal Work. / p.283 - "S.A.D", 2004, Malmas Recordings. / p.284 - "Dead Cert", 2003, Personal Work. / p.285 top - "S.A.D" used in context as the cover for the album 'Dark Skies' by Malmas, 2004, Malmas Recordings. / p.285 bottom - "Dreamlands" used in context with the album 'Dreamlands' by Horizon, 2002, Malmas Recordings.

LOMAX, Liz: p.286 - "Jeru the Damaja", Ground Original, record cover for Brooklyn rapper Jeru the Damaja. / p.287 - "Christina Aguilera", Rolling Stone Magazine, editorial for an article on the Richest Rock Stars. / p.288-289 - "The Rolling Stones", Rolling Stone Magazine, editorial double page spread for an article on the Richest Rock Stars. / p.290 - "Bush Buddies", Golf Digest, for the contents page for an article about famous fathers and sons that golf together. / p.291 - "Greg Norman and friends", Golf Magazine, advertorial double page spread for an article on the PGA tour dominated by Australian Golfers featuring Greg Norman.

LOOS, Mike: p.292 - editorial illustration "Aufschwung", Hannoversche Allgemeine. / p.293 - Cover Illustration for pocket book series, Rowohlt Verlag.

LÓPEZ, Brigitta Garcia: p.294 - "Flengel", book "Flieg, Flengel Flieg!", Atlantis Verlag. / p.295 - "Tante Sofie", book "Flieg, Flengel Flieg!", Atlantis Verlag. / p.296 top - "ballermann", personal work. / p.297 - "Superwomen", personal work.

LUCKHAUS, Iris: p.298 - "Fräuleinwunder", Icons for MacOSX, cooperation with Formfaktion, 2004; girls: Jolene, Ginger, Astrud, Marguerite, Shirley, Scarlett, Rhea, Nana, Emily, Grace, Rosemarie, Molly. / p.299 - "Piquenique", Artwork for an Exhibition, 2003.

LUNDBERG, Bo: p.300 - Promotional piece. / p.301 - "Milk Woman", Originally a promotion piece but later used by Time Inc. USA as a calendar image, 2004.

MACÉ, Margot: p.302 - "The woman with red hair and glasses", Boots, England, 2004. / p.303 - "The profile of a girl with purple top", Clarins, 2004.

MARTÍNEZ, Berto: p.304 - Paris, 2004, Custo Barcelona. / p.305 - Adidas Y, 2005, Woman Magazine. / p.306 - Japanese Art, 2005, Takashi Murakami Man. / p.307 - Cour des miracles, 2003, Paper Chic Exhibition.

MATEO, Matt Dineen: p.308 - The Crop Circle Culprit. / p.309 - Huddled In His Ghost.

MATEO, Miguel Berthelot: p.310-311 - Personal Work.

MATSUZAWA, Satoshi: p.314 - "Nina Simone", Soulful Anthology, The RCA Years, 2004, BMG Funhouse Inc. / p.315 - Goldfinger, 2005, personal work.

MCPHERSON, Tara: p.316 - The Witching #8, 2004, DC Comics. / p.317 - The Witching #1, 2004, DC Comics. / p.318 - New York is Book Country, 2004, DC Comics, New York is Book Country. / p.319 - The Witching #5, 2004, DC Comics. All images ©DC Comics.

MENDOZA, Rafael: p.320 - Skater duck Notebook cover, Cia. Papelera Moterrey. / p.321 - "My favorite summer", U-foria Magazine, Art Director: Maru Guzman.

MERINO, José Luis: p.322 - New Yorker. / p.323 - "Pedro Almodóvar", 2004, The New Yorker. / p.324 - "Wool", 2004, Personal artwork. / p.325 - "Substances", 2004, Estudio Rosa Lázaro, The Creator Studio.

MIA: p.326 - "ART", Lumiere de printemps, 2004. / p.327 - "ART", Self Promotion, 2005.

MICCA: p.328 - "Melon Hat", 2005. / p.329 - "ART Black", 2005.

MITSUMI, Mari: p.330 - "Blackbirds, Bluebirds", 2002, personal work. / p.331 - "Bird on the wire", 2002, personal work.

MORGAN, Patrick: p.332 - Tom Dixon, Habitat Creative Director, Afternoon Tea, Japan. / p.333 - Carling, WRSC Euro, Ad Promo. / p.334 - Three Mobile, Agency Thirty Three, Recruitment Campaign. / p.335 - Levi's, Agency Boxer, Pop Campaign. / p.336-337 - Selfridges, Agency Corporate Edge, Annual Report 03.

MORSE, Joe: p.338 - Spike Lee. / p.339 - Clint Eastwood. / p.340 - Illustration for the LA Times. / p.341 - Illustration for Vibe Magazine.

MURPHY 'BEE', Belinda: p.342 - "US Animals, Los Angeles", 2004, Agency Promotion, Kate Larkworthy. / p.343 - "Paradise Garden", 2003, Cover: Hemispheres Magazine (United Airlines), Art Director: Jaimey Easler. / p.344 - "Plaid", 2004, World (Qui Est La!), Japan, Art Director: Keino Uno. / p.345 left - "Iggy Pop", Flaunt Magazine, 2004, Art Director: Jim Turner. / p.345 right - "Jean Paul Gaultier", Flaunt Magazine, 2004, Art Director: Jim Turner.

NAKAGAWA, Gaku: p.346 - "Kobe City", Magazine DRAFT!2, 2004. / p.347 - "Assembly", SYUE (buddhism term), 2001.

NAKAJIMA, Miya: p.348 - "January moon", 2004, personal work. / p.349 - "It's a sunny day", 2003, personal work.

NICO: p.350 - CD cover, TOSHIBA EMI (Aiko Okumura) CD, 2005. / p.351 - "Poptune Tokyo", SUNDRY goods store, 2005.

NIEMANN, Christoph: p.352 - (Griechische Vase) Olympics 2004, Cover, The New Yorker, 2004, AD Francoise Mouly. / p.353 - "Hand mit Karten", book "100% EVIL" (Princeton Architectural Press), 2005. / p.354 - "The World is Flat", Cover, The New York Times Book Review 2005, AD Steven Heller. / p.355 - "Frauen moegen Schokolade lieber als Sex", Men's Health Deutschland, 2004, AD Andreas Schomberg. / p.356 - "FrauenReden sich um Kopf und Kragen", Men's Health Deutschland, 2004, AD Andreas Schomberg. / p.357 - Infographik fuer Ernaehrungstatistik, Greenpeace Magazin Deutschland, 2003, AD Kerstin Leesch. / p.357 right - Fall Chores, Cover, The New Yorker, 2004, AD Francoise Mouly.

NOLTE, Anja: p.358 - "Science of Media and Communication", DIE ZEIT Magazin, 2005. / p.359 top - "Kitchentools", 2004, free work, self promotion. / p.359 bottom - "Gemäldegalerie Kulturforum", 2003, Staatliche Museen Berlin-Stiftung Preußisches Kulturgut. All images © Anja Nolte

OHMORI, Seiko: p.360 - UMACHI, 2004, Ajimar Ltd. / p.361 - Flower that Blows in Winter, 2003, KIRIN Ltd.

OXMAN, Karen: p.362 - "Girl in Black", One of a suite of 8 illustrations for John Milton's Paradise Lost, July 2003. / p.363 - "Crow Twins", Empty Magazine, November 2004, Art Director: Andrew Johnstone. / p.364 - Cover of WYWS Magazine, November 2004, Art Director: Matt Ostrom, Editor-in-chief: Pete Cobus, (Issue 31, Big Holiday issue). / p.365 - Covers, Flaunt Magazine, June 2004, Creative Director: Jim Turner, Editor-in-chief: Luis A.Barajas. (Male and Female variants made for the Youth issue, n° 55).

PAGE, Dan: p.366 - The New York Times Magazine, AD: Christie Grotheim, "Winning With Diversity". / p.367 - Technology Review, AD: John Sheppard, "Out of the Lab Into the World". / p.368-369 - Pitcture Mechanics, "Why". / p.370 - Government Executive, AD: Kelly Martin, "Flushed Out". / p.371 - Cover, Time, AD: Edel Rodriguez, "Are the Great Lakes for Sale?".

PARDO, Carlos: p.372 - "Ash" (Naughtiness), 2001, Personal work. / p.373 - "Soba", 2003, Personal work. / p.374 - "Cassiopeia" (detail), 2004, Personal work. / p.375 - "Cold Fear - Creatures designs", 2004, UBI Software, Darkworks.

PASCHKE, Susanne: p.376 - "Winter Collection 2004/05", Animo Fashion (www.animo-fashion.de), 2004. / p.377 - "October", Personal work: Kalender von Lounge72 (www.lounge72.com/calendar), 2004.

PÉAULT, Frédéric: p.378-379 - Personal work.

PERSSON, Stina: p.380 - "2005 Horoscope Special", 2005, German MADAME magazine. / p.381 - Holiday Greeting Card, 2004-2005, CWC International. / p.382 - Horoscope spread, 2003, ELLE, UK. / p.383 - Versace Haute Coutured, 2004, AMICA Germany.

PFENDLER, David: p.384 - "Shout", 2004, Voices for Children website/logo. / p.385 - "Blown", 2004, Flaunt Magazine.

PILAR, Bella: p.386 - "English Bulldog", 2004, personal work. / p.387 - "Peacock Hat", 2004, personal work. / p.388 - "Snowflake Gown", 2004, personal work. / p.389 left - "Gemini Girl", 2004, CosmoGirl. / p.389 right - "Pisces Girl", 2004, CosmoGirl.

PINS, Arthur de: p.390 - Poster for WOMBAT-France (urban communication, flyers), 2002. / p.391 - Poster for WOMBAT-France (urban communication, flyers), 2003. / p.392-393 - Poster for WOMBAT-France (urban communication, flyers), 2003.

PIVEN, Hanoch: p.394 - "Albert Einstein". / p.395 - "Woody Allen". / p.396 - "Hommer Simpson". / p.397 - covers of the CD collection "The Artist Collection" for BMG.

POEPPERL, Yvonne: p.398 - CD Cover "Body & Soul", Sony Music, 2005. / p.399 - "Eyes wide", Personal work.

PONZI, Emiliano: p.400 - "Portrait of Courtney Love", 2005, Personal Work. / p.401 - "Sushi!", 2004, Personal Work. / p.402 - "Gioielli Etnici: Filippine", 2004, De Agostini Publishing. / p.403 - "Stalin's Suppers", 2004, Waitrose Food Illustrated.

POTTS, Andy: p.404 - Design Week Top 100, cover. / p.405 - Computer Arts.

RAE, Shonagh: p.406 - "Deadly Kin", author Tom Eslick, publisher Viking. / p.407 - "Genetic Sexual Attraction", article written by Alix Kirsta, Weekend Guardian magazine. / p. 408-409 - "Becoming Strangers", author Louise Dean, publisher Scribner.

RAMBLER, Calvin: p.410 - Small Spaces, 2005, Dwell Magazine. / p.411 - Texture, 2003, Weyerhaeuser. / p.412 - BASS maximizes the manufacturing process by using it all, 2003, Continental Magazine. / p.413 - Comparing Train and Plane Travel, 2004, Sierra Magazine.

RED NOSE STUDIO: p.414 - "Shane" from the book "Hey Fred! Nice Red Thread", 2004, Joint, promotional piece with Quality Printing, Planet 10 & Red Nose Studio. / p.415 - Assault on Education, 2003, The Progressive. / p.416 - Star Gazing: Winter DVD Guide, 2005, The New York Times Magazine: Special Advertising Section. / p.417 - Cafe Power Outlets, 2005, The New York Times.

RENDÓN, Maria: p.418 - Piano, 2003, CASE, Currents Magazine, Art Director: Angela Carpenter. / p.419 - Pigeon, 2004, The Warren Group, Art Director: Linda Warren. / p.420 - Contraceptives, 2002, U.S. News & World Report, Art Director: Darren Smith. / p.421 - Abacus, 2002, Bloomberg Publications, Art Director: Evelyn Good. / p.421 below - Horse, 2004, The American Lawyer, Art Director: Joan Ferrell.

ROGERS, Paul: p.422 - The four jazz portraits are from a book I did with Wynton Marsalis titled "JAZZ ABZ" published by Candlewick Press, Cambridge, Mass. October 2005. / p. 423 - The "Doing Our Part" poster was done for the Pixar Pictures feature film "The Incredibles" 2004.

ROPER, Kerry: p.424 - "LOVE", June 2004, Personal Work. / p.425 - "I Love Cake", October 2003, The Big Issue. / p.426 - "Cover for Digital Creative Arts Magazine", November 2003, Digital Creative Arts Magazine. /

sample book, 2005. / p.506 - "Bun", personal work done for "Boys Club" a traveling gallery exhibition, 2004. / p.507 - "Snowboard", art by: Gina Triplett and Matt Curtius, art director: Nuno Ferreira, Lamar Snowboards, 2005.

ULRIKSEN, Mark: p.508 - "Moab", 2004, Commissioned portrait. / p.509 - "New Hampshire Primary", 2004, Personal piece. / p.510 - "Gangsta War", 2003, The New Yorker. / p.511 - "Love the One You're With", 2000, The New Yorker.

ULVE, Kirsten: p.512 - Licorice Skunk, 2004, Hint Mint (concept). / p.513 - Zero Gravity, 2004, personal promotional piece.

VERHOEVEN, Julie: p.514 - Mixed media cover artwork for publication, Unit F, 2004. / p.515 - Detail view of decoupage mural in The Bellini Bar, The Hospital, London, 2004, photography: Andy Keate. / p.516 - Installation view of decoupage mural in The Bellini Bar ,The Hospital,London, 2004, photography: Andy Keate. / p.517 - Gibo by Julie Verhoeven, Autumn Winter 2004/5, "The Pleasure Garden", Cameo print swing coat and outsized beret.

VERHOYE, Annabelle: p.518 - "Spring is in the air", 2005, Vibe Vixen, New York. / p.519 - "Love Triangle", tote bag design for special promotion, 2004, Soap Net division of Walt Disney Co.,USA. / p.520 above - "Snow Angel",holiday greeting card, 2004, Nobel Works, New York. / p.520 below - "Languishing for Love", personal piece, limited edition C-Print. / p.521 above - "Je t'aime", Valentine's day greeting card, 2004, Nobel Works, New York. / p.521 below - "Miu, Miu", "Yves Saint Laurent", fall fashion, 2002, City Magazine, New York.

WIEBE, Gordon: p.522 - Platform Rankings, 2004, Bloomberg Wealth Manager. / p.523 - Liquid Assets, 2003, Attaché. / p.524 - The Big Dig, 2003, Attaché. / p.524 - Positively Charged, 2002, Selling Power Magazine.

WINSEL, Lars: p.526 - Wirtschaftswoche, Düsseldorf. / p.527 - So managt die Natur: Rhesusaffen, "Junge Karriere", Düsseldorf.

WU, Yihsin: p.528 - "Ways of Dating", The libertytimes of Taiwan, 2005. / p.529 - "Fortune Telling", The libertytimes of Taiwan, 2005.

YOSHII, Hiroshi: p.530-531 - Personal work.

YUKINORI, Tokoro: p.532-533 - Personal work.

Thanks

Making a reference book like this is not easy at all. Making it credible, is even more complicating. For that, we were all lucky to work with the best advisors that have great knowledge about illustration. Our best advisor and supporter Jim Heimann from LA has done an amazing job in putting up a list with the best names for us. Unfortunately we couldn't feature everyone we wanted, since we didn't have space anymore in the book, but I am confident that other volumes will come and will keep bringing the excitement we have all had to make this book happen.

For the two masters, Steven Heller and Brad Holland, my many thanks for the great texts introducing all readers to the book and inviting them to have the same pleasure with it that we had doing this illustration bible. Your words have illuminated the publication.

I have also to thank Daniel Siciliano for our joyful work together on the design of this book. Our constant discussion led us to a clean and still different layout. His tireless work contacting the names we have been filtering for months, and his good care with all the data we have received were fundamental to get all organized and in time.

On the production front, I have to thank thousand times Stefan Klatte for his expertise and patience going though all images and details, and tireless working to improve the quality of the book. He has also helped me and Daniel to work in a more dynamic and efficient way.

Moreover I want to thank Margerethe Hubauer from Hamburg for giving us access to her illustration library, and her insights about names that should have been published. Thanks go also to all other agents that have been in touch with us and have put so much material available. At last, and fundamentally, I thank all illustrators for their effort and enthusiasm to take part in the publication, giving us so much material to see. They are the heart and soul of the book, and their ideas and works illuminate not just the publication itself, but also our daily life. These 150 Illustrators presented here have all a special meaning for me. The book starts with them, and ends with the beauty of their images.

From the beginning we decided to have an independent selection for the names. None of the Illustrators published in the book has made any payment to publish their works. We always thought that this way of working would give us the necessary freedom to make a good selection that could satisfy a worldwide public interested in the subject.

Julius Wiedemann

Imprint

© 2005 TASCHEN GmbH
Hohenzollernring 53, D–50672 Köln
www.taschen.com

Design: **Daniel Siciliano Brêtas**
Layout: **Daniel Siciliano Brêtas** & **Julius Wiedemann**
Production: **Stefan Klatte**

Editor: **Julius Wiedemann**
Assitant-editor: **Daniel Siciliano Brêtas**
French Translation: **Anna Guillerm**
German Translation: **Heike Lohneis**
English Translation: **Daniela Thoma**

Printed in Italy
ISBN 3-8228-4033-5

To stay informed about upcoming **TASCHEN** titles,
please request our magazine at **www.taschen.com**
or write to **TASCHEN**, Hohenzollernring 53,
D—50672 Cologne, Germany, Fax: +49-221-254919.
We will be happy to send you a free copy of our magazine
which is filled with information about all of our books.